Talk of Power,
Power of Talk

Recent Titles in the
Praeger Series in Political Communication
Robert E. Denton, Jr., *General Editor*

Political Communication in America, Third Edition
Robert E. Denton, Jr., editor

Reelpolitik: Political Ideologies in '30s and '40s Films
Beverly Merrill Kelley, with John J. Pitney, Jr., Craig R. Smith, and Herbert E. Gooch III

World Opinion and the Emerging International Order
Frank Louis Rusciano, with Roberta Fiske-Rusciano, Bosah Ebo, Sigfredo Hernandez, and John Crothers Pollock

Seeing Spots: A Functional Analysis of Presidential Television Advertisements, 1952–1996
William L. Benoit

Political Campaign Communication: Principles and Practices, Fourth Edition
Judith S. Trent and Robert V. Friedenberg

Losing Our Democratic Spirit: Congressional Deliberation and the Dictatorship of Propaganda
Bill Granstaff

Communication Patterns in the Presidential Primaries: A Twentieth-Century Perspective
Kathleen E. Kendall

With Malice Toward All?: The Media and Public Confidence in Democratic Institutions
Patricia Moy and Michael Pfau

Making "Pictures in Our Heads": Government Advertising in Canada
Jonathan W. Rose

Videostyle in Presidential Campaigns: Style and Content of Televised Political Advertising
Lynda L. Kaid

Political Communication Ethics: An Oxymoron?
Robert E. Denton, Jr., editor

Navigating Boundaries: The Rhetoric of Women Governors
Brenda DeVore Marshall and Molly A. Mayhead, editors

Talk of Power, Power of Talk

The 1994 Health Care Reform Debate and Beyond

Michael W. Shelton

Praeger Series in Political Communication

Westport, Connecticut
London

Library of Congress Cataloging-in-Publication Data

Shelton, Michael W., 1957–
   Talk of power, power of talk : the 1994 health care reform debate
and beyond / Michael W. Shelton.
     p. cm.—(Praeger series in political communication, ISSN
1062–5623)
   Includes bibliographical references and index.
   ISBN 0–275–96751–4 (alk. paper)
   1. Health care reform—United States—Political aspects.
2. Political oratory—United States—Case studies. 3. Language and
languages—Political aspects—Case studies. I. Title. II. Series.
RA395.A3S475 2000
362.1′0973—dc21   99–43114

British Library Cataloguing in Publication Data is available.

Library of Congress Catalog Card Number: 99–43114
ISBN: 0–275–96751–4
ISSN: 1062–5623

First published in 2000

Praeger Publishers, 88 Post Road West, Westport, CT 06881
An imprint of Greenwood Publishing Group, Inc.
www.praeger.com

Printed in the United States of America

The paper used in this book complies with the
Permanent Paper Standard issued by the National
Information Standards Organization (Z39.48–1984).

10 9 8 7 6 5 4 3 2 1

This book is dedicated to the memory of my late brother Mark—who really was the better debater.

Contents

Contents

Illustrations

Series Foreword

Those of us from the discipline of communication studies have long believed that communication is prior to all other fields of inquiry. In several other forums I have argued that the essence of politics is "talk" or human interaction.[1] Such interaction may be formal or informal, verbal or nonverbal, public or private, but it is always persuasive, forcing us consciously or subconsciously to interpret, to evaluate, and to act. Communication is the vehicle for human action.

From this perspective, it is not surprising that Aristotle recognized the natural kinship of politics and communication in his writings *Politics* and *Rhetoric*. In the former, he established that humans are "political beings [who] alone of the animals [are] furnished with the faculty of language."[2] In the latter, he began his systematic analysis of discourse by proclaiming that "rhetorical study, in its strict sense, is concerned with the modes of persuasion."[3] Thus, it was recognized over twenty-three hundred years ago that politics and communication go hand in hand because they are essential parts of human nature.

In 1981, Dan Nimmo and Keith Sanders proclaimed that political communication was an emerging field.[4] Although its origin, as noted, dates back centuries, a "self-consciously cross-disciplinary" focus began in the late 1950s. Thousands of books and articles later, colleges and universities offer a variety of graduate and undergraduate coursework in the area in such diverse departments as communication, mass communication, journalism, political science, and sociology.[5] In Nimmo and Sanders's early assessment, the "key areas of inquiry" included rhetorical analysis, propaganda analysis, attitude change studies, voting studies, government and the news media, functional and systems analyses, technological changes, media technologies, campaign techniques, and research techniques.[6] In a survey of the state of the field in 1983, the same authors and Lynda Kaid found additional, ore specific areas of concerns such as the presidency, political polls, public opinion, debates, and advertising.[7] Since the first study, they have also noted a shift away from the rather strict behavioral approach.

A decade later, Dan Nimmo and David Swanson argued that "political communication has developed some identity as a more or less distinct domain of scholarly work."[8] The scope and concerns of the area have further expanded to include critical theories and cultural studies. Although there is no precise definition, method, or disciplinary home of the area of inquiry, its primary domain comprises the role, processes, and effects of communication within the context of politics broadly defined.

In 1985, the editors of *Political Communication Yearbook: 1984* noted that "more things are happening in the study, teaching, and practice of political communication than can be captured within the space limitations of the relatively few publications available."[9]   In addition, they argued that the backgrounds of "those involved in the field [are] so varied and pluralist in outlook and approach, . . . it [is] a mistake to adhere slavishly to any set format in shaping the content."[10] More recently, Swanson and Nimmo have called for "ways of overcoming the unhappy consequences of fragmentation within a framework that respects, encourages, and benefits from diverse scholarly commitments, agendas, and approaches."[11]

In agreement with these assessments of the area and with gentle encouragement, in 1988 Praeger established the series entitled "Praeger Series in Political Communication." The series is open to all qualitative and quantitative methodologies as well as contemporary and historical studies. The key to characterizing the studies in the series is the focus on communication variables or activities within a political context or dimension. As of this writing, over seventy volumes have been published and numerous impressive works are forthcoming. Scholars from the disciplines of communication, history, journalism, political science, and sociology have participated in the series.

I am, without shame or modesty, a fan of the series. The joy of serving as its editor is in participating in the dialogue of the field of political communication and in reading the contributors' works. I invite you to join me.

Robert E. Denton, Jr.

NOTES

1. See Robert E. Denton, Jr., *The Symbolic Dimensions of the American Presidency* (Prospect Heights, IL: Waveland Press, 1982); Robert E. Denton, Jr., and Gary Woodward, *Political Communication in America* (New York: Praeger, 1985; 2d ed., 1990); Robert E. Denton, Jr., and Dan Hahn, *Presidential Communication* (New York: Praeger, 1986); and Robert E. Denton, Jr., *The Primetime Presidency of Ronald Reagan* (New York: Praeger, 1988).

2. Aristotle, *The Politics of Aristotle*, trans. Ernest Barker (New York: Oxford University Press, 1970), p. 5.

3. Aristotle, *Rhetoric*, trans. W. Rhys Roberts (New York: The Modern Library, 1954), p. 22.

4. Dan Nimmo and Keith Sanders, "Introduction: The Emergence of Political Communication as a Field," in *Handbook of Political Communication*, eds. Dan Nimmo and Keith Sanders (Beverly Hills, CA: Sage, 1981), pp. 11–36.

5. Ibid., p. 15.

6. Ibid., pp. 17–27.

7. Keith Sanders, Lynda Kaid, and Dan Nimmo, eds. *Political Communication Yearbook: 1984* (Carbondale, IL: Southern Illinois University: 1985), pp. 283–308.

8. Dan Nimmo and David Swanson, "The Field of Political Communication: Beyond the Voter Persuasion Paradigm," in *New Directions in Political Communication*, eds. David Swanson and Dan Nimmo (Beverly Hills, CA: Sage, 1990), p. 8.

9. Sanders, Kaid, and Nimmo, *Political Communication Yearbook: 1984*, p. xiv.

10. Ibid.

11. Nimmo and Swanson, "The Field of Political Communication," p. 11.

Acknowledgments

I have three types of acknowledgments to offer. I would first like to acknowledge the valuable and insightful commentary on earlier drafts of this work provided by Professors Joachim Knuf and Ernest Yanarella.

I must also offer an acknowledgment to Professor Enid Waldhart. Enid, often unknowingly, provided me with continued assistance in the motivational process so essential to the production of any scholarly work.

I must also note that a portion of the research expenses for this project were covered by the Wayne Brockriede Memorial Research Grant, presented by the American Forensic Association.

Chapter 1

Introduction: A Framework and Overview

Talk is power. That is my *general* argument. Talk is power. I also have a *specific* argument—the talk/power connection—ultimately determined the outcome of the 1994 debate over comprehensive health care reform. That specific argument will be developed in great detail throughout this entire work, but the central focus of this introduction is to present my general argument that talk is power. I must acknowledge that this is not an entirely new argument. Indeed, I will examine works drawn from the fields of rhetorical studies, general communication, political science, and other areas that tend to concur with my general thesis. I will, however, assert that general thesis more directly than any of these earlier sources. I will also, as noted, apply that general thesis to the specific case of the 1994 health care reform debate.

It is important to explain how I have reached my general claim that talk is power. The development of that argument could take many paths, as the talk/power relationship is actually a relatively intrinsic and instinctive process. For example, the cognitive scientist Phillip Lieberman (1991) noted, "to paraphrase René Descartes, we are because we talk" (p. 4). The innate or instinctive nature of talk as power is, though, only one ingredient in the structure of the overall proposition. As the focus of much of this introductory chapter, I will draw connections to literature in a number of disciplines, discuss the general importance of power to both discourse and politics, and elaborate upon my own perspective on the argument. I close this introduction with an overview of my treatment of the specific case of the health care reform debate on the floor of the U.S. Senate in 1994, which dramatically illustrates the exercise of power through public discourse.

TALK IS POWER

Chesebro (1976) has reported that "Symbol-using and symbol-arrangement have traditionally been viewed as potential instruments in the acquisition and exercise of political power" (p. 289). Such a longstanding view does not, however, go far enough. Symbol-using or discourse is not merely a "potential instrument" in regard to power, it is the necessary agent for the development and exercise of power. Talk is power. The only means of ensuring the interaction and the relational behavior that so many others associate with power is discourse, either direct or mediated. Talk is power because it establishes agency for the development and exercise of influence and control. That is, absent talk, power could not exist in any socially meaningful way. A simple counterfactual claim attests to this point: but for talk, power would not be possible. As Kreps (1986) has noted, no one is "endowed" with power. It is not something that exists in a vacuum. It only exists in situations where others acknowledge that another possesses power. The inarticulate do not possess power.

To better contextualize my argument, it is useful to look briefly at some of the literature in rhetorical and communication studies, political science, and some other disciplines that point in the "talk is power" direction. For example, rhetorical studies and communication scholars have long recognized the interconnection between politics and public discourse. It only seems logical that scholars interested in the ability to employ words as a means of mobilizing citizens, defining problems, and carrying out the other practices associated with the establishment and maintenance of representative democracy would be drawn to the speeches of Abraham Lincoln, Franklin Roosevelt, Winston Churchill, and other notable historical figures. Additionally, most scholars who investigate discursive behavior generally acknowledge that virtually all discourse is suasory in nature, and that the suasory discourse of those such as presidents, prime ministers, leaders of social movements, and others playing out such roles command attention due to the potential consequences and effects of their persuasive appeals. The motivation that compels rhetorical studies and other communication scholars to examine political discourse should be obvious; political discourse is the most public and most significant form of discursive behavior that takes place in American society.

Students and scholars of rhetoric often trace their interest in political discourse to the classical foundations of the discipline as developed by Aristotle. Paraphrasing Aristotle, Wallace (1955) proclaimed that rhetoric would "sometimes masquerade as political science and the professors of it as political experts" (p. 198). In fact, Wallace went on to say that rhetoric could be "entangled" with politics. Similar positions have been developed by a great many rhetorical scholars. Wasby (1971) suggested that rhetoric and political science were conjoined by various areas of interest and concern. Washburn (1968) noted that politics is the "cultural matrix" which "any theory of speech communication must comprehend" (p. 3). In their seminal work on rhetorical criticism, Thonssen, Baird, and Braden (1970) put forth this claim and challenge to future critics of public discourse: "Rhetoric has long been the handmaiden of politics. Its association should be made even closer, more direct" (p. 466). A good many have taken up that challenge and have further asserted the inherent relationship that exists between public discourse and politics.

The Cold War era and its aftermath have permitted many rhetorical scholars to define the role of rhetoric as it specifically is played out in American democracy. Over forty years ago, Hedde and Brigance (1955) stated: "Democracy, in fact, has been described as a 'government by talk,' in that its problems are not settled by force but are 'talked out of existence or talked into solution' " (p. 8). In fact, like so many scholars who have been influenced by the cultural dynamics of that historical period, Hedde and Brigance go on to note that "dictators know that free speech is a dangerous form of power" and that "unless the people of a democracy are articulate, they cannot long maintain their democracy" (pp. 5–6). More contemporary scholars have echoed these views. O'Donnell and Kable (1982) have proclaimed that persuasion is often the only available means of influence in a free society. In a piece notable for its directness and some would say its hyperbole, Hart (1993) explains his view of how the argument works: "Freedom goes to the articulate. After all, with effective communication I decide who will pay me or love me, or vote for me " (p. 10).

Subdisciplinary elements of rhetorical studies and general communication have been even more explicit and direct about the connection their specialties, particularly, persuasion and argumentation share with politics. Simons (1976) makes clear, for instance, that his persuasion text is largely a book about "political communication." In developing his theoretical and practical stance regarding persuasion, Bettingham (1973) has argued that any "social"—which may just as easily be read as "political"—change that takes place in the United States is entirely dependent upon persuasion. Chesebro (1976) has quoted Edwin Black at length, who contends that "all persuasion is political." Black contends that this is particularly true of

persuasion that seeks to alter ratios and relationships of power. Indeed, on a societal level, I think that persuasion is wholly explainable in terms of its bearing on ratios and relationships of power. And, of course, anything having to do with the organization of power is within the province of politics. (p. 289)

Chesebro and Black's allusion to power helps demonstrate a connection between communication studies and political science perspectives regarding the talk/power relationship.

Several politicians and political analysts have drawn the conclusion that symbols and persuasion play a major role in the campaign process and the operation of government. Kellerman (1984) has, for instance, quoted Harry Truman who once noted, in a less than gender-neutral expression, the great force of suasory discourse as he explained that "A leader is a man who has the ability to get other people to do what they don't want to do, and like it" (p. 71). Truman's remark is often cited as illustrative of "leadership as persuasion." Several other authorities have made the connection between political leadership and the use of persuasion and other symbolic or linguistic activity. In fact, Rosen (1984) has defined leaders as "those persons or groups who can mobilize human, material, and symbolic resources toward specific ends" (p. 42). In a review of leadership literature, Hart (1984) has gone one step further to trace the historical development of leadership theory through the works of Simmel, Mead, Weber, and others who have placed great emphasis upon the ability of individuals playing the role of leader to construct social meaning or reality in some manner.

Some political writers have been rather direct and to the point regarding the role of discursive behavior in American politics. Shapiro (1981) sees politics and language as "intimately commingled" (p. 233). Shapiro has gone so far as to contend that "innovative political action . . . *consists in* linguistic action" (p. 233). Dryzek (1990) has more recently drawn upon the work of the European philosopher Habermas to argue that discourse should be at the heart of political discussions and investigations. Dryzek suggests that discourse is an essential ingredient in politics if society is to strive toward a robust, open public sphere as envisioned by Habermas: "*discourse* or free and open communication in political life [is] oriented toward reciprocal understanding, trust, and hence an undistorted consensus" (p. 38).

Most notable among all political writers who have embraced the centrality of discourse in the political world is Murray Edelman. Edelman (1965; 1971; 1977; 1988) has written a great many works based on the same general thesis—that discourse or language plays a central role in the political arena. In their elite-orchestrated view of political power, Dolbeare and Edelman (1985) have expressed the power of language as they explain that "how we define the major terms we use will shape what we see and how we understand it" (p. 3). Edelman (1965) has more directly stated: "The employment of language to sanctify action is exactly what makes politics different from other methods of allocating values. Through language a group cannot only achieve an immediate result but also win the acquiescence of those whose lasting support is needed" (p. 114). Edelman has gone even further to underscore the value of discourse in politics by noting that "It is the talk and the response to it that measures political potency" (p. 114).

Parallels between and across politics and discourse begin to emerge as one examines how many political scientists define the concept of power. Many political observers base their interpretations of power on the idea that it is grounded in behavioral or relational activity. Rosen (1984), for example, looks to the work of Weber and others to contend that power is developed through the relational process of building legitimacy for the exercise of that power with some constituency. Edwards and Wayne (1990) have noted simply that "Power is a concept that involves relationships between people" (p. 431). Isaak's (1975) account of power is most direct on this point:

It cannot be over emphasized that if power is to be a useful concept in political research, it must be viewed in relational and behavioral terms. That is, the research focus is on the behavior of one political actor insofar as it influences the behavior of others. (p. 237)

Most political writers clearly see power as a human activity that is carried out through some form of interaction among political actors.

Some in the communication discipline who specialize in the applied study of political discourse and other communicative behavior have defined their sub-disciplinary interest in regard to the relational or behavioral process that shapes power. Kendall (1990), for example, has defined *political communication* by concluding:

Politics is about power, about the contest over the allocation of scarce resources. Anyone who is working in politics is constantly involved in negotiations to secure, maintain, and strengthen power, and most of that negotiation requires skillful communication. (p. 239)

Kendall sees political communication as a study embedded on the understanding of the relational nature of power as played out through political negotiation.

Several others in the communication discipline not directly concerned with the study of communicative behavior in the political arena have similarly defined power in terms of its relational development through human interaction. Although not directly defining power, Thonssen, Baird, and Braden (1970) have indicated that all rhetorical study is intimately concerned with the process of social control. They note, "Ancient and modern authorities on rhetoric agree that the fundamental purpose of oral discourse is social coordination or control" (p. 6). Their argument is grounded in the logic inherent in the belief that absent oral discourse, chaos would emerge and the exercise of "coordination," "control," or "power" for that matter, would be impossible. Persuasion theorist Bettingham (1973) has defined power and has gone on to explain it is a "dyadic term and depends on the interaction of people" (p. 240). In his assessment of organizational communication, Kreps (1986) has been most direct on the relational nature of power. He notes that "Power is a social construct, it is gained through interaction. No person is endowed with power. People are given power by others based on the messages they exchange and the relationships they develop" (p. 184).

Additional ammunition in drawing parallels between power and discourse can be seen when one examines standard definitions of power and persuasion. *Webster's* (1979) has offered a standard denotation of the term *power* as "possession of control, authority, or influence over others" (p. 895). Virtually every attempt to define persuasion makes a similar connection to control and influence. Fotheringham's (1966) definition of persuasion is typical of this connection to control and influence. He notes: "The development of comprehension, feeling, belief, retention, confusion, uncertainty is instrumental to the goal of persuasion. These function to influence, direct, and control the actions of others" (p. 32). O'Donnell and Kable (1982) have gone directly to the point by concluding that "The key word in defining persuasion is influence" (p. 9). Apparently, in terms of control and influence, power and persuasion are basically interchangeable and can function as equivalents of one another. Indeed, Rosenfield (1968) has explicitly defined power as influence. In addition, many early social scientists, including Wickert (1940), have defined power and influence jointly as important basic societal goals. Freeley's (1962) discussion of argumentative and persuasive discourse has extended this view by suggesting that Americans view power and influence as desirable and that is what interests many in the study of debate and formal argumentation. The parallels are abundant and the connections can be developed even more closely and directly.

I arrive at my claim about talk and power both deductively and inductively. The review of literature presented here suggests that one can extend that previous, general, and broad research to draw the conclusion that talk is power. In addition, one can also work from an examination of the specific case of the 1994 debate over comprehensive health care reform to draw the same conclusion, and that is the focus of the remainder of this book. There are, however, several general questions or concerns that may arise regarding the general argument that talk is power that may impinge upon the specific case study to follow. Those questions will be addressed presently.

When one asserts that talk is power, that does not mean that all talk is *very* powerful. Talk is power runs along a spectrum or continuum much like any other element of substance. Just as "pain" may be severe or "pleasure" may be intense, there are also many different levels of talk as power. The simple continuum found in Figure 1.1 is illustrative of the range of talk as power. Little power or influence is exercised when someone says "It's a nice day." The power here is limited to defining their own reality and perhaps influencing the reality of others. The statement "pass the salt" is slightly influential in that it may well command the desired response. Telling a child to "leave your sister alone" is more influential as some degree of previous interaction has established a pattern of message—power—response. The governor's proclamation to "put the prisoner to death" is very influential as it is grounded in a complex social and cultural matrix of patterned interactions and responses. The same is true of talk as power in all political contexts. Additionally, intent is important here. A speaker may intend a statement to carry certain weight, but its actual impact will depend upon discursive interaction. "Pass the salt" is a good illustration here; the other person may reject the request if previous interactions have proven problematic in some manner. It is the actual pattern of talk that is important, not merely the intent of an individual speaker.

Figure 1.1
Talk as Power

Very Uninfluential	Slightly Influential	More Influential	Highly Influential

Several observers may say that to define talk as power ignores other agents of power. Some argue that the possession of extensive military resources empowers a nation or that the possession of great wealth grants power to a particular economic class. This argument has been addressed in large part by Isaak (1975) as he has explained the relational or behavioral nature of power. Isaak contends that wealth or military resources can only be thought of as power when they are exercised in some interactions. Unless the president "declares war," for example, military resources are merely so much inordinate hardware. Even a gun to the head lacks power unless the holder says "give me your money" or the intended victim recognizes the potential pattern of interaction and does so without the explicit request.

There are some who may say that talk as power is a confusion of ends and means, that talk may be a means to power but it does not represent that end in and of itself. Such a contention fails to hold water on several grounds. First, it obviously must dismiss the vast evidence that confirms the behavioral and relational nature of power. Additionally, this argument is grounded on the assumption that power can be defined in some formulalike manner whereby means and ends can be clearly separated. Such an assumption is far too simplistic. Means and ends blur together in the social construction of power in that the end—power itself—is bound up in the means—talk or discourse—that is used to achieve it. One cannot easily slice away the outcome of a power interaction from the process and pattern of interaction itself.

Cultural and environmental factors may well impact the talk as power relationship as they do all communicative activity. Once again embracing the view that emerged during the Cold War, it is important to acknowledge that talk as power is universal only in the type of political system that permits some degree of open, discursive interactions among citizens and political actors. The American political arena is far from the idealist public sphere as envisioned by Habermas, where the only force is the gentle force of the better argument, but it is a context where discursive interaction is robust and at the core of politics. Additionally, situational variables may be very important to the talk as power relationship. Such situational variables may include the various "argument fields" in which interaction participants reside, the unique public forums employed, and the nature of established rules and norms of behavior. All of those situational variables and others come into play in regard to the special case of the 1994 health care reform debate. In that case, and in every case, there are also interfactional features that emerge as social constructs largely due to patterns of discursive behavior. Indeed, it is the examination of the specific case of the 1994 debate that best illustrates and illuminates these issues and others germane to the general conclusion that talk is power.

OVERVIEW OF THE BOOK

The remainder of this book is devoted to critical examination of the 1994 comprehensive health care reform debate, particularly the U.S. Senate floor debate of August that year. That debate not only illustrates the contemporary concern and controversy surrounding health care issues in the United States, it is also the most recent dramatic example of talk as power. There are a great many ways to approach an investigation of the discourse that shaped and ultimately determined the outcome of the health care reform debate. I have elected to divide my examination into four mutually dependent sections of material: the context, the text, the discourse, and the implications. Those four sections, as outlined below, provide a framework for analysis of the 1994 debate and a vehicle for development of my general claim.

As with all social enterprises, the 1994 debate over comprehensive health care reform occurred within a unique context. That context was shaped by a number of different structural and social features. Chapter Two examines the nature of the health care system in the United States, which includes attention to resources, facilities, and other structural variables. A brief historical survey of health care reform in the United States is developed in Chapter Three. Chapter Four follows that historical account with specific attention to the nature of the 1994 comprehensive reform debate.

The second part of the book turns to the text for examination. As all rhetorical analysis is in some way textual, I define the text for examination of the 1994 debate broadly enough to encompass all those features that are necessary for an understanding of the discourse that framed the debate. Chapter Five details the unique features of the U.S. Senate as a discursive battleground for the struggle that ultimately ensued. The *Congressional Record* is embraced as a specific database, and its historical and textual features are explored in Chapter Six. Chapter Seven turns attention to the importance of investigating specific discursive features such as narratives, evidence, and metaphors in order to produce a robust assessment of the 1994 debate.

Discourse receives special attention in the third section of the book. The examination and analysis of discursive behavior that emerges is fueled by extensive citations from the actual Senate floor debate. Chapter Eight explores the exercise of several specific discursive features and the overall patterns of interaction that develop. Chapter Nine turns to a more general examination of the deliberation that took place on the floor of the U.S. Senate as the status of comprehensive health care reform was hotly contested. The triumph of the "big government" argument is the focus of Chapter Ten and the success of this particular claim is tied directly to the failure of the United States to initiate comprehensive health care reform.

Part Four closes the book with consideration of the most salient implications to be drawn from this case study. Chapter Eleven employs Toulmin's (1958) concept of argument fields as a framework for an ethical appraisal of the 1994 comprehensive health care reform debate. Chapter Twelve examines both the theoretical and practical implications associated with the 1994 debate specifically, and the contention that talk is power, generally. The contemporary currents that can be tied to the 1994 debate are illuminated in Chapter Thirteen.

Part I

The Context

Chapter 2

The U.S. Health Care System

Several years ago, Ivan Illich (1976) made a remarkable and radical claim regarding health care. Illich suggested that it is often the process of being drawn into the medical establishment with its host of iatrogenic maladies that renders individuals sick or unhealthy. Indeed, Illich, writing in his well-known text, *Medical Nemesis,* noted, "That society which can reduce professional intervention to the minimum will provide the best conditions for health" (p. 1). If Illich was right, then one might well argue that the United States has developed the very poorest conditions for health. In the early 1990s, spending on health care had reached an all-time high, there was an explosion in medical technology, and "professional intervention" seemed to abound. In fact, there were many who came to the conclusion that the U.S. health care system itself was sick—that it was too costly and that it left far too many individuals without the protection of health insurance. This was a different type of systemic illness than Illich had articulated, but it did become the focal point of a heated political debate, and it helped to establish an overall context for investigation of that controversy. The specific structural context for the 1994 health care reform debate can best be explored by examining the nature of the health care system in the United States.

The term "system" suggests notions of various parts, interrelated in many ways, working to produce a larger whole that is somehow more than the mere sum of those parts. Railroad systems have multiple tracks and destinations. A health care system may be somewhat similar to the latter. It runs along several tracks, has many stops and starting points, and—in the case of the United States—the occasional derailment along the way.

Although the railroad analogy conjures up several initial thoughts about the status of the U.S. health care system, some additional context and framework for understanding are necessary. In fact, some comparative context helps to better place the status of the U.S. health care system in its rightful place on a global scale. A great many United Nations task forces, governmental reports, and scholarly authorities have generated volumes of information regarding comparative health care systems. One particularly insightful and interesting perspective was produced by Milton Roemer (1993) of UCLA. Roemer's construction of comparative framework structures also helps to facilitate detailed assessment of the U.S. health care system itself.

Historical development, economics, and ideology obviously contribute to the status of health care systems in more than 165 sovereign nations around the globe. Roemer argues that almost every health care system can be classified according to the degree of market intervention exercised in each nation. He goes on to argue that there are primarily four types of health care systems, based upon this standard of market intervention, around the globe—entrepreneurial, welfare oriented, comprehensive, and socialist. A brief examination of each serves to further the contextualization process.

The entrepreneurial type of health care system represents those systems characterized by the least amount of governmental intervention into the marketplace. An entrepreneurial system is characterized primarily by a *fee-for-service* payment structure, wherein individuals pay physicians, hospitals, and other health care providers for the services that are provided. The United States is, of course, the chief illustration of an entrepreneurial system of health care, and detailed examination of that system will receive the vast majority of my attention in this chapter. Suffice it to say, however, that the U.S. entrepreneurial system is driven primarily by a private-sector, market orientation that has generated both enormous resources and problems.

As Roemer notes, "Many health systems of Western Europe are welfare oriented as are the systems of Canada, Japan, and Australia" (p. 698). Indeed, Roemer holds up Germany as a classic example of a welfare-oriented health care system. Germany, much like the other welfare-oriented systems, is characterized by a mix of private and public sector resources and funding, with extensive assistance programs for individuals provided by the national government. The vast majority of these systems predate the contemporary U.S. health care system. For example, Roemer notes that Germany enacted mandatory insurance policy measures in 1883. Although many physicians in such systems are paid by government salary programs, many others are not and their payment schedules vary a great deal from country to country and often are highly complex. Roemer (1991) and others have concluded that Germany and the vast majority of similar welfare-oriented systems have worked rather well at providing coverage for the bulk of their populations' health care needs.

Great Britain, the Scandinavian countries, and several other nations have established comprehensive health care systems, in which government intervention into the market is more direct and more widespread. In fact, Roemer (1993) notes that, "This has meant that 100% of the national population has become entitled to complete health service, and the financial support has shifted almost entirely to general tax revenues" (p. 701). Roemer goes on to tout the British National Health Service (NHS) as a prime illustration of comprehensive health care systems, principally because of its worldwide impact. The British NHS expanded in an evolutionary manner, covering low-wage workers at one step, providing limited insurance for general care and prescription medications at another, and ultimately working through a series of steps that have generated comprehensive coverage for most health care needs of the population. A number of other systems followed a similar evolutionary process, but there are systems in such lesser-developed nations as Costa Rica and Sri

Lanka that have established comprehensive systems directly. Some complaints about long lines and waiting periods have recently characterized some of these systems, but Roemer has concluded overall that "The results have been impressive" (p. 701).

Those systems with the greatest degree of market intervention by the government are the socialist health care systems. Roemer points chiefly to the now largely collapsed Russian systems of the former Soviet Union as a typical illustration of socialist health care systems. Despite the fact that it took several decades to put the system fully into practice following the 1917 revolution in Russia, the health care system was subserved totally by the government. This is the opposite extreme of the entrepreneurial type of system, as the private sector is essentially abolished and absorbed by the state. Some former communist nations still maintain health care systems that largely socialist in practice, even though market economies are being developed. Many of these systems including the former Soviet system, seem to unravel when sufficient government funding is not fully available; however, "from the historical experience of the socialist countries we learn that government-organized systems can function quite satisfactorily in the health sector" (p. 705).

The United States is, in many ways, set apart from much of the rest of the industrialized world. The bulk of health care systems in other industrialized nations clearly rest further along the market intervention continuum than does the United States. Despite such differences, Roemer's work does help to provide a robust framework for the examination and assessment of the working of the U.S. system itself. Roemer (1993) of UCLA. Roemer suggests that all health care systems have five principal components: resources, organization, management, economic support, and delivery of services. If one were to envision the U.S. health care system as a pie, these five components would comprise the five slices that contain the various "fillings" essential to the provision of health care (see Figure 2.1).

Health care systems tend to be complex. Unlike the United States, other nations typically have a principal governmental authority and a number of secondary agencies with some responsibility for health care. In addition to this, there are voluntary health agencies and enterprises as well as private health care markets with some variation in the organizational control exercised by each of these elements.

A variety of processes characterizes the management of a health care system. Roemer (1993) notes that these include "health planning, administration (supervision, consultation, coordination, etc.), regulation, and legislation" (p. 695). This points to the importance of authority in a health care system. Such authority may be established in a legal sense or it may simply emerge from other structures within the system.

Financing mechanisms will often define the economic support of a health care system. They include the use of tax revenues and social insurance by the government, private or voluntary insurance, charity programs, and financing by individual households. Many features of a health care system can be influenced by the relative proportions among these various forms of economic support (Roemer, 1991).

Figure 2.1
The U.S. Health Care System "Pie"

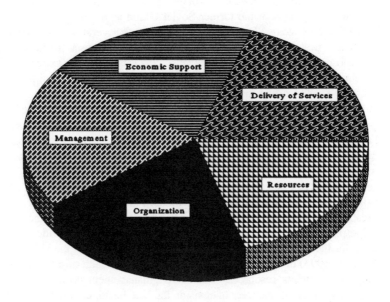

Roemer (1993) argues that these four components of a health care system work to produce a fifth, vital part of the system, the delivery of health care services. Preventive and curative primary health care, secondary care, and tertiary care are each important for the delivery of services within a health care system. In addition, special care options for the indigent, aged, and others may be important as well. Taken together all of these five components—resources, organization, management, economic support, and delivery of services—provide the framework for the examination of a health care system to which I will turn next.

RESOURCES
The U.S. health care system has no shortage of resources. The number of personnel engaged in health care services, facilities devoted to health care activities, and commodities consumed for health care needs are all abundant. Indeed, the U.S. health care system is unique in the global community in this regard. For instance, there have been occasional claims that there is an "oversupply" of physicians and hospitals in the United States. Evidence indicates that the actual resources devoted to health care are impressive.

The U.S. Department of Health and Human Services (HHS) (1990) has reported that physicians are relatively plentiful in the United States, with about twenty physicians for each 100,000 population across the nation. HHS has also reported that for each physician in the United States there may exist an additional fifteen to twenty associated health personnel, including nurses, pharmacists, dentists, technicians, physical therapists, administrators, and so on. Simple addition then indicates that for each 100,000 population throughout the nation, there are between thirty-five and forty health care providers of one sort or another. And, these personnel figures do not reflect the large number of unreported caregivers who also perform health care tasks.

Roemer (1993) has argued that health care professionals in the United States are trained and prepared for service in a variety of ways through both governmental and private enterprises. Training centers such as universities and hospitals are sponsored about half and half by governmental and nongovernmental agencies. The specific structure of the private hospital network and the development of the physician training system in the United States have been discussed at length by Paul Starr (1982). Starr's historical analysis of the transformation of medicine in the United States illustrates the many rigid guidelines, gatekeeping procedures, and other standards that predominate in the training of health care personnel in the United States.

Medical personnel in the United States are also uniquely specialized. Most physicians tend to favor specialization in a particular subfield of medical care, so that only about 15 percent of all doctors are generalists (Roemer, 1993). Further, a relatively large number of physicians practice in group clinics with three or more physicians. The HHS (1990) reported that nearly half of all physicians are in such group practice settings in order to share operational expenses and to provide a number of specialized services.

A large number of medical facilities exist throughout the United States. Of all hospitals, two-thirds are in nongovernmental institutions (HHS, 1990), and 10 percent of all hospitals are operated for profit. These figures are generally representative of all health care facilities in the United States.

Medical personnel in the United States have access to a host of advanced medical technologies. In addition to the traditional X-ray machines, clinical laboratories, and similar medical apparatuses, there is an abundance of more exotic medical equipment available. Randal (1993) has noted that "The nation already has more mammography machines, open heart surgery suites, magnetic resonance imagers, and other big-ticket items than can be used efficiently" (p. 24). Without question, medical equipment abounds in the United States health care system. Not even included are non-institutional features such as health food stores, exercise programs, and so forth. Indeed, Micozzi (1996) has argued that more and more Americans are turning to what the medical profession call "alternative" or "complementary" treatment modalities. Suffice it to say that overall resources within the United States health care system are quite impressive.

ORGANIZATION

"The United States is an entrepreneurial health system in a highly industrialized country" (Roemer, 1993, p. 696). This is an accurate characterization. Health care in the United States is not organized in a clear, governmental fashion directed at the national level. Rather, as Grogan (1993) has noted, the U.S. health care system is highly decentralized. Although decentralization is widespread, it is possible to point to both governmental and nongovernmental elements of the system that are responsible for the organization of medical and other health services.

At the national level, the chief governmental health care system authority is the Department of Health and Human Services (HHS). The primary aim of the HHS is to promote disease prevention and to give medical care to selected segments of the total population (Roemer, 1993). Throughout the 50 states and approximately 3,100 counties in the United States, there are a host of public health authorities "engaged in environmental sanitation, communicable disease control, preventive services for mothers and infants, and certain other functions" (Roemer, 1993, p. 696).

Grogan (1993) has noted that governmental health care programs are largely viewed as supplements to the private sector. Most notable among these government programs, however, are Medicaid and Medicare. Medicaid is a joint federal-state program that is designed to protect selected groups of low-income individuals and families who meet state-specific eligibility criteria (Grogan, 1991). Iglehart (1992) has reported that Medicaid financed care for 42 percent of persons with incomes below the federal poverty level. Medicare is a federal program designed primarily for older adults, typically defined as persons over sixty-five years of age (Grogan, 1993). Medicare also covers individuals who are permanently disabled and those who have end-stage renal disease. There are also special federal programs which provide health care coverage beyond Medicaid and Medicare. The Federal Employees Health Benefits Program is designed to provide benefits to federal employees, retired federal workers, and their families (Major Federal Health Care Programs, 1994); it is supported through annual congressional appropriations. The U.S. federal government also provides benefits to veterans for health care (Grogan, 1993; Major Federal Health Care Programs, 1994).

Within the U.S. health care system there are numerous voluntary health agencies. These agencies tend to focus on certain categories of persons, diseases, or services (Roemer, 1993), for example, providing services for cancer patients or for Native American families.

"The largest channel for providing health care," notes Roemer (1993), "is the private market of thousands of independent medical practitioners, pharmacies, laboratories, and so on" (p. 696). Indeed, there is a very heavy reliance upon employer-provided, private health insurance in the United States (Intriligator, 1993). This employer-provided insurance is highly decentralized with limited governmental regulation. In fact, there are thousands of payers, administrative procedures, and policy-making costs across these programs, which "vary dramatically" (Grogan, 1993). Iglehart (1992) has reported that those programs offer varied benefits with different usage review mechanisms, modes of delivery, funding sources and reimbursement methods.

Employer-provided insurance within the U.S. health care system is largely the result of historical developments. Nixon and Ignagri (1993) have argued that "World War II would prove to be the defining event in the construction of the nation's peculiar system of health insurance coverage" (p. 815). The federal government had taken action to freeze wages and prices at the outset of the war. Then, in 1942, the War Labor Board ruled that moderate increases in fringe benefits were not inflationary and could be permitted. Following this ruling, unions began to press for health benefits, and employers who faced wartime labor shortages began offering them to attract workers. This employer-provided mechanism for insurance has largely prevailed ever since that time.

In many ways, it is difficult to refer to "organization" or a health care "system" within the United States. As noted, there are really many different levels and types of organization and many different types of health care structures within the United States. Indeed, the organization of health care the United States might be thought of most accurately as a patchwork of governmental and nongovernmental elements largely directed by the private, entrepreneurial sector.

MANAGEMENT

The management of the health care system in the United States is similar to its organizational structure. Health planning, administration, and so forth is largely decentralized, with most authority concentrated in the private sector. The United States is one of the few industrialized nations without a central governmental system with authority for management of health care.

Many critical observers believe that authority over much of the system is exerted at other levels. Most notable among these observers is Paul Starr. Starr (1982) has argued that the medical profession—one of what he calls the "sovereign" professions—exercises enormous authority over health care in the United States. Here I will offer highlights of his argument.

Starr argues that the medical profession in the United States exercises a level of dominance that is unparalleled in American society. This dominance is not merely rooted in the medical profession's control of specialized information and knowledge, for the medical "profession has been able to turn its authority into social privilege, economic power, and political influence" (p. 5).

Starr argues that authority is largely dependent upon the development of some status or claim that compels trust or obedience. He notes that the medical profession has obtained such authority through the conjoined features of dependence and legitimacy. The medical profession, Starr goes on to note, has developed dependency upon the part of the general population through the preclusion of alternative sources of health care and other market-regulatory devices. He suggests that legitimacy is maintained via the gatekeeping procedures and other "professional" activities largely controlled by the American Medical Association. Starr feels that this has been a very effective combination for the medical profession, as "the twin supports of dependence and legitimacy introduce a stability into authority relations" (p. 10).

The authority of the medical profession is most unique. In fact, Starr argues that its authority goes well beyond the practice of control of the external environment to the very construction of social reality. Starr notes, "Authority, then, also refers to the probability that particular definitions of reality and judgments of meaning and value will prevail as valid and true" (p. 13). He labels this component "cultural authority."

The medical profession exerts such cultural authority as doctors are forced to define and characterize their patients' condition and the very meaning of "ill" and "well."

Ultimately, Starr believes that medicine in the United States is best defined by the exercise of authority through professionalism. Such professionalism has been employed by physicians as a means to retain the reins of power over health care. Starr elaborates:

Professionalism serves, among other functions, as a basis of solidarity for resisting forces that threaten the social and economic positions of an occupational group. In the nineteenth century, professionalism served physicians as a basis for resisting competition from other practitioners. Late in the nineteenth century, it began to serve doctors and others as a means of resisting corporate competition and control. And in the twentieth century, in addition to these two earlier functions, it has become the ground for resistance to government. (pp. 27–28)

Thus, Starr argues that if any particular source of management or authority can be identified the U.S. health care system it would most certainly be the medical profession.

It is important to acknowledge that Starr's assessment is grounded in and resembles much of the rich diversity of literature that has been written on authority more generally. Scholars and social commentators have long been interested in the subject. Weber and Foucoult were among the most notable political and social critics to take up appraisal of the processes of authority. In a review of relevant political literature, Chesebro (1976) has noted that authority is the very definition of contemporary politics: "Authority (the maintenance of an influential and manipulative relationship between leaders and interest groups) is generally conceived to be the most relevant definition of politics today" (p. 290 n.6). More recently, Lincoln (1994) has extended the work of Weber by arguing that "legal-rational authority" is essentially the only "viable game in town" (p. 2). Lincoln also contends that much of the power associated with any type of authority relates to how agents of that authority employ discourse. Starr makes this connection between discourse and the practice of authority in many of the ways noted. Such perspectives on authority are also consistent with the wealth of literature that I have reviewed earlier regarding the parallels between politics, power, and persuasion. These views also add further weight to my general contention that talk is power. The exercise of this particular power or authority is more directly highlighted later in the examination of the discourse that characterized the 1994 reform debate.

ECONOMIC SUPPORT

Rosenau (1993a) noted, "No one at any place in any historical period, has ever invented a more expensive health care system than that observed in the United States today" (p. 871). This rather accurately points to the enormous economic resources devoted to health care in the United States. Rosenau goes on to note that the United States spends a larger share of its Gross National Product (GNP) on health care than virtually any other nation. Nearly 12 percent of the United States GNP is spent on health care. Indeed, Peterson (1993) has suggested that the American health care financing and delivery system is one of the single largest economies in the world. He goes on to state that "At $838 billion in 1992, the U.S. health care system is about the size of Great Britain's entire economy" (p. 798).

The enormous amount of economic resources spent on health care in the United States is not likely to diminish. In fact, most estimates and trend analyses predict that spending devoted to the U.S. health care system will continue to escalate through the turn of the century. Nixon and Ignagri (1993) argue that without some control mechanism in place costs will continue to climb "until the end of the decade, at which point health care costs will consume 18% of the gross domestic product, 17% of all federal revenues, and 12% of state revenue" (p. 821).

Roemer (1993) has noted a trend within the U.S. health care system toward increased financing through collective mechanisms. These mechanisms include the various government social support programs such as Medicaid and Medicare, but also the full range of private insurance options that have replaced out-of-pocket payments. As indicated, the great bulk of private insurance is employer-provided. Intriligator (1993) adds that business and industry spend billions of dollars annually to maintain funding for private insurance programs.

Economic support and resources are not well balanced or distributed the U.S. health care system. In fact, Intriligator (1993) has explained that administrative costs are rising particularly fast and that they have been estimated to consume some 20 percent of overall health care spending. These costs appear to be similar for both governmental and nongovernmental programs. The sources of revenue in the system are also rather unbalanced. Although households accounted for the largest share of expenditures at 37 percent, business was a close second, providing some 30 percent of total health expenditures for services and supplies, excluding research and construction (Bergthold, 1993).

There can be little doubt that enormous economic support is devoted to the health care system in the United States. Indeed, this complex of economic support is huge by any standard and is summarized in Table 2.1. This level of spending and the escalation of costs has not gone unnoticed by critics. As will be explained at some length later, the costs of health care in the United States became a focal point of calls for systemic reform in the 1990s.

DELIVERY OF SERVICES

As has been noted, the health care system in the United States is very diverse, decentralized, and largely entrepreneurial. Due to its pluralistic nature, primary care is not delivered in any uniform manner. Roemer (1993) argues that the United States has the "dubious distinction of being the only industrialized nation on earth whose people lack the protection of a social insurance program for general health service" (p. 698). There is, simply put, no guarantee of universal health care coverage in the United States. And Intriligator (1993) has noted that there is no populationwide delivery system for services in the United States health care system. Overall access to health care services also varies from state to state (Hanson, 1993).

Despite the lack of any universal program to guarantee delivery of health care services in the United States, most of the population does have some level of access

to care. As noted, the bulk of insurance in the United States is employer-provided and
this mechanism serves to cover a good proportion of the working population. Grogan
(1993) has reported that 75 percent of American workers have access to employer-
provided group health insurance.

Table 2.1
U.S. Health Care Economic Support

1992 Estimates	
Dollar amount	$838 billion
Percentage of GNP	12%
Year 2000 Trends	
Percentage Gross Domestic Product	18%
Percentage Federal Resources	17%
Percentage State Revenues	12%
Sources of Health Spending	
Households	37%
Business	30%

Many of the individuals and households in the United States not covered by
employer-provided insurance receive some level of access to health care through the
supplemental programs operated by the federal government. Medicare, Medicaid, and
veterans' programs provide some medical services to many of these individuals.
Additional services are provided on a piecemeal basis by free clinics, emergency
rooms, and other delivery mechanisms.

Despite all this, millions of individuals in the United States, perhaps 35 million
to 40 million, lack access to affordable health care. This, much like the escalation of
health care system costs, has attracted the attention of critics and social reformers.
Indeed, the conjoined issues of health care cost and access would become the central
features of a heated debate regarding reform of the U.S. health care system in the early
1990s. It is important to keep analysis of that debate focused within the context of the
health care system itself. The health care system in the United States is a vast complex
of personnel, resources, and other components that provides an array of services to
much of the population. Contemporary American society has, however, seen the rise
of medical, social, and political issues connected to that system. The advocacy
surrounding those issues is ripe for scholarly investigation, as is the discursive
treatment of the present health care system in the reform debate. Prior to my analysis
of discursive behavior it is, however, important to continue to illuminate the context
that shaped the 1994 debate including the history of health care reform in the United
States.

Chapter 3

The History of Health Care Reform

Judith Randal (1993) recounted a rather grim bit of humor regarding demands for comprehensive health care system reform in the United States: "A durable joke has it that the late Wilbur Cohen, an architect of Social Security and later Lyndon Johnson's Secretary of Health, Education, and Welfare, once asked God whether the United States would ever have national health insurance. 'Only if I live long enough,' God replied" (p. 22). Although rather hyperbolic, this odd bit of humor sums up the past several decades of attempts to achieve national, comprehensive reform of the U.S. health care system. Indeed, the history of health care system reform in the United States is marked more by tombstones than milestones. Each and every comprehensive national attempt at reform has met with failure.

Accounts of attempted reform efforts of the health care system in the United States during this century are interesting from a historical perspective, but they are also illuminating in other ways. The history of health care reform during this century helps provide an important context for examination of reform efforts during the 1990s. The failure of comprehensive reform elements points to the substantial obstacles confronting contemporary reformers and policy makers, and to the enduring nature of health issues as major components of national, political, and rhetorical appeal. Further, the incremental responses that have tended to emerge from previous health care debates set the tone for the measure of effectiveness of reform calls.

There are many places to turn for such historical data. Perhaps the most extensive collection of information available on the subject is the work of sociologist Paul Starr (1982). Starr has constructed an award-winning account of the rise and fall of health care system reform efforts in the United States from the very early 1900s through the 1970s. The following, though laced with that of others, draws heavily upon Starr's work.

"For decades, presidents and members of Congress have struggled with the question of how to assure health security for all Americans" (Health Care Reform, 1994, p. 225), and that struggle has had several periods of drama, interest, and attention. Early in the 1900s, into the period of World War I, during the Truman administration after World War II, and during the Nixon era of the 1970s, calls for comprehensive reform of the health care system in the United States have garnered considerable attention and have earned a place on the national agenda. It is worth taking a brief look at each of these episodes, and considering the tendency of U.S. policy response to take the form of incremental, rather than comprehensive reform.

REFORM DEMANDS IN THE EARLY 1900s

One particularly important ingredient in early calls for comprehensive health care system reform was the trade union movement. Nixon and Ignagri (1993) have noted that trade unions, since their inception in this country, have wrestled with the question of how to secure health security for their members and workers in general. Early on, unions established national sick funds similar to the immigrant fraternal orders of the time, and in 1877 the Granite Cutters established the first national sick benefit plan (Starr, 1982).

The interest of trade unions and the labor movement in the issue of health care system reform persisted into the 1900s. In fact, Starr (1982) has argued that the most important player in demands for health care system reform in the early 1900s was the American Association for Labor Legislation (AALL). Although the American Socialist party had begun to make demands for health care system reform, the AALL was able to play a more centralist role with calls for the reform, rather than the abolishment of capitalism. The AALL was not officially a "union" organization, nor did it take a position on the role of unions in the marketplace. Yet, many prominent union leaders worked within the organization and many of its members supported unions.

The AALL can best be described as a collection of "social progressives." These were individuals who viewed a positive and reform-oriented role for the government and who embraced such political figures as Teddy Roosevelt. Indeed, Roosevelt's failure to reclaim the presidency as the candidate of the Progressive party in 1912 struck a blow against most major social reform efforts of the time, including health care system reform.

The AALL, the Progressive movement, trade unionists, and others were able to help place comprehensive health care system reform on the national agenda in the days leading up to World War I. Major conferences were conducted and extensive reports released regarding health care issues. Meetings, marches, and rallies occurred, which often included discussion of health care issues and reform of the health care delivery system. This level of attention was about as far as reform efforts would go in the early 1900s. No system of national health care insurance was established. No guarantee of health security was obtained. And no comprehensive health care system reform was ever implemented. Starr offered this overall assessment:

In America health insurance first became a political issue on the eve of the first World War, after nearly all major European countries had adopted some sort of program. The rapid progress that workmen's compensation laws made in the United States between 1910 and 1913 encouraged reformers to believe that if Americans could be persuaded to adopt compulsory insurance against industrial accidents, they could also be persuaded to adopt compulsory insurance against sickness which caused poverty and distress among many more families. . . . As would happen repeatedly in the next several decades, advocates of reform had the impression that victory was close at hand, only to see it vanish like a mirage. (pp. 236–237)

This pattern of inflated expectations was repeated during later health care reform efforts, but there were also other specific factors at work that produced failure for this first early attempt at comprehensive health care reform.

Starr traces the failure of these early reform efforts to a myriad of factors characteristic of the social, political, and cultural times. He suggests, for instance, that there was no major governmental instability spurring reform as had existed in Europe. A tradition of adherence to charity and volunteerism at the state and local levels also worked against reform, as did the failure of conservative unions and the Socialist party to merge as a unified labor front on the issue. The variety of special interests, most notably doctors, also had some role to play in the defeat of these early reform efforts. Among the factors contributing to the failure of reform, Starr has identified two as being of utmost importance: The entry of the United States into World War I and the success of the Communist revolution in Russia. The entry of the United States into World War I not only changed the national agenda for a period of years, but it also consumed enormous resources and attention that otherwise might have been devoted to the pursuit of domestic policy concerns. The victory of Lenin and the Communists in Russia generated a powerful "red scare." The "scare" concerning the advance of communism cast an ugly shadow on both "socialized" medicine and the trade unionist movement, two elements often connected to the pursuit of comprehensive, national health care system reform. Starr elaborates on this ideological assault against demands for comprehensive health care reform: "Defeating health insurance in toto by opening up the ideological issues . . . was a safer strategy for the opponents than working within the framework of reform in the hope of turning it to their advantage" (p. 257). Thus, reform became a zero sum game that advocates could not win.

REFORM DEMANDS FOLLOWING WORLD WAR II

The years just after World War I and those leading into the second were not totally lacking in concerns for and interest in comprehensive health care system reform. In 1935, for example, President Franklin Roosevelt's Committee on Economic Security issued a report endorsing national health insurance. And in 1943 Senator Robert Wagner of New York and Senator James Murray of Montana, along with Representative John Dingell, Sr., of Michigan introduced the first national health insurance legislation in the U.S. Congress (Chronology of Federal Involvement, 1994). Neither of these initiatives, however, gained much ground. The next major effort toward comprehensive health care system reform came in the period just after World War II during the Truman administration.

Peterson (1993) noted that Harry Truman was the first U.S. president to actually take an active role in calls for reform of the health care system. In fact, shortly after taking office in 1945, Truman called for compulsory national health insurance funded by payroll deductions and providing every citizen with medical and hospital services

(Chronology of Federal Involvement, 1994). Truman garnered some valuable support for this proposal. Once again, organized labor and allied associations seemed to enthusiastically embrace reform demands (Starr, 1982).

"Truman found himself relatively alone among elected officials challenging the central precepts of American medicine" (Peterson, 1993, p. 786). And the ultimate defender of the medical establishment—the American Medical Association—stood firmly in his way (Poen, 1979). The AMA worked with its allies to challenge and stifle the development of Truman's initiative in many ways, but it was most successful in use of the "red scare" card once again. The "red scare" in this case was connected to general American concerns about the expansion of global communism, especially in China and Eastern Europe, following World War II. There was a general belief that such expansion threatened traditional American values, and political figures such as Wisconsin Senator Joseph McCarthy capitalized on these fears to advance their own agendas. Labeling proposals for comprehensive health care reform "socialized medicine" and "creeping socialism" cast them in a very negative light (Starr, 1982). Campion (1984) and others have argued that working with a Republican Congress, the AMA succeeded in raising fears of "creeping socialism" associated with national health insurance during the early years of the Cold War.

Peterson (1993) has argued that the Republican Congress, which was influenced heavily by the AMA during Truman's health care system reform effort, also functioned to help defeat that effort in its own right. Peterson contends that the Congress had developed an oligarchical rule system that was dominated by either a hostile Republican majority or a conservative coalition of Republicans and Southern Democrats. Indeed, the ability of the AMA to use the structure, process, and governing of Congress in this case has made the period a notable illustration of government held hostage by "iron triangle" relationships (Peterson, 1993).

Several attempts have been made to summarize these first two failed attempts during the first half of the century. Neufield and Greenfield (1972) identified the extensive force of the medical profession as being the principal agent of defeat: "National health insurance was first seriously proposed by Franklin Roosevelt in 1935; it was raised next by Senator Robert Wagner, Sr. in 1943 and again by Harry Truman in January of 1948. Each time the AMA mobilized its forces and managed to kill the idea" (1982, pp. 162–163). Starr has also assigned great force to the impact of the medical profession and its allies, but he has gone one step further to characterize that force as the practice of "symbolic politics." He contends:

The burial of national health insurance during the cold war was only the culmination of a long process of treating it in symbolic terms. . . . [T]hroughout the debate over health insurance in the United States, the conflict was intensely ideological. . . . The interest groups opposed to health insurance repeatedly found it useful to cast the issue in ideological terms. By accusing the supporters of health insurance of being the agents first of German statism and then of Soviet communism, they meant to inject a meaning into health insurance that the reformers deeply resented. (pp. 286–287)

Such shaping or framing of meaning is yet another example of talk or discourse as power, and it is a strategy that is re-emerging in future reform debates.

REFORM DEMANDS IN THE 1970s

Although the 1960s saw passage of both Medicare and Medicaid, these incremental measures did not add up to comprehensive health care system reform. Media attention in the early 1970s had increasingly turned to health-related issues. As Starr (1982) reports, headlines and stories were addressing escalating health care costs, limited access, and the imminent "crisis" in health care confronting the nation. National, comprehensive health care system reform was once again on the public agenda, this time with some renewed vigor.

There were important changes in the status of health care in the United States by the early 1970s and changes in political dynamics. As noted, considerable attention was being paid to a national health care "crisis." Medical cost inflation was running well ahead of the general inflation rate, and serious concerns were emerging regarding the ability of millions of Americans to secure access to health care (Starr, 1982). Indeed, this period was the first to be popularly constructed as a time of health care "crisis." Starr has suggested that the popular discourse of "crisis" was fueled by complaints from both the left and the right. Liberals felt that too many of the poor and infirm lacked adequate access to delivery of health care services. Conservatives, particularly the business community, felt that health care costs posed dramatically negative economic consequences. It is also important to remember that this was a historical period ripe with "crisis" alarms—there had been a civil rights crisis, the crisis in Vietnam, a growing environmental crisis, and others. It should not be surprising that when elements from both sides of the political aisle became alarmed about health care, it too would be labeled a "crisis." All of this helped prompt Republican President Richard Nixon to call for substantive reform of the health care system. In 1971 Nixon proposed expansion of health maintenance organizations (HMOs) and incentives for employers to provide health insurance to their employees (Chronology of Federal Involvement, 1994).

It should be noted that Nixon's proposal was only one of many at the time, and it was among the most conservative of options. The many bills and options did differ significantly, but Davis (1975) did suggest that the bulk of them held many features in common. She noted, "They try to (1) ensure that all persons have financial access to medical care, (2) eliminate the financial hardship of medical bills, and (3) limit the rise in health care costs" (p. 166). Neufield and Greenfield (1972), reform proponents themselves, have reported that dozens of bills were introduced into Congress proposing some form of national health insurance, however, "most of these bills will never ever be the subject of a public hearing, much less a floor debate" (p. 162). Indeed, the only floor debate on the issue would not come for another two decades. All of these proposals, including the one offered by Nixon, were largely responses to some claim of health care crisis. One appeal hoping to prompt legislation was stated "logically": "One simple syllogism seems to sum up health care in America. The poor get sick. The sick get poor. And the medical-industrial complex gets richer all the time" (Neufield & Greenfield, 1972, p. 154).

Despite the fact that it was somewhat remarkable that a conservative Republican political figure like Nixon would endorse any major national health care system reform effort, many more liberal advocates of reform were not satisfied with his heavy reliance upon a public-private mix of responses. Peterson (1993) explains rather clearly that, "The organized advocates of reform also had developed so much political presence that they were cocky enough to reject Nixon's employment-based plan and later compel President Carter to adopt, although reluctantly, the mantle of national health insurance" (p. 787). What these groups had in political presence, they lacked in capacity to succeed (Starr, 1982).

Health care reform during the 1970s also faced many of the ideological obstacles that similar reform efforts encountered during the Cold War. Although not directly appealing to fears of communist domination, opponents of reform did suggest that reform proposals were too extreme and that they were tilted to the political left. Neufield and Greenfield (1972) report one incident during which one AMA representative was so outraged by the "liberal" criticisms of Senator Ted Kennedy, that he raised the threat of withdrawing all organized medical support for any Democratic party candidate. Redman (1973) writing primarily about Senator Warren Magnuson's proposal for the establishment of a National Health Service, noted that "socialized medicine" of any sort would raise ideological hackles at the White House and throughout the administration. He notes that, for example, "for the government actually to employ doctors was out of the question" (p. 62).

Advocates of national health insurance and other comprehensive reform measures in the 1970s were not up to the challenge of defeating the conjoined power of organized medicine and their business allies (Starr, 1982). Although business and industry had grown generally concerned about the rising cost of health care in the 1970s, they tended to favor maintenance of the status quo with health benefits as a component for collective bargaining and with tax code benefits attached to health plans (Starr, 1982). Further, the AMA and other elements of organized medicine maintained their longstanding opposition to government regulation of the national health care system. "Together," wrote Peterson (1993), "they had the clout to forestall any major public sector interventions, especially when reform proponents grew more confident about their own influence than wisdom may have dictated" (p. 787). As Starr (1982) has explained so well, these forces caused the collapse of comprehensive health care system reform on yet another occasion.

GENERAL IMPLICATIONS

Despite the many differences among demands for comprehensive health care system reform throughout this century, some common elements, general implications, and overall conclusions may be gleaned from this historical account. Peterson (1993) has argued that each of the previous reform efforts had "ended with reform advocates soundly defeated and the status quo firmly in place" (p. 784). And this is the most significant of all conclusions regarding comprehensive efforts at reform of the health care system from the early 1900s to the late 1970s. They have all failed. This suggests that reform of the sort advocated in each case may confront unique obstacles in the U.S. political, policy, and rhetorical arenas.

Organized medicine and its chief agent, the American Medical Association, have played a key role in the defeat of each attempt to ensure comprehensive reform of the U.S. health care system. As previously noted, Starr (1982) has written at great length about the power and authority of organized medicine in the United States as a "sovereign profession." The medical establishment has generally seen demands for government intervention into the health care sector—particularly those comprehensive in nature—as a threat to that power and authority. The medical establishment has also been able to employ its considerable political clout—often coupled with that of like-minded allies—to derail reform efforts.

Comprehensive health care reform in the United States has also developed as a focal feature of debates regarding the role of the government in regulation of the private marketplace and the appropriate extent of government intervention on behalf of social goods into that marketplace. As noted, raising concerns about the "red scare" and "creeping socialism" has worked in the past to help paint comprehensive health care system reform as a product of the big-government loving–"liberal" left. Opponents of reform have tended to color themselves as champions of free enterprise, private markets, open competition, and the American way.

The health care system status quo has remained rather firmly in place throughout the century, but it has not escaped multiple approaches to reform it that have resulted in "band-aid"–type incremental responses. Indeed, Starr (1982), Peterson (1993), and others agree that some type of incremental health care system reform has engulfed the periods leading up to and following demands for comprehensive reform of the system in the United States. The national treatment of health care issues has tended to be incremental in nature; helping specific target populations, responding to specific health maladies, and generally working in small steps to change the health care establishment.

The *Congressional Digest* (Chronology of Federal Involvement, 1994) has offered a useful summary of the most notable national legislative measures to reform health care in the United States. Many of these measures were designed to assist the poor, workers, and the aged. In 1960, the Kerr-Mills Act was enacted to provide federal support for state medical programs for the older adult poor. In 1965, Congress passed, and President Johnson signed into law, Medicare and Medicaid, providing publicly funded health insurance for poor older adults and disabled citizens. President Gerald Ford, in 1974, signed into law the Employee Retirement Income Security Act (ERISA), the first comprehensive law regulating employee pension and health plans. Other, less noteworthy, health care legislation has been passed by Congress and signed by U.S. presidents for many decades.

One other incremental measure deserves some special note to the Medicare Catastrophic Coverage Act. Julie Rovner (1995a) and others have written about the rise and ultimate demise of this particular health care legislation, and their general conclusions regarding the episode tend to agree. The Act was passed by Congress and signed into law by President Ronald Reagan in 1988. It was designed to expand Medicare coverage for catastrophic costs and prescription drugs, and to help cover rising premiums. Although originally backed by many advocates for the aged, the Act did not remain on the books very long. The 1989 Congress passed the fiscal year 1990 budget reconciliation bill that replaced the 1988 Medicare Law with a new physician payment system to be phased in from 1992 to 1996, based on the amount of work involved in a treatment, geographical area, and a variety of other incentive factors. It seems that the American Association of Retired Persons and other groups representing the aged found that the potential cost of the 1988 measure left such a bad taste in their mouths that they spearheaded its ultimate repeal.

The tendency toward incrementalism that characterizes the American health care system has also resulted in fragmentation and some degree of disarray within that system. Starr's (1982) assessment is most explicit in this regard:

The political failure of universalism also had its reflection in the fragmentation of public policy. Each government agency . . . provided its own agenda. The hospitals sought relief through and for construction, and the medical schools through aid for research. The culmination of this piecemeal approach was categorical legislation on behalf of constituencies organized around specific diseases, such as cancer and heart disease. The opposition to compulsory insurance did not prevent a steady growth on state intervention in medical care. Government funding increased, but it was channeled into avenues that did not . . . threaten professional sovereignty. (p. 289)

The feared growth of government tended to follow incremental reform, but it occurred on a small step-by-step scale that did not pose a "threat" or an alternative "crisis."

One closing note regarding the tendency toward incremental rather than comprehensive health care reform is important in assessing the apparent up and down status of reform on the political agenda. There were, of course, situational features associated with each of the calls for comprehensive reform that contributed to its failure in each case, as noted. Further, certain common—themes including the power of the AMA, fears of "creeping socialization," and concern about the appropriate role of the federal government—have factored into the demise of reform demands. Incrementalism itself may have also played an important role. As the implementation of Medicare, Medicaid, and other measures suggest, the health care system has been "patched" or treated with "band aid" approaches from time to time. Although not specifically discussing health care issues, Murray Edelman (1965) has posited a theory regarding the consequences of such incrementalism. Edelman argues that incremental measures associated with major policy issues have tended to win over disparate interest groups. This view seems to make sense in terms of health care. There has been an ongoing series of limited reforms of the health care system and such reforms may have "bought off" those groups and interests that have occasionally called for comprehensive reform. Given some small reward from time to time, reform groups may have been effectively demobilized.

The Catastrophic Care Act discussed above became a hot pocketbook issue. When confronted with responsibility to pay for expanded health care protection, many found that the cost would simply be too great. Costs, the question of who shall pay for care, and many similar issues would become prominent features of the next major national debate regarding comprehensive reform of the health care system in the United States. Examination of the discursive construction of such issues represents a vast potential for investigation. The ability to compare and contrast those issues and their discursive construction during the most recent reform debate with earlier periods would also be of interest. Let us examine in some detail the nature of the most recent reform effort.

Chapter 4

Health Care Reform in the 1990s

Over forty years ago, Democratic presidential candidate Adlai Stevenson suggested that sickness and health should be treated in the same way that a war is, because they are both matters of life and death. Sickness and health have not always been treated like a war, but the question of health care reform in the early 1990s did have many similarities to martial scenarios. Battle plans were drawn up on each side. Offensive and defensive strategies were developed. Considerable resources were marshaled in order to wage vigorous campaigns. And, ultimately, there were winners and losers.

As previously indicated, the issue of developing some type of comprehensive reform of the health care financing and delivery systems in the United States was not a new one. Major reform proposals had worked their way onto center stage on several different occasions over the last eighty years or so. That issue emerged in full force once again in the early 1990s. Although some scholars like Luann Aday (1993) felt that the central features of any debate or discussion regarding health care and reform should focus on improvements in preventive care and public health services, most would agree that the real focus of attention in the early 1990s revolved around issues of cost and access. Indeed, reform advocates painted a dismal picture of both rising costs and reductions in access to delivery of health care in the United States. Opponents of comprehensive reform efforts often focused on the risk of expanding the role and scope of the federal government to implement and carry out reforms. One can shed much light on the situation in the early 1990s by examining both the case for and the case against comprehensive reform of the health care system in the United States.

THE CASE FOR COMPREHENSIVE REFORM

Advocates of comprehensive reform of the health care system in the United States have long charged that the status quo is simply inadequate. Millions of individuals and families lack basic health care coverage, and the costs associated with financing the present system exclude millions of others. Hanson (1993) summarized the overall position of advocates for comprehensive reform:

There is a health care crisis in the United States, and its dimensions are depressingly familiar. As many as 39 million people have little or no access to basic medical services because they lack any form of health insurance. Another 70 million have inadequate insurance, and although they can obtain routine services these people and their families face financial risk if they contract a catastrophic illness or disease. To make matters worse, the costs of medical care, hospitalization, and institutionalization are rising very rapidly. In 1970, Americans spent about 9% of their income on health; now they spend 14%. That is nearly twice the rate paid by citizens in other industrialized democracies in the West. For many in the United States, health care is becoming prohibitively expensive, the technological wizardry of American medicine notwithstanding. (p. 760)

Virtually all of the elements raised by Hanson were common themes in the call for reform.

Advocates of comprehensive reform of the health care system did not simply feel that "serious" or "significant" problems existed in regard to health care. Most proponents for reform would contend that there was a health care "crisis." Indeed, the phrase *health care crisis* became a fixed part of the vocabulary of reform advocates in the early 1990s. Although it would be impossible to identify the exact moment at which the health care issue came to be characterized as a crisis, it is possible to assess its development. Much like the crisis claims of the 1970s, the reform demands in the 1990s came from both interests on the left and the political right that were concerned about access and cost, respectively. These common sense concerns certainly contributed to the development of a "critical mass" of social critics, advocates, and others who labeled the situation a crisis. In addition, many respected and prominent social commentators helped to popularize the characterization. Michael Intriligator (1993) of UCLA noted, "The current crisis in health care financing and delivery in the United States has made health care reform once again a subject of considerable interest and debate" (p. 709). More recently, a physician used a medical analogy to express the state of crisis that existed: "Health insurance is part of the basic financial skeleton on which health care is structured, and there are bones missing" (Shecter, 1996, p. A5). Some reform advocates even suggested that *crisis* understated the dimensions of the problem. Rosenau (1993a), for example, suggested that many health care providers knew that the system was in a state of "national emergency."

Advocates of comprehensive reform of the U.S. health care system also suggested that a consensus existed regarding the state of the health care crisis. In fact, the conclusion of Nixon and Ignagri (1993) was typical: "It is no longer disputed that the health care system in the United States needs a major overhaul" (p. 813). This appeal to consensus would suggest that everyone would agree that the health care system in the United States was facing a crisis and that substantive reform would be necessary. Rovner (1995b) elaborated on the nature of that consensus appeal by suggesting that virtually everyone agreed that it was the conjoined features of rising costs and limited access that undergirded that consensual concern. Intriligator (1993) held a similar view, arguing that both cost and coverage were central to the issue of reform. The *Congressional Digest* (Health Care Reform, 1994) reported that the large number of uninsured people in the system and the escalating cost of care were the "two most serious problems in the health care delivery system" (p. 225). Each of these factors had its own unique dimensions.

As indicated previously, enormous financial resources have been devoted to the health care system in the United States. Further, data generally suggest that costs the system were escalating at an enormous rate. A variety of sources have generated the same general statistics regarding the parameters of the cost issue. "The United States spends 14.3 percent of its gross domestic product on medical care, with expenditures expected to double over the next ten years absent reform" (Health Care Reform, 1994, p. 225). The statistical data on the growth of health care costs in the United States are impressive:

Between 1965 and 1980, national health expenditures grew by almost 500 percent from $42 billion per year to $250 billion per year. By 1993, national health expenditures had ballooned to $900 billion. Health spending amounted to only 5.9 percent of gross domestic product (GDP) in 1965, but totaled 14.3 percent of GDP in 1993. In the next ten years, health spending is expected to more than double without reform, reaching a total of $2.1 trillion—20.2 percent of GDP. (Health Care Overview, 1994, p. 230)

These data are also summarized in Table 4.1. Figures from the Congressional Research Service also indicated that the United States spent more on health care on a per capita and aggregate basis than any other nation (Health Care Overview, 1994, p. 230).

Table 4.1
Growth of Health Care Costs

Year	Expenditure	Percentage GDP
1965	$42 billion	5.9%
1980	$250 billion	11%
1993	$900 billion	14.3%
2000 (projection)	$2.1 trillion	20.2%

Many of the individuals and households in the United States not covered by employer-provided insurance receive some level of access to health care through the supplemental programs operated by the federal government. Medicare, Medicaid, and veterans' programs provide some medical services to many of these individuals. Additional services are provided on a piecemeal basis by free clinics, emergency rooms, and other delivery mechanisms.

Despite all this, millions of individuals in the United States, perhaps 35 to 40 million, lack access to affordable health care. This, much like the escalation of health care system costs, has attracted the attention of critics and social reformers. Indeed, the conjoined issues of health care cost and access would become the central features of a heated debate regarding reform of the U.S. health care system in the early 1990s.

It is important to keep analysis of that debate focused within the context of the health care system itself. The health care system in the United States is a vast complex of personnel, resources, and other components that provides an array of services to much of the population. Contemporary American society has, however, seen the rise of medical, social, and political issues connected to that system. The advocacy surrounding those issues is ripe for scholarly investigation, as is the discursive treatment of the present health care system in the reform debate. Prior to my analysis of discursive behavior it is, however, important to continue to illuminate the context that shaped the 1994 debate, including the history of health care reform in the United States.

According to reform advocates, these abstract financial figures also had real world economic impacts, particularly on business and industry. For example, Rovner (1995b) reported that survey data revealed that a large number of businesses spend one-fourth of their net earnings on health care costs for employees. It is important to remember that health care coverage primarily works through an employer-provided system of voluntary insurance. Business and industry most often have heavy financial burdens to ensure that coverage to workers.

Intriligator (1993) noted: "In many industries health care costs are among the highest reported costs and these costs have risen to the point where some companies simply cannot afford to include the cost of health care as part of their cost of business" (p. 710). One result of this, according to Intriligator, was a rise in the number of "restructuring" layoffs by huge corporations in the 1990s. Intriligator further summarized a number of the financial costs to industry and the economy of rising health care costs. He noted, for instance, that huge reported losses by General Motors, Ford, and other major manufacturers could be traced to the costs of paying long-term health care benefits to employees. He further argued that rising health care costs have played a major part in limiting the recent growth of small business in the United States compared to earlier periods. Intriligator even argued that health costs are "also a factor in the lack of competitiveness of U.S. made products and services" as U.S. firms must bear the costs of health care coverage, while their competitors in many industrialized nations do not directly do so, because health care coverage is provided by the government in those nations.

A number of health care reform advocates, including President Bill Clinton, felt that rising economic costs associated with health care financing had broader consequences for social and economic policy in the United States. Writing in a rather critical retrospective piece, Kaus (1994) noted that the Clinton administration was convinced that welfare reform would be impossible without first implementing comprehensive health care reform. Kaus explained that many in the Clinton administration argued that a very large number of individuals are forced to remain on the welfare rolls simply to be able to have some means of coping with rising health care costs for their families.

A variety of congressional sources have also argued that rising health care costs were the main engine driving the federal deficit. They further contend that these costs are also squeezing out resources that could be spent by the federal government on other social programs. "Between 1995 and 1998, half of all federal spending growth will be for health care, even though health care only accounts for 19 percent of total federal spending" (Health Care Overview, 1994, p. 256).

The rise in health care costs in the United States also had clear implications for the other major problem pointed to by advocates of comprehensive health care reform—limited access. As costs began to rise, simple economic forces led to limitation of the number of individuals who could afford health care. The rising costs to business and industry meant that employers would be compelled to reduce insurance coverage for workers and their families. And these and other uninsured individuals would find it increasingly difficult to pay for expensive health care resources in the private market.

Randal (1993), for example, argued that some 37 million individuals were not covered by any form of insurance in the United States. Some estimated that the number of uninsured individuals approached 40 million (Health Care Reform, 1994). Rovner (1995b) noted: "Estimates vary, but most analysts put the number of uninsured Americans at between 30 and 35 million" (p. 181). Some congressional sources concluded that one in every six Americans lacked any form of insurance coverage (Health Care Reform, 1994). Further, recent information (Shecter, 1996) suggests that the number of uninsured Americans continued to grow at a rate of 1 million individuals a year. Weil (1992) has gone on to estimate that 60 million people in the United States are without health insurance benefits at some time during each year.

Those totally lacking health insurance coverage only comprised a portion of the access problem. Millions of other individuals were "underinsured." In other words, they lacked adequate insurance protection to cope with a major accident or some catastrophic disease or illness. "According to a survey of more than 1,600 households, one in five families reported problems paying medical bills. Three-quarters of the families struggling with these costs were insured" (Health Care Overview, 1994, p. 236). Thus, the access problem was further compounded by large numbers of people who had some form of health care insurance, yet could not meet the total costs of medical care.

It is also important to remember, as Roemer (1993) and others have reported, that there has never been a guarantee of access to affordable health care in the United States. The United States does not currently have any system or program that ensures health services for all citizens. The result of this was simply another component of the access problem: "Those Americans who do have health insurance today cannot be certain that it will be there to protect tomorrow. Over half of all Americans say they worry that they might lose their health insurance at some point in the next five years" (Health Care Overview, 1994, p. 230). Clearly, a job change or job loss, a layoff, rising premiums, or exclusions for certain medical problems could force many out of the safety of insurance coverage.

There were real costs to be paid by those who lacked access to the health care delivery system. They simply were unable to obtain health care services they needed. Intriligator (1993) has argued that "real problems" result for those who lack health care coverage in the United States. Often, diseases go undetected, illnesses untreated, and medical conditions are left to worsen. Rosenau (1993) has suggested that the "costs" of illness and disease that result are great: "They represent lost potential and are a deficit on any society's balance sheet" (p. 885). Based upon data gleaned from Senate reports, the Congressional Research Service, and information from the Library of Congress, the *Congressional Digest* (Health Care Overview, 1994) provided this summary of the consequences of being uninsured:

Because they lack coverage for routine care that could detect and cure health problems before they become serious, uninsured individuals generally receive medical help when a condition is much more advanced. According to the Office of Technology Assessment, uninsured patients are up to twice as likely as insured patients to be at risk of dying when they reach the hospital door. Other studies have found that once hospitalized for care, the uninsured experience poorer medical outcomes than those with insurance, including higher rates of mortality. The uninsured also have less access to high cost technology and to services that involve significant physician discretion, such as diagnostic tests, elective surgery, and different courses of treatment for cancer. (p. 231)

According to these various data, the consequences of a lack of insurance coverage could be fatal.

While advocates of health care reform would probably not have agreed upon a single causative agent for the rise in health care costs and the large number who lacked access to the system, they did clearly agree upon a single type of cure—comprehensive reform of the U.S. health care system at the national level. There was a general consensus among proponents of reform that piecemeal, incremental measures had failed and would no longer be sufficient to deal with all that ailed the health care system. Intriligator's (1993) claim was typical: "Rather than patchwork fixes, the problems with employer-provided health insurance call for fundamental reform, with the current system replaced by a new system of national health insurance" (p. 713). The concern that emerged regarding a state of crisis obviously fueled the calls for comprehensive reform. It was the call for such fundamental and comprehensive change that spurred on many of the opponents of health care reform.

THE CASE AGAINST HEALTH CARE REFORM

Although Bergthold (1993) and others have reported that the majority of Americans do receive some kind of health care coverage provided by their employers, this was not the central argument cited to challenge demands for comprehensive reform of the health care system in the United States. Much of the opposition to comprehensive health care reform was rooted in political, ideological, and philosophical concerns. As will soon be seen and as they played out in the congressional debate, these concerns related to such matters as how much should be spent in public funds and the appropriate scope and power of the federal government as an agent to implement and manage any comprehensive system. Rovner (1995b) effectively summarized much of this opposition when she reprinted the contents of a memo written by Republican political adviser Bill Kristol that was circulated widely among opponents of comprehensive reform and the media. It read:

Any Republican urged to negotiate a "least bad" compromise with the Democrats, and thereby gain momentary public credit for helping the president "do something" about health care should also be resisted. Passage of the Clinton health care plan [a comprehensive reform measure] in any form, would guarantee and likely make permanent an unprecedented federal intrusion into and disruption of the American economy—and the establishment of the largest federal entitlement program since Social Security. Its success would signal a rebirth of centralized welfare state policy at the very moment we have begun rolling back that idea in other areas. And, not least, it would destroy the present breadth and quality of the American health care system, still the world's finest. On grounds of national policy alone, the plan should not be amended; it should be erased. (pp. 200–201)

Kristol's advice was part of the battery of attacks on all measures advocating national comprehensive health care system reform in the early 1990s.

Many general arguments can be attached to all plans or proposals for comprehensive health care system reform, and they could each be addressed based upon the complexity and detail contained in each. Given the scope of the problems and the size of the system, it became apparent that every proposal for national comprehensive reform would be very detailed and highly complex and complicated. This complexity merely increases the opportunity to mobilize opposition. Shecter (1996), for instance, cites one medical expert who argued that comprehensive reform proposals tend to have something for everybody to hate.

One particular approach to national comprehensive reform attracted considerable opposition. A number of reform advocates tended to embrace use of an expanded managed care option. Managed care operates primarily through use of Health Maintenance Organizations (HMOs) and strives to both enhance access and control costs. Many viewed such managed care approaches as too bureaucratic and cumbersome. Randal (1993) argued that managed care options, such as HMOs, often control costs by limiting access to certain treatment options and techniques, thus reducing the ability to obtain quality care. Kasper, Mulley, and Wennberg (1992) noted that such terms as "cost containment," "effectiveness," and even "rationing" were becoming increasingly popular as a means of characterizing the consequences of managed care and other reform plans.

Americans have tended to favor decentralized government and often express fear of growth in the size and scope of the federal government. This was an important value position in regard to proposals for comprehensive health care system reform. Grogan (1993) explained: "At the heart of the health care reform debate are philosophical differences concerning the appropriate degree of government involvement in (or centralization of) the financing and administration of health care policy" (p. 741). Grogan goes on later to explain that Americans continue to favor a decentralized approach to the health care system. Morone (1990), Tallon and Nathan (1992), and other researchers have concluded that the general public shares a common lack of faith in the federal government as an administrator. Ongoing jokes about the U.S. Postal Service exemplify this belief. And Americans tend to scorn the thought of the federal government as a provider of their health care (Grogan, 1993).

Although business and industry often suffered serious economic consequences associated with the current employer-provider system of health insurance, many tended to oppose federal action to regulate the system. Indeed, the *Congressional Digest* (Health Care Reform, 1994) reported that opposition to comprehensive health care system reform among business and industry tended to reflect the fact that reform plans represented a challenge to established interests. Further, the regulatory nature of reform was also viewed with considerable concern on the part of business and industry. Bergthold (1993) reported, for example, that virtually all small businesses were united in their opposition to governmental regulatory schemes that mandated health care coverage for workers.

Concerns regarding calls for comprehensive health care system reform also arose among advocates of many particular populations in need of specialized care or health coverage. Binstock (1993) explained that many representatives of older adults were concerned about the nature of care that these persons would receive under plans for comprehensive reform. Hafner-Eaton (1993) expressed great concern that women's health needs might be marginalized in an overall, comprehensive approach to reform. A similar concern for the unique needs of homeless individuals was expressed by Cousineau and Lozier (1993).

Procedural and operational matters also became central to concerns about what implementation and operation of comprehensive health care system reform might entail. Many critics point to "welfare cheats" and others who have taken advantage of current entitlement programs as illustrative of the risk that comprehensive health care system reform measures might pose. Rosenau (1993a) noted that fears of government fraud and cheating were not uncommon in discussions of proposals for comprehensive reform.

As indicated, many concerns were raised about the proposals for comprehensive health care system reform in the United States. These disparate concerns often fragmented groups that would otherwise have tended to support reform measures. That was not, however, the case with the opposition. Hanson (1993) offers this detailed explanation of the opposition, writing:

If the proponents of new health care policies are divided, their opponents are not. Small businesses have organized against any proposal that imposes increased costs on employers. Hospitals, clinics, and other health care institutions are opposed to limitations or changes as regulations on expansion and investment in new technology. Many . . . physicians and health care professionals are against limitations or fees or restrictions on services that are expensive but useful in diagnosis and treatment. Insurance companies resist mandates that increase risks and oblige them to make larger payments, thereby jeopardizing profits. Seniors oppose policies that would be financed by savings from restricting Medicare. And middle-class citizens everywhere object to policies likely to increase their taxes. (p. 774)

Hanson's assessment clearly highlights the difficulty of uniting the diverse elements interested in reform. Specific proposals contained features that were in some way unacceptable to business, older adults, and other specific interests. Further, Aday (1993) and others have pointed to division regarding the appropriate focus for reform as a cause of fragmentation. There may, indeed, be something for everyone to hate in comprehensive reform proposals.

It should also be noted that much retrospective analysis has suggested that most Americans were generally satisfied with their present care and did not support any specific reform measure. Rovner (1995b), for example, has argued that most

Americans in the early 1990s were simply "spoiled." She suggests that most citizens enjoyed access to high quality care and did not favor anything that might diminish their opportunities to receive expensive medical treatment as quickly as they desire. Schick (1995) has also argued that proponents of comprehensive reform had misread public opinion and the public mood. He notes that most Americans generally favored "reform," but they could not be mobilized to embrace the type of specific detail that would necessarily accompany reform measures. And Miller (1993), after conducting a rather detailed analysis of public opinion data, found that to the average voter the budget deficit and other economic issues were of far greater concern than health care reform.

CONCLUSION

The case for comprehensive reform of the health care system in the United States during the early 1990s can be summed up fairly simply. Proponents of comprehensive reform agreed that American health care was in a state of "crisis." The crisis had largely emerged as social commentators, opinion leaders, and reform advocates became increasingly dissatisfied with more limited reform initiatives. That crisis was characterized by two conjoined problems. The first was the escalation of health care costs and the multiple economic consequences that those costs generated. The second was the issue of access to the system for the uninsured and the underinsured. Reform advocates concluded that only comprehensive reform efforts would be sufficient to resolve these two issues.

The case against comprehensive health care system reform was in many ways more complex. Many Americans felt generally satisfied with their care, and it was difficult to mobilize support for comprehensive reform proposals. It was not, however, difficult to generate opposition to comprehensive reform proposals. Such reform proposals were often viewed as an unnecessary and risky expansion of the power of the federal government. Business and industry feared regulation and government mandates. Many specialized health care populations felt that they might come up short in the reform process. And concern about the risks of bureaucracy, higher taxes, and other negative consequences of reform were abounded.

Analysis of the discursive features—narratives, use of evidence, and more—of this debate offers an opportunity to further illuminate this unique argumentative dispute. In addition, it is important to note that this debate did not simply occur as an abstract public policy concern on the part of medical experts and health care analysts. It soon became a political and discursive dispute by policy making bodies, especially the U.S. Congress. Rosenau (1993b) noted: "Health services is at a crossroads in the United States. Years of federal government inattention and even neglect of policy in this sector mean that today it is the concerted focus of attention" (p. 689). Rosenau was right. Health care reform was the focus of attention in the early 1990s. And the debate on the issue would play out in a unique political arena that functioned as part of an overall text. It is to an explication of that text that I next turn my attention.

Part II

The Text

Chapter 5

The Senate Battleground

Much as the context for the 1994 debate regarding comprehensive health care reform was treated with a wide brushstroke, so too must the text for examination of that debate be developed in a very broad sense. All rhetorical criticism and much of qualitative social scientific research is concerned with "textual" analysis and such analysis has employed "texts" as diverse as historical documents, family conversations, and film. All such interpretations of "text" strive to accomplish the same goal I pursue here—to clearly lay out the broad slate upon which a given discourse event occurs. In pursuit of that goal, I think that it is first necessary to define the structure of the text, what document, stage, or other forum employed and what it actually is. The quiddity or essence of the structural nature of a text may be elusive in many ways, but it is possible to provide an explication of the forum where a debate plays out. Although the 1994 health care reform debate touched upon fixtures running from the White House to the backers of television spots, the specified forum where the debate regarding a specific proposal to actually implement health care reform was the floor of the U.S. Senate.

To explore the "textual" nature of the U.S. Senate, it is important to take three interdependent steps. First, it is necessary to lay out several practical reasons for turning to that specific forum for the investigation of my particular case study of talk as power. Next, the rich history of rhetorical study of the U.S. Senate needs to be illuminated in order to display the keen interests that scholars and students of public discourse have long held regarding that venue for interaction. Finally, to better place the U.S. Senate within the realm of a text, or at least one layer of a text, it is essential to define the forum through the concept of an argument field based upon Toulmin's (1958) original notion, discussed and elaborated by many others, and extended here in an operationalization that helps facilitate the investigation of power as talk. Most casual observers would point to the election of Bill Clinton in 1992, the creation of a special health care reform task force chaired by Hillary Rodham Clinton, and the many meetings conducted by Mrs. Clinton and Ira Magaziner, who was in charge of staff resources for the President's Task Force on Health Care Reform, as the watershed events in health care reform in the 1990s. Those actors did play a significant role, yet the actual "debate" regarding comprehensive health care system reform was played out in the halls of the U.S. Congress. The Congress, and specifically the U.S. Senate, became the focal point for the debate in 1993 and especially in 1994. Many reasons speak to the importance and value of looking to the U.S. Senate for examination of the comprehensive health care reform debate. They are grounded in both practical political matters and those associated with the scholarly interests of those who study such discursive behavior as debates.

PRACTICAL REASONS

There are, indeed, a number of practical reasons for looking to the U.S. Senate for examination of the debate regarding comprehensive health care reform in the early 1990s. It is first important to note that the overall Congress, both the House and Senate, was important to the health care reform issue. Mann and Ornstein (1995) have recently edited a collection of essays that explain in great detail that the U.S. Congress plays a pivotal role in the shaping of health care policies. They note that a variety of congressional committees have a hand in what happens in regard to any health care policy, and that all significant policy decisions on the subject have in some way been tied to the Congress.

President Clinton did play a significant role in the ultimate development of a congressional battleground for the resolution of the comprehensive health care reform debate. Aaron (1996) noted, for example, that President Clinton committed himself to congressional approval of a comprehensive health care reform proposal. On September 22, 1993, President Clinton expressed his desire for such action to a joint session of Congress and introduced details of his own plan (Recent Action in the Congress, 1994). Peterson (1993) has explained that Clinton's proposal and the overall issue of comprehensive health care system reform would have to be resolved in the "national legislature"—the U.S. Congress.

The U.S. Congress was also to play a substantial role in the debate on comprehensive health care reform beyond merely dealing with a proposal from the president. Congress, at the time, was increasingly becoming an arena for health care reform advocacy and a center of information on the subject. A variety of sources (Kosterbitz, 1991; Peterson, 1992; Peterson, 1993) have argued that as of the early 1990s, a significant number of rank and file members of both the House and Senate had become health care reform policy entrepreneurs, crafting and promoting their own plans for restructuring the sharing and delivery of medical services. These health care reform policy entrepreneurs seemed to have an effect upon the entire Congress. Peterson (1993) has noted that "the activities of these policy entrepreneurs . . . have elevated the overall knowledge base in Congress about the intricacies of the health care system" (p. 794).

The U.S. Congress, in addition to comprising several members interested in the subject of health care reform, also possessed rather unique information resources. Peterson (1995) has noted that, over the last several decades, a number of important institutional structures and programs were developed to provide members of Congress with information on such subjects as health care. He cited the creation of the Congressional Budget Office (CBO), the Office of Technology Assessment (OTA), and the expanded role of the General Accounting Office (GAO) as illustrations. In a discussion of such offices as the CBO, OTA, and GAO, and other information outlets, Peterson (1993) concluded:

Together with the significantly expanded professional committee, subcommittee, and personal office staffs and the information available from executive branch officials and the diverse community of interest group lobbyists, Congress has an unprecedented potential to evaluate rather complex social policy initiatives. (p. 795)

If past history was an accurate indicator, comprehensive health care reform should certainly be counted among the most "complex social policy initiatives" that policy makers could confront.

Congress was not only an important legislative body with valuable information resources and concerned individual members, it was also designed to shape health care policy. A wide number of committees and subcommittees in both the House and Senate had some interest in health care reform and health care–related policies (Peterson, 1993). Mann and Ornstein (1995) have edited an illuminating volume of essays that has developed this central theme. They and the individuals writing in their volume argue that Congress was—institutionally—responsible for shaping health care policy. Aaron (1996) has argued that "it behooves anyone interested in health care or American political life to examine the effort to reform health care that began so energetically in 1993 and ended so ignominiously in 1994" (p. 11). That 1993–1994 reform effort and debate was concentrated in the 103rd session of the U.S. Congress (Mann & Ornstein, 1995).

Even within the U.S. Congress, the focus of the debate concerning comprehensive health care reform can be narrowed. Although there was general interest and some level of action in both chambers of Congress, that interest and action was not identical. Further, Murphy (1995) has stated what may be fairly obvious to some observers but nonetheless important to note: "In both historical design and contemporary practice, there is no monolithic Congress; the House of Representatives and the Senate are two very different institutions" (p. 90). It is to the unique institution of the U.S. Senate to which we must first turn to best examine the most recent national debate on comprehensive health care reform.

Initially, the differences between the House and Senate warrant some elaborations. Most obviously, the Senate is a smaller body than the House, with participation in the chamber limited to two representatives from each state. This smaller size and comparatively limited participation has contributed to the Senate being viewed as somewhat of a more elite institution than the House. Indeed, Katznelson and Kesselman (1975) have argued that the House has typically been viewed as representing "the people" at large, the Senate had been thought out as a more exclusive environment that is somehow elevated over the mass representation of the House. Kane (1995) has more recently suggested that this perceived difference between the two chambers has contributed to a "slowness of pace" in the Senate that prevents a sudden rush to judgment regarding important legislative decisions.

Beyond the more "elite" nature of the Senate, it also departs from its sibling chamber in important structural and leadership features. Dolbeare and Edelman (1985) have explained the principal features of the leadership difference:

Although the position of President Pro Tem of the Senate corresponds in form to that of Speaker of the House, in practice it is no more than an horrific title. The actual managerial functions performed by the Speaker in the House are in the hands of the Senate Majority Leader. The Senate Majority and Minority Leaders serve informing, scheduling, and conveying functions for their perspective parties, and in effect, they combine the duties of Speaker, party leader, and Rules Committee in the House. (p. 234)

These leadership features often tend to render the Senate a very partisan institution, yet one more open for debate and deliberation than a chamber where the joint power of the Speaker and the Rules Committee impose a number of limits in the process.

The Senate is a unique type of institution. It is not only smaller in size than the House of Representatives, it is also viewed as a very different sort of place. Kane (1995) has recently written, "There remains a sanctifying quality to the institution, selfishly protected by the one hundred men and women who hold membership in what they collectively regard as the most exclusive legislative body in the world" (p. 57). Members of the Senate itself also feel that it is a very special place. Senator Robert Byrd (1995) has reminded other members that they were fortunate "to have been selected by the American people to actively participate as their representatives in this miraculous experiment in freedom which has set the world afire with hope" (S18967). Byrd's statement might be a bit hyperbolic, but the Senate does have unique traditions and procedures and it might be thought of as "an important place where history itself needs protection" (Kane, 1995, p. 58).

This view of the Senate as a special place was even more intensely held in earlier years, and it has received a great deal of critical attention. Sinclair (1989) has, for example, argued that the Senate of the 1950s held firmly to institutional standards that limited its role as an important public forum. She notes that "It was an inward looking institution, which was reinforced by the institutional patriotism norm . . . and norms mitigated against using the floor, a public forum, for decision making" (p. 213). Katznelson and Kesselman (1975) also saw the earlier Senate as functioning in an "enclosed world" characterized by complex and conflict-limiting 'institutional norms" (p. 306). Dolbeare and Edelman (1985) have argued that the overall effect of these institutional standards or norms was to "maintain the functional status quo" (p. 222).

Perhaps the most critical appraisal ever offered of the Senate was Donald Matthews's (1960) landmark volume, *U.S. Senators and Their World*. Matthews noted that a sense of institutional royalty and superiority was instilled in members of the Senate, as "Senators are expected to believe that they belong to the greatest legislative and deliberative body in the world" (p. 101). Matthews went on to explain that a complex schema of "folkways" worked to instill and maintain this attitude. Among these "folkways" were apprenticeships for new members, a willingness to engage seriously in legislative work, courtesy toward fellow Senators, reciprocity, and institutional patriotism. Senators were, therefore, educated in the ways of the Senate and expected to be good pupils and ultimately good members who adhered closely to the institution's "folkways." Matthews went on to note that Senators "are expected to revere the Senate's personnel, organization, and folkways and to champion them to the outside world" (p. 102).

Kane (1995) has argued that traditions and appeals to "the old Senate" have become largely ritualistic. Indeed, many observers feel that the Senate has increasingly developed as a vital public forum for decision making and debate on issues of national substance. Kane (1995) has argued that a series of changes—including the more widespread emergence of two-party politics in the South, the greater willingness of Northern liberals to take risks in matters of importance, and the expansion of mass media attention—have worked to help make the Senate an important place to argue about national issues. Sinclair (1989) has also argued that the Senate has emerged as a place where individual members can use its floor debates, committee hearings, and other features as public arenas. Foley (1980) has written at some length about the contrast between the "old" Senate of the early part of this century and what he characterized as the "new" Senate. He notes:

The new Senate came to assume a prominent position in the general flow of problems and policy ideas. Increasingly, senators appeared on the front line of political controversy—investigating problems, highlighting irregularities and injustices, arousing public concern, mobilizing interest-group support, formulating innovatory proposals, tapping the political resources of the White House, and forcing issues onto the agenda of political debate. (pp 254–255)

Indeed, Butler (1995) has noted that the United States Senate has become "one of America's most celebrated forums for public argument" (p. 62).

Beyond such historical and institutional characteristics, the U.S. Senate is uniquely important to the issue of comprehensive health care reform in the early 1990s. The election of one particular member—Harris Wofford of Pennsylvania—helped set the stage for special attention on the subject of comprehensive health care reform to be received in the U.S. Senate. Rovner (1995b) has argued that Wofford's come-from-behind victory in a special election in 1991 was instrumental in propelling the issue of health care reform into the national arena. Wofford had taken the need for comprehensive health care reform as the centerpiece of that 1991 campaign. His election helped place the issue on the agenda of both the national Democratic and Republican parties (Rovner, 1995b). Wofford's upset victory was also a sign that grassroots interest and support for comprehensive health care reform was building (Heclo, 1996). Heclo (1996) has also argued that Wofford's election helped garner significant media attention for the issue. And, Skopol (1996) has concluded that it was the election of Wofford that brought health care reform to the forefront in Washington, D.C.

As action began to take place in the 103rd session of the U.S. Congress, particularly in the U.S. Senate, floor debate developed very differently in the two chambers. Proposals regarding comprehensive health care reform remained bogged down in committee in the House of Representatives throughout the 103rd Congress. This was not to be the case in the Senate. Rovner (1995b) has noted that late in the summer of 1994 the U.S. Senate actually held a floor debate regarding comprehensive health care reform. A plan proposed by Senate Majority Leader George Mitchell was introduced on August 9, 1994, and twelve days of intense floor debate ensued. This was an important first not only for the health care reform effort, it was also "the first floor debate in United States history on comprehensive health care reform" (Health Care Reform, 1994, p. 225). It would seem natural to examine that unique historical event as a way of illuminating the issue of comprehensive health care reform. Although that particular discursive event has thus far received very limited attention from scholars, there is a rich history of rhetorical investigation and analysis connected to the Senate.

SCHOLARLY INTEREST IN THE SENATE

Rhetorical critics and other communication scholars have long been interested in the discourse that takes place in the U.S. Congress, and, particularly, the debates held on the floor of the U.S. Senate. Speech making in the U.S. Congress has garnered attention from rhetorical scholars for a good many years. Voorhis (1948) was one of the earliest rhetorical critics to offer commentary on speech making in the U.S. Senate. Indeed, Voorhis was chiefly concerned with providing a descriptive assessment of effective speech making in the Congress. Many other scholars would follow Voorhis's lead and look to the Congress as a site for examination of public discourse. The process and practice of congressional debate has, for example, received critical attention from both Fitzpatrick (1941) and Cain (1954).

In addition to a general rhetorical assessment of speech making within the chambers of Congress, a number of scholars have focused more specifically upon argumentative disputes. Rives (1967), for instance, provided a detailed account of the type of argumentative strategies that are often characteristic of congressional hearings. Camp (1983) turned his attention to the arguments that framed the Senate expulsion trial of Senator Jesse D. Bright in his analysis of that 1862 episode. Schuetz (1986) has examined a number of specific language strategies that tend to be employed on a fairly regular basis in the construction of congressional arguments.

The discursive behavior of members of the U.S. Senate has been examined at some length over the past several decades. For instance, the speech behavior of U.S. senators has been examined in a series of articles in *Today's Speech*, which is now *Communication Quarterly* (Tompkins & Linkugel, 1959; Tompkins & Pappas, 1967; Cahn, Pappas, & Schoen, 1979). In many respects this series of articles served two important functions. First, it was somewhat of a public service effort by the communication discipline as it attempted to provide a contemporary account of discursive behavior within the confines of the Senate. Additionally, the series also provided a critical appraisal of the increasingly important role of the Senate as a public forum. That series was not, however, alone in providing critical appraisal and assessment of discursive behavior in the Senate. Various persuasive appeals employed by U.S. senators were explained by Rosenwasser (1969). The unique strategic device of the filibuster and its role in Senate discourse was explicated and evaluated in some detail by Borman (1962). And Peterson (1957) turned both a rhetorical and historical eye upon a number of Senate speeches that focused on the issue of slavery.

Debate in the U.S. Senate has received some specialized attention from rhetorical scholars interested in the way in which discourse is utilized in such a deliberative process. Chester (1945) was one of the first rhetorical scholars to examine debate in the U.S. Senate. Chester worked to establish a generic assessment method for the evaluation of Senate floor debates. A similar generic approach was undertaken by Cain (1955) who provided a rigorous examination of both the process and practice of Senate debates. The potential effects of the unique institutional rule structure of the Senate upon the practice of debate and deliberation was examined in some detail by Kane (1971), who found debate in the chamber uniquely rule-governed and heavily procedural in nature.

A good many of those rhetorical scholars who have looked to the debates that occur on the floor of the U.S. Senate as an arena ripe for investigation have focused upon the critical assessment of particularly significant historical debates. In addition to the much earlier slavery debates, scholars have been very attracted to assessment of the Senate debate regarding the League of Nations that took place over three-quarters of a century ago. Braden (1960) and Micken (1951, 1952) were two of the leading scholars to provide a rhetorical assessment of that important historical deliberation.

In recent years, the discourse and debates have received less attention from rhetorical scholars. That trend was breached in 1995 with a special issue of *Argumentation and Advocacy* that provided a contemporary forum for the assessment of Senate discourse and debate. That special issue was introduced by Kane (1995) who authored a concise, yet valuable, assessment of the evaluation of the U.S. Senate as a public forum. Butler (1995) developed the first detailed argumentative account of the discourse of a female entry into the Senate with his treatment of Illinois' Carol Mosley–Braun's discussion of race in America. The Clarence Thomas–Anita Hill hearings and, specifically, the role of Senator Arlen Specter, received critical approval by Armstrong (1995). And Murphy (1995) grounded his examination of a recent Senate debate regarding the role of the filibuster in the context of assessing American political mythology.

It should be apparent that a good many rhetorical scholars and others interested in discursive behavior and public argument have examined the U.S. Senate and the unique argumentative battles that take place there. Examination of the comprehensive health care reform debate that took place during the summer of 1994 in the U.S. Senate would thus be an important addition to such a line of scholarly investigation. The examination of that particular debate is also the most striking example of talk as power in a contemporary public forum regarding an issue of national social and economic significance. To further explicate the Senate as part of the text for that debate, however, it is important to establish the U.S. Senate as a specialized argument field.

THE SENATE AND ARGUMENT FIELDS

Most contemporary scholars trace the conceptualization of argument fields to the 1958 publication of *The Uses of Argument* by the British logician and philosopher Stephen Toulmin. Toulmin conceived of argument fields as those specialized discursive groups and forums where argumentation took place, following specific rules, norms, and standards for reasoning, testing claims, and the evaluation of knowledge. Toulmin actually hinted at the notion of argument fields in an earlier work (1950) by alluding to the idea that logical form dictates discursive argument from one discipline to another. Indeed, the notion of "disciplines" provided the chief basis for Toulmin's 1958 metaphorical reference to argument fields. Essentially, Toulmin reasoned that the pursuit of knowledge and its testing and evaluation argumentatively varied from field to field or from discipline to discipline. The legal discipline would receive particular attention from Toulmin and he was clear on the point that what might count as "sound" reasoning in the medical profession, for instance, would not necessarily be deemed so by those in the legal profession. Toulmin felt that different professions and different disciplines were engaged in attempting to solve different problems and that engagement in that problem-solving process varied from one specialty to another.

Toulmin elaborated upon his notion of argument fields in later works and came to view fields more as differing enterprises than differing disciplines, viewing disciplines as a too narrow interpretation of the unique contexts in which arguments take place. Indeed, Toulmin not only felt that arguments occurred in different contexts, but that each context developed its own guidelines for the acceptance of claims and appraisal of reasoning:

The trains of reasoning that it is appropriate to use vary from situation to situation. As we move from the lunch counter to the executive conference table, from the science laboratory to the law courts, the "forum" of discussion changes profoundly. The kind of involvement that the participants have with the outcome of the reasoning is entirely different in the different situations and so also will be the way in which positive outcomes of the argument are tested and judged. (Toulmin, Rieke, & Janik, 1979)

When Toulmin (1972) initially extended his concept of fields as enterprises, he clearly placed emphasis upon the notion that various communities of reasoning and discourse exist.

Many writers have attempted to further interpret Toulmin's meaning of an argument field. One of the best in the way that it simply illustrated and explained Toulmin's position rather than going beyond it was offered by Crable (1976). Crable argued that one argument field is distinct from another primarily because of the type of claims presented and the warrants as reasoning advanced in support of them:

At the point that we as receivers have ascertained the meaning of the claim and decided that it is worthy of our consideration, we should demand that we be presented with reasons to accept the claims that are field-related. We may be told . . . that "You cannot play the piano," and we may discover that our arguer means that "Legally, you cannot play the piano." Our demand that the arguer state the criteria (legally) has done more than simply enhance the clarity of the claim;

in addition ... it has revealed to us the kind of *reason* we should demand in order to accept the claim. (pp. 209–210)

Thus, Toulmin's notion as explained by Crable suggests that arguments are always field-related; that is, the manner by which we test an argument depends upon in which field it is presented or framed. To expect legal reasons for an argument framed as a theological construct would, therefore, be absurd and meaningless.

Virtually every argumentation theorist and scholar who has assessed Toulmin's work would agree that arguments take place in different contexts or fields and that those fields provide specific parameters for the type of reasoning and warrants to be offered by an arguer. That is, however, about as far as consensus regarding argument fields runs. For the last two decades, argumentation scholars have batted different interpretations of fields back and forth in the literature. This disagreement has largely centered around Toulmin's failure to precisely define the boundaries of specific fields, to explain what places one in field A rather than in field B. Ehninger and Brockriede (1963) focused upon defining fields in regard to subject matter. Klump (1981) has provided a dramatic approach to a sociological/psychological view of fields. McKerrow (1990) has defined fields as argument or discourse communities. And Prosise, Miller, and Mills (1996) have recently extended the meaning of fields to account for collectives of power and the arena for discursive struggles, fueled by their application of a critical theory perspective.

The disagreement regarding the exact boundaries of fields has not prevented scholars from applying the concept of fields to specific forums or arenas for argument. In fact, Schuetz (1986) has described the legislative arena of Congress as an argument field. Schuetz argues that political decisions in the Congress are representative of several general functions of argument, particularly the strategic use of language, and that constitutes mail, public hearings, and floor debates serve as differing "overlays" of argument in the legislative arena and that operates independently to some extent, while also producing a broader complex or "web" of arguments. Schuetz concludes her assessment of Congress as an argument field by noting:

To understand the complexity of argumentation in legislative process, observers must separate one species from another. But after separating the species, the observer then should discover how these species are drawn together in a web by the corroboration and congruence between arguments and arguers. (p. 233)

Again, Schuetz is stressing that there are several different overlays or species of argument in the legislative field, yet they are interconnected largely due to the fact that they occur within that particular arena.

Schuetz made several valuable contributions in connection to the examination of discursive behavior in the U.S. Congress. As I shall explain and incorporate into my own discursive assessment later, Schuetz does a particularly good job of identifying language strategies that are unique to the specialized political and legislative arena of the Congress. In addition, Schuetz does an excellent job of extending the use of generic research associated with examination of the discourse and debates that take place in the chambers of Congress. Additionally, Schuetz was the first of the argumentation scholars to attempt to define the Congress as an argument field. Despite these valuable contributions, Schuetz's conceptualization is too limited for the utilization of argument fields envisioned here. She fails to account in any way for the various interpretations of the meanings of argument fields presented by other scholars, nor does she provide her own clear operationalization of the concept as it applies to the Congress. Schuetz also fails to provide explicit criteria for how one should view the chambers of Congress as an argument field. She does, as noted, explain that several different overlays or species of argument are involved in congressional deliberation and that multiple functions of argument occur. Such an explanation does not, however, provide a clear set of elements that must be present in order to define the Congress as a field. And Schuetz's notion of a complex or web of congressional arguments only scratches the surface of a very complicated interconnection and interdependence of different fields all examining the same issue or claim.

My own discussion of the Senate and argument fields begins with the identification of four criteria for the understanding of an argument field. The first is the existence of a community of discourse. This criterion draws upon the works of Wenzel and Kneupper (1981), who view fields as universes of discourse, and McKerrow (1990) who has explained that citizens of the same society, members of the same group, and so on inhabit differently constituted rhetorical communities characterized by "the discourse in which they engage" (p. 29). The second criterion is drawn from Rowland's (1982) view that argument fields are composed of individuals sharing the same purpose. Although Rowland claims that "all defining characteristics of fields can be traced to shared purpose" (p. 228), I think that for that view to be truly useful one must simply limit shared purposes, goals, and responsibilities to the category of one defining characteristic and not the sole essence of fields. Third, I think that Dunbar's (1986) "common sense" standards for fields work well to explain the nature of the more metaphorical concept of argument fields. Both an argument field and a field of crops occupies some ground or covers an expanse, they both have limits or boundaries, they both have particular standards or guidelines for what takes place within them, and certain expectations are associated with both. One could think of the Congress in this light as an argument field. The Congress occupies the ground we refer to as the legislative branch of the federal government. It clearly has boundaries or limits—it cannot legislate policy on intrastate commerce, it cannot debate the behavior of the courts, and so forth. As will be demonstrated in this chapter, Congress has guidelines or procedures that set it apart from other institutions. And the opportunity to function as a forum for the resolution of important public policy issues and to act as an arena for discussion of contemporary political issues are among the most important expectations associated with the Congress. Finally, one can take from Prosise, Miller, and Mills (1996) the view that fields play a role in the process of power distribution. Indeed, as I view talk as power, argument fields are the basic units of power as they provide a site for discursive behavior to reside.

As noted, the Senate would clearly meet Dunbar's (1986) common sense guidelines for a field: It has a shared purpose or many in regard to serving as a national legislative arena, it functions through the exchange of discourse much like other rhetorical communities, and it provides a place or site for the exercise of power. The Senate itself is not, however, the only argument field that impacts the discursive behavior that occurs within the chamber. There are, in fact, multiple layers of fields constantly interconnected and interdependent associated with discourse in the U.S. Senate. There is certainly something of a "supra-field" on a number of levels that help to frame the deliberative discourse of the Senate. There is, as with any public forum, a larger supra-field of "the public," as well as a larger supra-field of "the government." There are several passive sub-fields that operate within the Senate such as committees, sub-committees, and caucuses. The two most significant sub-fields are, however, the two major political parties; the Democratic and Republican sub-fields. Figure 5.1 partially illustrates this distribution of fields and the flow of discourse connected to them. Those layers of argument fields and flows of discourse also work in a circular manner in that the public field produces discourse that also flows directly to the sub-fields of the two political parties.

Figure 5.1
Layers of Argument Fields

> *The Public Field*
> ↕
>   *The Government Field*
>   ↕
>   *The Senate Field*
>   ↕
>   *The Democratic Field*   *The Republican Field*

Note: ↕ = discourse flows

This conceptualization of argument fields associated with the Senate is valuable on several levels. It helps to place the discourse of the Senate in a very clear context for examination. It also provides a clear framework for better understanding the unique discursive behavior associated with the Senate that others have examined. Indeed, Butler (1995) has spoken of "a certain *rhetoric of the Senate by the Senate*" (p. 103) that takes a greater meaning when one recognizes that the Senate can be thought of as an argument field. The notion of fields associated with the Senate also facilitates later analysis of the ethical quality and debate in the chamber and the ability of the Senate to influence behavior far beyond its own confines. It also makes clear that consideration of the general rule that talk is power cannot be productively explored in a vacuum; talk is power is assessed differently based upon differing standards for arguments in different fields. And for more immediate purposes, argument fields help to explain why the Senate should be thought of as an element of the text for this investigation. Just as the use of film instead of the written word changes a text, so too does the selection of an argument field for analysis. It is, however, important to examine the other elements that help to construct that text for analysis.

Chapter 6

The *Congressional Record*

To add to the layering of elements or features for the particular text being developed here, it is important to turn to the *Congressional Record* as a textual database. As noted, the actual debate regarding comprehensive health care reform took place on the floor of the U.S. Senate, and the most appropriate data source available for the examination of that discursive dispute is the *Congressional Record*. Scholars interested in the textual analysis of rhetorical events have long turned to the *Congressional Record* as a primary database. Indeed, textbooks on rhetorical criticism contained explicit and often detailed discussions regarding the *Congressional Record* as a mainstay for cities throughout a period of forty or so years (Auer, 1959; Borman, 1965; Clevenger, Parson, & Polisky, 1968; Thonssen, Baird, & Braden, 1970). Although more recent textbooks on rhetorical criticism have turned to other sorts of texts as mainstays for criticism, the *Congressional Record* remains a vital source for those interested in the process and practice of congressional discourse and debate. To better illustrate that vitality, it is necessary to take a brief look at the historical evolution of the *Congressional Record*, to explore the case that has been raised regarding the usefulness of the *Record* as a textual database, and to fully explicate the value of the *Record* as a textual source for congressional discourse.

HISTORICAL BACKGROUND

Although the *Congressional Record* has been employed as a textual database for the examination of discourse in both chambers of the U.S. Congress by rhetorical scholars for decades, it has not always been available, nor has its use lacked controversy. For a good many years, there was no official recording device for speeches, debates, and other actions in the U.S. Congress. An excellent summary of the history of textual recording of discourse in the U.S. Congress was developed by Thonssen, Baird, and Braden (1970) in their landmark text on rhetorical criticism. It is informative to take a brief look at the historical development of the *Congressional Record* as presented by Thonssen, Baird, and Braden.

Thonssen, Baird, and Braden note that official recording of speeches was not always an institutional feature of the U.S. Congress. Verbatim reporting of speeches was not attempted in the Senate until 1848, and in the House of Representatives until 1850. Prior to that time, reporting of speeches in the U.S. Congress was what Thonssen, Baird, and Braden have called "haphazard and irregular." In fact, until 1802 the Congress often met behind closed doors and no more than a loose journal of the proceedings was maintained. Daily accounts of discourse in the Congress were rare. Two early historians attempted to piece together a volume of addresses that covered the Congress between the years 1789 and 1824. Such work was largely a collection of random journalistic reports and the recollections of previous members of Congress.

Beginning in 1824, a publisher started to release reports of discourse in the Congress at the end of each session in a report called the *Register of Debates*. The *Register* was not really much of an improvement over earlier, more informal reporting efforts. Speeches were often not directly reported or recorded and the general level of textual accuracy was in great doubt. A similar publication, the *Congressional Globe*, began publication in 1833 and continued producing reports for about fifty years. The *Globe* was often in competition with the *Register* and suffered from many of its rival's shortcomings. In fact, Thonssen, Baird, and Braden (1970) argued that both "were often accused of misrepresenting the remarks of the speakers, particularly those in the opposition party" (p. 328).

Although the *Congressional Globe* developed as a semi-official publication of the House and Senate after a period of time, it was not yet an official recording device that would generate an ongoing account of discourse in textual form. In 1873, report Thonssen, Baird, and Braden, the United States officially launched the *Congressional Record*. The *Congressional Record* has thus been available for a period of well over one hundred years as a textual source for the discourse that has occurred in both chambers of the U.S. Congress. It records deliberation daily, is ongoing, and represents one of the best such official publications of legislative activity available. Most scholars readily admit to the technical proficiency of the *Congressional Record*, but many have raised questions regarding its value as a textual database.

THE CASE AGAINST THE *CONGRESSIONAL RECORD*

Despite the allure of a text that purports to provide an account of some of the most significant public policy discourse available, a number of critics have suggested that the issue of textual accuracy must be more closely examined before embracing the *Congressional Record* as the chief source for analysis of rhetorical practice by Representatives and Senators. Over half a century ago, Robinson (1942) developed a very detailed examination of the textual accuracy of the *Congressional Record*. Robinson laid out factors that worked in favor of accuracy as well as factors that tended to work against the accuracy of the *Congressional Record*. I will return to his discussion of factors favoring accuracy later, but first it is worthwhile to summarize those features that he saw as limitations to the value of the *Congressional Record*. Robinson felt that there were five factors mitigating against the textual accuracy of the *Congressional Record*. He first noted that there is always a possibility for error in the transcription of any textual document. The practice of editing employed by reporters, Robinson noted, extended well beyond simple corrections of grammar and syntax to include efforts designed "to improve the style of the speeches" (p. 11). His most striking concern revolved around the ability that members of Congress possessed to revise remarks. Robinson identified this ability to revise remarks as "the greatest single factor contributing to the discrepancy between speeches as spoken and the same speeches as they appear in the *Record*" (p. 12). Robinson also argued that the ability of members of Congress to expunge remarks that may be viewed as offensive by others and to insert materials unspoken on the floor into the "Extension of Remarks" section further limited the utility of the *Congressional Record* as a textual database.

Some other critics of the *Congressional Record* went beyond the balanced approach taken by Robinson and found the *Record* lacking for several reasons. Hendrix (1965), for example, displayed great distrust of the *Congressional Record* suggesting that it was "a source of dubious value for evaluation of the intrinsic factors of inversion, disposition, and style" (p. 153). The *Congressional Record* should not be accepted on a wholesale basis by rhetorical critics. Hendrix maintained an overall distrust of textual accuracy within the *Congressional Record*, but as will be indicated later, he did provide a means for "testing" the textual value of the *Record* and that method tends to support the value of the *Record* as a textual source.

In a manner akin to that employed by Robinson, Reid (1940) also identified specific features that he felt worked against the textual accuracy of the *Congressional Record*. First, Reid suggested that a resistance to verbatim reporting of speeches on the part of legislators served to limit the textual utility of the *Congressional Record*. Reid also felt that the ability to revise remarks contributed to excessive corrections, deletions, and revisions. Reid felt that the ability to revise remarks made by members of Congress produced what "is the strong, almost instinctive desire of speakers to make their speeches read as well as possible" (p. 40). Finally, Reid suggested that there were "mechanical possibilities for error" associated with the use of dictation and shorthand recording on the part of reporters.

The harshest of all criticism launched against the *Congressional Record* arose not from rhetorical scholars at all. Rather, it emerged as an outgrowth of consumer advocate Ralph Nader's Congress Project. Green, Fallows, and Zwick (1972) produced the book *Who Runs Congress?*, which included an assault against the *Congressional Record*. Among other specific charges, Green and his colleagues suggested that the *Congressional Record* often served primarily as a "Xeroxing service" for members of Congress to campaign with their printing privileges and produce enormous political benefit for incumbents. Green, Fallows, and Zwick also painted the "Extension of Remarks" portion of the *Congressional Record* as little more than a repository for anecdotes about barbers, baseball players, and other "hometown celebrities."

Green and his colleagues also leveled serious charges against the value of the *Congressional Record* as a textual source. They charged that the document was replete with inaccuracies. They offered this critique regarding the *Congressional Record*:

In purely technical terms, the *Record* is an impressive operation. . . . But while the production of the *Record* may be impressive, its content is not. The *Record* is a subsidiary Xeroxing service for congressmen, producing by the thousands whatever item they choose. The back section of the *Record*—often half or two-thirds of its bulk—is made up of various insertions: articles from *Reader's Digest*, speeches boosting some favored constituent, clever items from the home-town paper which have caught the member's eye. (p. 183)

Green, Fallows, and Zwick have gone on to say, "Even the parts of the *Record* which appear to be chronicles of the day's debate are far from accurate" (p. 184). They back this further claim with accounts offered by congressional aides who suggest that members of Congress "are content to make a garbled statement so long as they later make the *Record* precise" (p. 184).

Robinson, Reid, and the Nader critics were not alone in challenging the textual accuracy of the *Congressional Record*. For example, Stevens (1964) has offered specific illustrations of inaccuracies and errors in the reporting of speeches in the *Congressional Record*. Other rhetorical scholars have raised similar concerns (McPherson, 1942, 1944; Cain, 1962). Despite what might appear to be a plethora of criticism, however, a very strong case can be made in favor of using the *Congressional Record* as a textual database.

THE CASE FOR THE *CONGRESSIONAL RECORD*

A large body of evidence suggests that the *Congressional Record* is a reliable database for those who wish to examine the discourse that takes place in the U.S. Congress. Robinson (1942), for example, has outlined a series of factors that work in favor of the textual accuracy of the *Congressional Record*. Robinson suggests that an effective and efficient reporting system is employed by the *Congressional Record*. Robinson also notes that there is a right of members to correct errors that might occur in the transcription process. Robinson further contends that multiple checks for accuracy exist within the recording system used by the *Congressional Record* and that a prohibition against striking "words spoken in order" precludes the wholesale exclusion of unpopular remarks. Robinson did, as noted, identify some factors that also work to mitigate against textual accuracy, but generally supported use of the *Congressional Record* as a database.

Earl Cain had raised similar concerns regarding textual accuracy of the *Congressional Record*, but concluded from his extensive research that revision and editing did not represent a serious threat to accuracy. In fact, he employed a comparative method of analysis and reported in 1954:

The speeches appearing in the *Congressional Record* are closer to reality than the editing privilege might imply. A comparison of speeches in the *Record* with reasonably complete day by day reports of the neutrality debates in the *New York Times* showed clearly that in spite of some editing, the basic argument, evidence, and appeals remained the same in the two sources. The order of the speeches and, in many cases, the exact words of the speech were identical. (p. 93)

Hendrix (1965) employed a similar process of comparative analysis of a particular collection of speeches and found a high degree of accuracy with regard to content and structure of the addresses. Thus, despite his overall concerns concerning accuracy, Hendrix's application of his comparative method of "testing" a database revealed the *Congressional Record* to be a valuable source of speech content material.

Most political scholars contend that the *Congressional Record* serves an important practical and symbolic function in the context of American democracy. One U.S. Senator, Robert C. Byrd (1982) of West Virginia, has spoken very highly of the *Congressional Record*: "The *Congressional Record* is a vital instrument of the legislative process without which our work would be nearly impossible" (p. 75). Byrd has outlined three arguments to bolster his claim. He argued that the *Congressional Record* is used to follow the movement of legislation from the introduction of a bill to its passage or defeat. He also argues that the *Congressional Record* provides a "complete account" of floor debates that members might have missed in order to attend to other business. Byrd further argued that the *Congressional Record* provides a rather detailed legislative history of laws that are passed, which is often employed by judicial officers who must interpret such legislative mandates. Byrd has concluded that "The *Congressional Record* is a symbol of our democracy through which the people may fully observe the making of their laws and may hold their lawmakers accountable for their words and deeds" (p. 75).

Although the many critics of the *Congressional Record* would not endorse it as warmly as Senator Byrd, many of them have been forced to acknowledge that it provides one of the best sources of its type available. Indeed, one of Robinson's (1942) principal conclusions was that "in comparison with the official records of the British Parliament and the American Congress a hundred and a hundred and fifty years ago, the *Congressional Record* is accurate and complete to a high degree" (p. 10). Even Green and his fellow harsh critics (1972) have been compelled to acknowledge the unique value associated with the *Congressional Record*:

The *Congressional Record* is printed daily while Congress is in session and purports to be a transcript of speeches and proceedings on the floor of the House and Senate. Despite the fact that many members hurriedly revise their speeches just before the *Record* goes to the printer, it is the most useful source of congressional activity. (p. 254)

Critics today would also have to agree that as a source of materials concerning the debates on the floor of the U.S. Congress, the *Congressional Record* is superior to any alternative database and, as will be noted, it is especially useful to the argumentation critic who seeks to examine the overall development and deliberation of a debate.

Perhaps the clearest endorsement of the *Congressional Record* as a textual database was developed by David Quadro (1977). Quadro offered an extensive review of literature on the subject of accuracy in the reports of the *Congressional Record*. He also pointed to a trend in the area of rhetorical criticism by scholars to utilize the *Congressional Record* as a textural database. Quadro reported that "practice in the field" confirmed the claim that the *Congressional Record* represents a valuable textual source for the examination of speeches in the U.S. Congress. He noted that dozens of doctoral dissertations, for example, had employed the *Congressional Record* in their attempts to provide insight into the rhetorical activity in the U.S. Congress. My own recent informal review of "practice in the field" confirms that a good many graduate students of rhetoric have turned to the *Congressional Record* as a database. In addition, both Kane (1995) and Murphy (1995) freely employ materials taken from the *Congressional Record* to build their cases regarding the role of argumentation in the Senate.

Quadro also provided a more "empirical" basis to support his belief in the textual accuracy and value of the *Congressional Record*. Quadro surveyed several members of the U.S. Congress and he asked them to verify information reported in the *Congressional Record*. The findings of his survey confirmed that the *Congressional Record* was largely accurate. In fact, Quadro offered this conclusion after conducting his review and research: "The evidence supports the claim that . . . in the main the *Congressional Record* is sufficiently accurate in matters of substance to allow full and complete rhetorical analysis and criticism of the invention and deposition processes" (p. 258). He further concluded that "rhetorical examination of congressional speeches can be pursued with reasonable confidence that the texts reflect the content and structure of the presentations" (p. 258).

Argumentation critics who examine the overall deliberation that takes place in a floor debate, such as the August 1994 debate regarding comprehensive health care reform, can feel particularly confident about their use of the *Congressional Record* as a textual database. As I have done for my investigation of the 1994 floor debate, excluding materials drawn from the "Extension of Remarks" section permits researchers to more closely associate data with the actual floor debate. A focus on the *meaning* of the arguments that are developed and not on the *style* of individual speakers also works to the advantage of the argumentation critic. Stylistic features may come into play at some level, but the overall practice of discourse employed to build a particular case—for or against comprehensive health care reform in this instance—is not heavily dependent upon examination of whether an individual speaker was a flowery or eloquent orator. There should be no mistake: Individual discursive features are quite important, as I will outline in the next chapter. Examination of those features need not, however, focus on how a term might seem to *sound*, but more on what it *means* and why the particular expression was selected.

In conclusion, I will briefly recount—in a manner similar to both Robinson and Reid—several specific features that help to build a strong case for use of the *Congressional Record* as a textual database. First, as Robinson has noted so well, there are specific technical and reporting factors that contribute to the accuracy of materials in the *Congressional Record*. Second, the *Congressional Record* serves an important symbolic and political function for contemporary American democracy as Senator Byrd has so well explained. Third, Cain (1954) and Hendrix (1965) have demonstrated that the value of the *Congressional Record* is easily confirmed when put through comparative "testing" against other sources. Fourth, even the harshest of critics acknowledge that the *Congressional Record* is a uniquely valued source of information for the very specialized discursive behavior that it reports. A fifth factor working in favor of the *Congressional Record* is its rich history of being employed on a widespread basis by scholars in the field of rhetorical criticism and argumentation. Quadro's (1977) investigation has been challenged based on its acknowledged limited rate of response to questionnaire items, but as the sole significant investigation of its type, it does provide a level of "empirical" support as a sixth factor working in favor of the *Congressional Record*. The seventh, and final, factor regarding militating in favor of the use of the *Congressional Record* rests upon the fact that those examining debates and overall argument development can feel comfortable looking to it for materials. Overall, the case for utilization of the *Congressional Record* as a textual database easily outweighs those factors mitigating against its utility and further suggests that it is a very vital component to the development of a larger text, as proposed here.

Chapter 7

Textual Features

A final layer must be added to the "text" of the 1994 comprehensive health care reform debate on the floor of the Senate. Just as rhetorical scholars and conversation analysts sometimes focus upon specific elements of a larger text, some focus here needs to be placed upon specific textual features of the discourse that helped to shape the overall debate. Let me make it clear, however, that such specific discursive features represent only one component of the larger text and they do not provide the only means for examination of the Senate floor debate. Indeed, as I examine the discourse of that debate in Part III of this work, the bulk of my focus will be upon the overall rhetorical and argumentative nature of the debate. A focus upon certain specific discursive features does, however, provide a richness of depth and detail that is helpful in illuminating just how talk is power in this dramatic case.

Although it would be possible to examine dozens of specific discursive features relevant to any argumentative activity, this investigation will focus upon five such features: (1) the development of "crisis" discourse, (2) the use of particular categories of evidence, (3) narratives, (4) a set of items that fall under the rubric of what Schuetz (1986) labels "language strategies," and (5) "medical metaphors." Selection of these particular features is warranted by both the individual value of each, as I shall explain, and by the scholarly indications that such features play a pivotal role in public policy discourse. Information regarding each of these discursive features and a method of investigation for each is developed in turn. In addition, I also report more formal analysis associated with examinations of those discursive features. The *Congressional Record* printed more than 450 pages of debate regarding Senator Mitchell's proposal for comprehensive health care reform, the "Health Security Act," in August of 1994. All speeches printed under the heading of the "Health Security Act" were included for analysis in this project. All of the speeches in this floor debate were coded for the five categories of discourse features. Each of these five broad categories of discourse features was divided into component parts for coding. The crisis discourse category included coding for use of the term "crisis" and the context given for construction of that usage. Evidence was coded as simple numerical instances, complex numerical instances, opinion-centered testimony, source-center testimony, and specific historical instances. Narratives were divided into three different types for coding: personal narratives, other-person narratives, and social narratives. Language strategies were coded for use of naming, blame, and categorizing. Medical metaphors were coded for the specific type of medical relationship made. Silverman (1994) has suggested that the "counting" of data can be helpful and informative by clearly laying out the number of data occurrences, identifying patterns and trends, and providing easy reference for later interpretation. I will now discuss and tabulate each of the five specific discourse features.

CRISIS DISCOURSE

Kasper, Mulley, and Wennberg (1992) noted, "The phrase *health care crisis* has become a major part of national rhetoric" (p. 183). Such an observation should not surprise given the power that scholars have attributed to language generally, and to specific expressions particularly. In his highly touted rhetorical analysis, Richard Weaver (1953) wrote eloquently of the social and cultural power that can be attached to what he termed "god/devil" terms. Such words could evoke nearly immediate positive or negative reactions, respectively, on the part of a listener. Further, Edelman (1965) has suggested that words often operate in a similar manner when used as political language. He contends that many words are used by politicians to spark particular connotative interpretations by listeners. The word *crisis* may be one term reflective of these perspectives and the present investigation will examine the use of such crisis discourse. In addition, as Weaver, Edelman, and the present work shall indicate, a term such as *crisis* can play a particularly important role in the overall development of talk as power.

It is possible to chart specific methods of investigating the crisis discourse employed in August 1994 during the U.S. Senate floor debate on comprehensive health care reform. The first simple step will be to identify how often the term "crisis" is used to refer to the issue of health care. Second, and more important, the nature of the development or context of crisis can be explicated in each case of usage. In the first speech during the debate in the Senate on comprehensive health care reform, Senator Mitchell, for instance, used the term "crisis" several times but in each case it followed an illustration of problems with the existing health care system. The present investigation will examine the process of crisis construction in each of the speeches presented during the 1994 debate by identifying how a "crisis" is developed, whether through specific illustration of a situation or direct statement of the crisis.

The first step in coding this specific discourse feature was to simply tabulate the number of times the term "crisis" was used during the August 1994 floor debate. Eighteen speakers used the term "crisis" a total of forty-two times for a mean (average) usage rate of the term at 2.33 per speaker. The context for the construction of a "crisis" was coded for each usage by all speakers. A total of twelve simple construction categories could be established for use of the term crisis throughout the Senate floor debate, as summarized in Table 7.1. The most frequent usage was in regard to the construction of a general health care crisis, with thirteen instances following that approach. Most other instances of usage also related to the overall construction of a health care crisis in some regard, such as coverage and access limitations (six instances) and personal health care crisis situations (four instances). There were two instances of usage of the term "crisis" regarding natural disasters (earthquakes, floods, and so forth) to demonstrate a comparison and contrast to alternative "crisis" scenarios. The term "crisis" was only used once to explicitly denote the risk of a crisis of "big government." I will return to a discussion of the role that use of term "crisis" played in the Senate floor debate as I examine all of this discursive features in Chapter Eight. Presently, though, it is important to turn to a discussion and tabulation of evidence as a specific discursive feature.

Table 7.1
Construction of Crisis

Construction Context	Number of Instances
General Health Care Crisis	13
Coverage/Access Crisis	6
Affordability/Price Crisis	4
Personal Health Care Crisis	4
Reference to Use of "Health Care Crisis"	3
Insurance Crisis	2
Crisis for Older Adults	2
Health Crisis in Rural America	2
Medical Malpractice Crisis	2
Natural Crises	2
Crisis of "Big Government"	1
Total	42

EVIDENCE

Most debate scholars and argumentation theorists agree that some form of supporting material or evidence is important to the process and outcome of debate. Evidence is often discussed with regard to specific forms that are used by advocates during debates—facts, testimony, statistics, examples, and so on. Although there is no general agreement on a definition of evidence in the communication discipline, McCroskey's (1969) operational definition is fairly typical. McCroskey suggests that evidence may be defined as "factual statements originating from a source other than the speaker, objects not created by the speaker, and opinions of persons other than the speaker which are offered in support of the speaker's claims" (p. 191).

Despite the fact that McCroskey's operational definition of evidence has been employed by many communication scholars, there is no universal agreement on the meaning of evidence. Indeed, ever since a special issue of the *Western Speech Communication Journal* in 1977 asked the question "What counts as evidence?" disagreement and discussion have been pervasive. Many argue that only those materials produced through quantitative and scientific methods can function as evidence. Others have argued that such things as personal experience might also count as evidence. There is clearly no consensus on the subject.

The situation with regard to political discourse is similar to that in the broader communication discipline. Some valuable and informative operational definitions have, however, been developed to examine political discussion. A typology of evidence was recently developed by Levasseur and Dean (1996) for their investigation of evidence usage during the past several presidential debates. That typology includes five specific forms of evidence: simple numerical instances, complex numerical instances, opinion-centered testimony, source-centered testimony, and specific historical instance. This typology appears to capture much of what counts for evidence in regard to political discourse. A brief explication of the five forms is thus in order.

Levasseur and Dean define simple numerical instances as "units of factual evidence which contain a numerical value which represents a concrete quantity" (p. 133). Such evidence would include units such as "100,000 uninsured" or a "$30 billion." This contrasts with complex numerical instances. Complex numerical instances involve figures based upon calculations, such as "19 percent of GNP" or "one-third of coverage."

Opinion-centered testimony is related to evidence that is derived from a source that makes an opinionated statement. Such opinion-centered testimony would include items such as, "The American Medical Association calls this reform proposal a multi–billion dollar loss of quality." Source-centered testimony is essentially a way to code evidence that offers some documentation as to a specific factual unit. One might identify a statement such as, "The *New York Times* has reported significant numbers of underinsured workers" as source-asserted testimony due to the use of a specific citation. Specific historical instance is used to refer to nonnumerical concrete actions or occurrences. This category includes such items as "The Senate passed the Social Security Act many decades ago based upon similar social conditions."

The present investigation will employ the typology developed by Levasseur and Dean. It was specifically developed for the examination of evidence in political campaign debates, but there is no reason that such types or categories of evidence would not also operate in floor debates in the U.S. Senate. Each individual address in the August 1994 U.S. Senate debate on comprehensive health care reform will be coded for the five types of evidence and overall usage will be tabulated.

A total of 1,850 instances of the usage of some form of evidence, as coded in this project, were tabulated from the Senate floor debate on comprehensive health care reform. Nearly two-thirds of that evidence usage (1,202) was numerical in some regard. There were 673 usages of simple numerical instances, closely followed by 529 situations where complex numerical instances were used. The use of opinion-centered testimony occurred a total of 75 times. Source-centered testimony was employed, on the other hand, a total of 379 times. Specific historical instances functioned as evidence in the Senate floor debate a total of 194 times. Evidence usage is summarized in Table 7.2. Next, I will discuss the role of narratives as a specialized form of discourse use during the Senate floor debate.

Table 7.2
Evidence Usage

Type of Evidence	Instances of Usage
Simple Numerical Instances	673
Complex Numerical Instances	529
Opinion-Centered Testimony	75
Source-Centered Testimony	379
Specific Historical Instance	194
Total	1,850

NARRATIVES

Narratives represent significant discursive behavior. Many authorities feel that most people explain ideas through stories and respond to and understand the stories of others. Walter Fisher (1987) has suggested that reasoning and discourse through stories can be regarded as a narrative paradigm of communication. Fisher (1987) offered a detailed summary of his perspective:

(1) Humans are storytellers. (2) The paradigmatic mode of human decision making and communication is "good reasons," which vary in form among situations, genres, and media of communication. (3) The production and practice of good reasons are ruled by matters of history, biography, culture, and character. . . . (4) Rationality is determined by the nature of persons as narrative relays—their inherent awareness of narrative probability, what constitutes a coherent story, and consistent habit of testing narrative fidelity, whether or not the stories they experience ring true with the stories they know to be true in their lives. . . . (5) The world as we know it is a set of stories that must be chosen among in order for us to live life in a process of continual re-creation. (p. 5)

People are thus storytellers who evaluate the good reasons offered in the competing stories of others.

Narrative, as a specific discursive feature, is particularly appealing with regard to argumentative discourse in a political context. Fisher's (1984) original treatment of the subject of narrative focused on public moral argument in regard to nuclear weapons. Fisher and others have extended this focus on narrative in argumentative discourse. In fact, Hollihan and Baaske (1994) have advocated the use of a narrative paradigm to frame discussion of all argumentative contexts, including political argument. Further, Toolan (1991) has shown that narratives and politics are inherently intermingled; narratives often display political or ideological preferences and narratives are often used to stimulate or motivate political action. Corcoran (1990) has provided a survey of theoretical perspectives for analyzing language and politics and has concluded that a narrative view is the best for examination of political discourse. More recently, Roe (1994) has argued that narrative may be employed as a device for the analysis of policy issues. Griffin (1994) has connected narrative to the construction of crisis rhetoric, which is particularly important to the rhetorical analysis that comes later. Griffin claims that crisis situations are best cast as narratives because "narrative form is well suited to resolve the informational, structural, and moral ambiguities of crisis situations" (p. 137). Given the connection of the discursive feature of narrative to political argumentation, it would seem appropriate to examine the narratives employed by members of the U.S. Senate in the August 1994 floor debate on comprehensive health care reform.

The present investigation will identify and examine the narratives that were employed by U.S. Senators during the August 1994 floor debate on comprehensive health care reform. In order to do so, it is necessary to provide some categories for the sorting and analysis of the various narratives that were presented. The first category is simply "personal narratives." This category includes all narratives defined from the personal experience of the speakers. If a member of the Senate were to say, "I never needed a government handout for medical care" and then offered an explanation of one adverse situation she endured, that would be a personal narrative. The second category is "other-person narratives." These are simply narratives that recount the experience of another individual. If a Senator explains how an unemployed auto worker in his state has suffered due to a lack of health insurance, that would be categorized as an "other-person narrative." One other category for this investigation would be "social narratives." Social narratives deal with social circumstances for many people, not a single individual. A Senator's explication of the treatment of homeless families without insurance would be an example of a social narrative. These three categories capture the most common narratives employed in the comprehensive health care reform debate.

The use of narratives in the Senate floor debate regarding comprehensive health care reform and the Mitchell proposal was coded according to the simple typology explained above, which can be recognized on an intuitive basis by the reader and further guided by the illustrations developed in the preceding discussion. The 253 narratives coded, using this typology, are summarized briefly in Table 7.3. Personal narratives accounted for the smallest category of usage, with a total of 55 such narratives recorded. By contrast, other-person narratives comprised the largest category according to the typology developed here, with 111 instances of their use. A total of 87 social narratives was also uncovered during study of the debate on the Health Security Act. Language strategies will now be discussed.

Table 7.3
Narrative Usage

Type of Narrative	Instances of Usage
Personal Narratives	55
Other-Person Narratives	111
Social Narratives	87
Total	253

LANGUAGE STRATEGIES

One broad category of discursive features will be examined in the present investigation. That is a category of discourse that Schuetz (1986) calls "language strategies." In a broad sense, all of the specific features thus far discussed—crisis discourse, evidence, and narratives—are language strategies, and the central role of language in political argumentation has been clearly established. However, Schuetz has identified three unique linguistic forms used by political arguers. These include naming, categorizing, and attributing blame. Some explication of these three forms is necessary.

Naming is a process of making some application of a label to a problem. Schuetz explains: "Political arguers name problems so that audiences perceive them as timely, distinctive, and important or as untimely, irrelevant, and unimportant" (p. 225). This might involve referring to a situation as a "new problem" or a "national concern." Such naming illustrates the process discussed by Schuetz. Categorizing simply places problems into distinct classes, such as social and institutional problems. Schuetz suggests that such categorizing is used to simplify complex problems. Attributing blame means that an arguer attempts to place blame for a problem on a particular party or group. One might claim, for instance, that the insurance industry is to blame for a crisis in the financing of health care services.

The three specific language strategies identified by Schuetz are clearly useful in an investigation of discourse that involves a problem situation. Problems are named. They are placed into categories, and blame for them is attached. The present investigation will further code discourse in the August 1994 health care reform debate in the U.S. Senate to identify usage of these three specific language strategies. This should help illuminate the most salient issues of controversy in the debate on comprehensive health care reform and to further demonstrate the inherent power of talk.

Use of the three language strategies as developed by Schuetz (1986) was also coded for the comprehensive health care reform floor debate in August of 1994. The naming strategy was employed a total of 240 times. There were 244 instances of the blame strategy used by Senators during the floor debate. The categorizing strategy was employed much less frequently by Senators. It was used on only 65 occasions. These totals are summarized in Table 7.4.

Table 7.4
Usage of Language Strategies

Language Strategy	Number of Instances of Usage
Naming	290
Blaming	244
Categorizing	65
Total	599

MEDICAL METAPHORS

Ever since Aristotle discussed metaphor as analogy, communication scholars have been keenly interested in this particular discursive feature. Rhetorical scholars such as I. A. Richards (1936) and Kenneth Burke (1952) have attested to the power of metaphor. More recently, Jorgensen-Earp and Staton (1993) have reported: "Metaphor analysis has a rich history in the field of communication studies, whether those studies are in rhetoric and public address, organizational communication, or relational communication" (p. 125). An examination of political discourse also warrants consideration of metaphor because Johnson (1981) and others have argued that metaphor is central to how language operates and also carries epistemological implications. Osborn (1967) was one of the rhetorical scholars to develop the notion that metaphor is not merely a linguistic device, but also a psychological and philosophical one.

Lakoff and Johnson's (1980) simple definition makes it clear how metaphorical discourse works: "The essence of metaphor is understanding and experiencing one kind of thing in terms of another" (p. 5). In other words, a metaphor asserts that $A = B$, when A and B are essentially different. The notion of understanding is also very important in recognizing the value of metaphor. Lakoff and Johnson (1980), for example, have noted that the human conceptual system is highly metaphorical. Indeed, Taylor (1984) contends that this relationship is so important that metaphor may be viewed as "an ubiquitous feature of our thinking" (p. 5). Deshler (1985) has further argued that as part of our conceptual process, metaphor functions in a "sense-making" manner, helping us to understand and interpret the world around us. Lakoff and Johnson (1980) have concluded that both the way we think and the way we act are guided by our conceptual system's metaphorical nature.

Metaphor and metaphorical expressions are replete in discourse, both ordinary and specialized. In fact, Goodman (1968) has argued that metaphor so permeates discourse that it is difficult to identify a phrase or statement that is not metaphorical. Given the pervasive nature of metaphor in discourse, it is essential to narrow or focus the type of metaphor to be examined in this investigation. Lakoff and Johnson (1980) have suggested that specific metaphors may be examined in relation to the larger conceptual metaphor that they represent. They explain, for example, that the conceptual metaphor *The mind is a brittle object* is present in such common expressions as "Her ego is very *fragile*," "He *broke* under cross-examination," and "She is *easily crushed*" (p. 28). Thus, it would be possible to identify a broad conceptual metaphor relevant to the health care debate and examine all of the specific metaphors that fall under that rubric.

The last category of this portion of the investigation will examine "medical metaphors" employed in the floor debate on health care reform. Broadly, a medical metaphor is one that asserts a relationship between the health care and health care reform issue and items drawn from the medical field, such as *health care reform is like medicine and medical practice*. Specific metaphors related to this broad conceptualization would include such statements as "American health care is a terminal patient," "This proposal will cut the heart out of the best health care system on Earth," and "The heavy doses of taxes doom this prescription for reform." All such medical metaphors employed in the August 1994 floor debate will be examined.

The conceptual metaphor of health care reform and medicine and all of the specific metaphors fitting under that rubric were coded for the Senate floor debate. There was a total of thirty-three explicit medical metaphors employed in the comprehensive reform debate. Those medical metaphors can be further sorted into five sub-categories. There was a total of thirteen medical metaphors that related to treatment or prescription. Six medical metaphors related to diagnosis and ills. Five

Table 7.5
Medical Metaphors

Medical Metaphors	Instances of Usage
Prescription/Treatment	13
Diagnosis/Ills	6
Physician/Patient	5
Miscellaneous	5
Process/Procedure	4
Total	33

such metaphors were linked to physicians and patients, while another five fit into a miscellaneous category. There were also four medical metaphors that concerned medical process or procedure. All of these medical metaphors are summarized in Table 7.5. As I turn to Part Three of this work, the specific discursive features discussed and tabulated here will be the first component of the Senate floor debate on comprehensive health care reform to receive attention and begin to further reveal the power of talk as displayed in this specific case.

Part III

The Discourse

Chapter 8

Discourse Patterns

The U.S. Senate is no exception to the general rule that talk is power, particularly in political deliberation and decision making. The rich history of rhetorical studies and other communication scholarship concerning the Senate certainly tends to confirm that view. The interpretation of the results of the present enterprise should also go a long way toward confirmation of the central role of a host of discursive features in the practice of political debate, in this case, the August 1994 Senate floor debate on Majority Leader Mitchell's Health Security Act proposal to assure comprehensive health care reform. In fact, many of the Senators who took part in the August 1994 floor debate made explicit reference to the "discourse" that was being used, the "language" that shaped the debate, and the tendency by some to use "semantics" for their own purposes and ends. It is, initially, wise to examine the results regarding each specific discourse feature: crisis discourse, evidence, narratives, language strategies, and medical metaphors. However, in addition to examining the general role of each of these specific discourse features, it is also important to note that in each case there was a distinctly different utilization of these features by advocates or proponents of reform and opponents of reform. Those speaking in favor of the Mitchell proposal tended to employ a very narrow, present-oriented approach to discourse. Those advocating reform spoke narrowly of the consequences, primarily to individuals, of inadequate health care. They tended to describe the nature of what they perceived to be an existing problem. Opponents of the Mitchell proposal employed a discourse that was broader and more future-oriented in nature. The opponents of the Mitchell proposal broadened their discourse beyond health care to point to the role of the government in general, and to construct a negative impact on the larger economy due to the governmental expansion that they saw as inherent in the Mitchell proposal. Each of the specific discursive features will be examined in this light.

CRISIS DISCOURSE
   It should not surprise us that a term such as "crisis" would be employed in a heated debate regarding an issue as widely disputed as comprehensive health care reform. Most standard dictionaries defines the word "crisis" as an unusually critical moment in time or as a period that entails existing or potential disaster. Such meanings would naturally seem to be powerful forces as discursive features in a political dispute or debate. Edelman (1965) has suggested that when such powerful meanings become widely acknowledged and familiar, they can have great political import. He notes, "A word or phrase which has become established as connoting threat or reassurance for a group thus can become a cue for the release of energy 'out of all proportion to the apparent triviality of meaning suggested by its mere form' " (p. 116). Given the potential connotative and emotive weight of a term such as "crisis" it is actually surprising that it was not employed much more frequently during the 1994 Senate health care reform debate. (The limited explicit use of the term "crisis" during the comprehensive health care reform debate in the Senate is further examined as part of the overall rhetorical analysis of crisis rhetoric in Chapter Nine.)
   Of the forty-two times that the term "crisis" was explicitly employed as a part of the discourse that shaped the August 1994 floor debate, the vast majority of these uses related to the establishment or description of a "health care crisis." In fact, the largest single context for usage of the term "crisis" (thirteen times) was in regard to a general "health care crisis." A few examples are illustrative of the point. Senate Majority Leader Mitchell invoked the notion of a "health care crisis" several times during his August 9 statement that introduced his Health Security Act as a means to establish comprehensive health care throughout the United States. For example, Mitchell stated, "There is a crisis in American health care. It is a crisis of affordability and more. It has to change" (S11006). The bulk of the other times that the term "crisis" was employed was also in some way related to the health care crisis. In fact, twenty-two other cases of use of the term "crisis" related to some health or medical matter (six for coverage and access, four for affordability and price, four for some personal health care crisis, and two each for a medical crisis for older adults, a health care crisis in rural America, a medical malpractice crisis, and an insurance crisis). As previously noted, a great many advocates of health care reform characterized the nature of health care in the early 1990s as being in a state of crisis.
   Advocates of comprehensive health care reform, like Senator Mitchell and many of his supporters, probably recognized—at least implicitly—one power of a term like "crisis." Use of the word "crisis" does not merely tell a listener that something is a problem or that something is fairly serious. Use of the term tells listeners that a situation is worthy of alteration and action, that it is a threat, and that it warrants a prominent place on the political agenda due to its critical nature. One must assume that those powerful connotations were the type of response that advocates of comprehensive health care reform were seeking to evoke when they invoked the term "crisis." Further, as Kasper, Mulley, and Wennberg (1992) reported, the phrase "health care crisis" had become a common feature of national discourse. It is not surprising that Senate advocates of comprehensive health care reform would latch onto

a phrase that has potentially powerful connotative effects, but also one that has become a common feature of discourse for those who share interest in their cause.

Senate opponents of comprehensive health care reform used the term "crisis" on three occasions as a point of reference to the claims made by the other side, those advocating legislation that would address the "health care crisis." The statement of Senator Hatch is illustrative: "I personally pay tribute to Mrs. Clinton in the efforts she has put forward in trying to come up with something that would help solve what many think is a health care crisis in our country" (S11834). Unlike advocates of reform, Hatch and other opponents felt that the health care crisis was only a perception or viewpoint held by some Senators. Indeed, advocates of reform seemed to have a clearly defined set of features which comprise the crisis—limits to access, accompanied by personal tragedies induced by the cost of the present system. Of course, Hatch, like the others who used such referential notations of a "health care crisis," did so only to help make a point for their case against comprehensive reform legislation. In fact, Hatch continued his statement by adding this after the reference to a "health care crisis" and potential solutions: "One of the problems, of course, is who is going to pay for all this?" (S11834). Thus, when the opponents of health care reform legislation employ the term "crisis" or the phrase "health care crisis," their goal was to discursively establish a point for clash or refutation.

Opponents of Senator Mitchell's proposal for comprehensive health care reform only invoked the explicit notion of a "crisis" once in regard to the role that government might play under such a reform proposal. In that instance, the term "crisis" was applied to the problems of big government that had recently plagued many nations of Western Europe that experimented with various forms of socialized medicine and other welfare state programs, such as heavy tax burdens, regulatory control, and diminished economic productivity. A casual observer might ask why opponents of the Mitchell proposal did not explicitly paint it as a path to a "crisis" of big government. Indeed, as the rhetorical analysis that follows demonstrates, opponents of comprehensive health care reform relied most heavily upon the rhetorical construction of a "crisis" of big government as a potential consequence of passing the Health Security Act. The preference for rhetorical construction of such a crisis, as opposed to explicitly labeling of the risk in that way, it will be argued, is due to the power of that rhetorical process.

It is worthy of note that many of those engaged in the August 1994 floor debate regarding comprehensive health care reform acknowledged the importance that an individual word might have. Senator Helms was one of many Republican foes of the Mitchell proposal who pointed to a specific word count made by Congressional staffers: "I would just like to mention that the Clinton-Mitchell bill contains the word "shall" 2,618 times. . . . [T]hat means there are 2,618 times when the government tells doctors, hospitals, businesses, states, and patients what to do" (S12166). This is proof that those Senators recognized that an individual term such as "shall" might be of importance and could carry discursive weight. It would seem fair to conclude that proponents of reform had a similar feeling about the term "crisis."

The examples utilized in the general discussion of crisis discourse point to the discursive behavior of both proponents and opponents of Senator Mitchell's Health

Security Act. Those who were advocating reform focused their discursive behavior almost exclusively on the narrow realm of health care, as in the description of a "health care crisis." Another example from Senator Mitchell is illustrative: "There is a crisis in American health care. It is a crisis of affordability and access to care. It must change" (S11007). Senator Mitchell and other proponents of reform simply said, "Here is a problem with health care, and we ought to do something about it." This was a discourse narrowly focused around a single issue and one that was not employed to "impact" the issue on a broader scale. Advocates of reform established the parameters of their advocacy squarely around health care, the "crisis" and its specific causes and consequences—restricted access and high costs resulting in individual tragedies. Further, they suggested that this current state of affairs meant that "it must change." Instead of pointing to future gains and benefits, they focused their discourse around the nature of the status quo.

Although they were much less likely to explicitly employ the term "crisis," opponents of the Mitchell proposal were successful in employing a more powerful discourse that carried out an implicit cost-benefit–analysis calculus, demonstrating that reform offered minimal rewards, but very high costs. When they spoke of "crisis" indirectly, it was to impact the negative consequences of endorsing the Mitchell proposal. Rather than simply saying, "This is how things are," they said, "This is *how bad* things will be if the Mitchell proposal is enacted." In an account of what his constituents had been telling him about health care reform, Senator Dole offered a statement typical of the opposition:

They were very determined in their view that the one thing we do not need is more Government, more Government control, more agencies, and some national board somewhere that is going to make their life miserable. (S11009)

Dole's discourse and the bulk of the opposition's rhetoric clearly identified a "crisis" and did so in a way that moves beyond the narrow parameters of health care. Dole's comment made it clear that the expanded role of government posed the real danger, not the more narrow issue of health care. Indeed, Dole maintained that the expansion of government would "make life miserable." He did not focus solely on health care in the status quo; rather, he painted a broader picture of what the *overall* negative consequences will be in the future. In addition, Dole's reference to "control" and "agencies" is a precursor to the more explicit claims of other opponents of the Mitchell proposal that economic ruin is the natural consequence of its enactment. Much of this specific discursive behavior is further illustrated in the examination of crisis rhetoric, which follows in the next chapter.

EVIDENCE
The August 1994 Senate floor debate on comprehensive health care reform was rich in evidence. According to the typology developed by Levasseur and Dean (1996) and employed here, nearly 1,900 individual incidences of evidence usage occurred during the debate over Senator Mitchell's Health Security Act. This abundance of evidence usage should not be surprising. Levasseur and Dean found much evidence

usage in all of the presidential debates that they examined, and there is a common-sensical belief that it is valuable to employ evidence as a means to establish credibility, build a case, and generally enhance the persuasive appeal of an argument. However, research may not be fully supportive of that view. In fact, in a comprehensive review of research regarding evidence usage, Reinard (1988) concluded that much more work is needed to establish the true value of evidence usage. It appears, though, that the Senators engaged in the comprehensive health care reform debate conformed to the more general or common view that evidence can be valuable. Indeed, some Senators in the comprehensive health care reform debate made explicit demands for evidence use by their opponents. The statement of Senator Gramm is illustrative:

What is amazing about their assertion . . . is that nowhere is there any data given to substantiate the claim. In all the world, not one example is given in 5,000 years of recorded history. I am not aware of a single case where government control of anything has made it cheaper, has raised the quality, and has broadened the access in real terms when considering the limits imposed to expand that access. (S11197)

Senator Gramm's challenge seems to point to the implicit belief that evidence is of importance.

The bulk of the evidence employed during the August 1994 floor debate was numerical in nature, consisting of either simple or complex numerical instances. Over 1,200 of the cases of evidence used during the floor debate fell into one of these two categories. Senator Mitchell's discussion of typical family costs for health care is illustrative of the use of simple numerical instances: "If we do not control costs, in 6 years' time, that family will be paying more than $900 a month for health insurance" (S11005). Other Senators spoke of the number of individuals lacking health insurance, the projected cost of the Health Security Act, and a host of other items that would fall under the rubric of simple numerical instances. Complex numerical instances were used just as frequently. Note Senator Kassebaum's statement as an example: "According to some estimates, there are as many as 250,000 underused hospital beds in the United States, about 30 percent of the total" (S11029). Many others pointed to the percentage of individuals who are underinsured, the potential numbers affected by the pending legislation, and numerous other cases regarding the use of complex numerical instances.

It is interesting to note that virtually every case of usage of either simple or complex numerical instances shared a common theme or relationship pattern with all of the other cases. The usage of numerical instances all revolved around the common theme of resources—the price for the availability of health insurance, numbers of hospitals or medical professionals, expenditures by government agencies, and so on. Further, these resource issues tended to be employed in an implicit cost-benefit relationship. Senator Mitchell's reference to the future cost of health care for families, for example, worked to suggest that in order to obtain any benefit, costs would escalate. Senator Kassebaum's account of underused hospital beds also works in this way. She indicates that potential benefits—hospital beds and the possible medical cases they represent—are being wasted, or imposing a cost on the system. This type of relational implication with simple and complex numerical instances should not be surprising. When people employ numerical instances in ordinary talk, they are typically pointing to gains and loses, prices and net rewards to cost-benefit relationships.

Some Senators seem to acknowledge that it might be difficult to fully assess and process large amounts of quantitative data, particularly complex numerical data. In response to this, some Senators attempted to interpret or simplify complex numerical data. For instance, many Senators pointed to the percentage of the GNP consumed by health care. Senator Dominici attempted to simplify those data this way: "This health care system will be so big that one of every five Americans will be taking care of you. ... [Y]ou can walk down the street and you can almost be assured that if five people have passed you, one of them is taking care of you" (S11095). Such statements appear to be discursive attempts to both illustrate complex numerical data and to make it more manageable for the listener.

The large amount of numerical evidence used during the August 1994 Senate floor debate is also probably related to the presumed value and power that such data hold for an audience. In reference to the testimony of a colleague, Senator Moynihan acknowledged the impact of numerical material: "I want to note that I was struck by the statistics, by the data he brought to us" (S11763). Many people seem to be "struck by" the power of numerical data, such as statistical reports. Indeed, the 1992 Presidential election two years earlier was noted for the public appeal and impact of displays of numerical data by Ross Perot. Edelman (1965) has discussed the general power of language to value important "abstractions" for listeners and he has noted that "They are often quantitative abstractions, lent prestige by the successes of science and by the preoccupation of business with profit and loss statements" (p. 117). He thus suggests that such numerical data have power due to their grounding in cultural and social experience. Numerical data also seems to have appeal as something more clear and concrete than the words that a speaker may use. Merriam (1990) noted: "The appeal of numbers as a source of rational order and harmony are derived in part from their perceived precision. In contrast to the inevitable ambiguities and abstractions of language, numbers seem to possess exactness and objectivity" (p. 338). The use of large amounts of numerical evidence by the Senators engaged in the August 1994 floor debate may therefore rest in an attempt to both capture the social power of quantitative data and the perceived precision of numbers. Indeed, many Senators attempted to enhance the appeal of numerical evidence by stressing relationships to specific quantities. Senator Mitchell spoke about individual family cost that would be "more than" $900 a month. Senator Kassebaum explained that "as many as" 250,000 hospital beds may be underused. In such cases, the numbers are "packaged" in a way to make them more compelling.

Advocates in the Senate debate regarding comprehensive health care reform also employed a large amount of opinion-centered and source-centered evidence. In fact, Senators would often submit the entire text of a letter, a news article, or an official report as proof into the record of the debate. Although paraphrase and interpretation of evidence was widespread, Senators would also often directly quote some other sources. This suggests that Senators assumed that some persuasive value would be garnered by being able to reinforce their own ideas with the testimony of others, whether another opinion or the findings of some other source.

Many Senators also made attempts to help establish the credibility of evidence they employed from other sources. Often, a Senator would offer detailed source qualifications for a particular piece of evidence that was to be presented. Although difficult to confirm, many believe that such a "buildup" for a source can aid in the persuasive power of the evidence that is presented. Senator Durenberger, for example, points to both the qualifications and the logic of the process used by a source he cites: "For whatever else you may think of Reisdmauer's estimating powers, I think he has been in health policy for as long a time as many of the rest of us. He worked trying to find a compromise by combining provisions from different bills might make the health system worse. He compared it to building an auto engine with incompatible parts" (S11092). It appears that much like trying to benefit from the perceived power of numerical data, Senators were also attempting to obtain the perceived authority of source credibility.

Specific historical instances were employed relatively infrequently as a form of evidence. Typically, when such evidence was employed, it functioned to help establish historical context and relationship to a specific relevant event. Reference was made by a number of advocates for comprehensive health care reform to the efforts of President Harry Truman in the 1940s. A number of other Senators spoke of the case of attempting to deal with catastrophic care in the late 1980s in order to link Senator Mitchell's Health Security Act to potential problems similar to those encountered with that legislation. In that way, specific historical instances seemed to function largely in a referential sense, while numerical data and evidence from other sources function in a more directly suasory sense. Further, the reluctance to employ specific historical instances may be grounded in the "linkage baggage" they carry. When Senators speak of Truman's actions in a specific historical instance they also provide connections to other actions and views associated with that instance. Senators may appeal to the interest Truman had in reform, but they also open the door to discussions of Truman's ultimate failure, fears of expanded government, and a host of other less desirable connections.

It should also be noted that use of evidence did not always occur in a single individual attempt to boost one's case. Evidence was used to build a countercase and often served as a direct point of contention. A number of Republican opponents of the Mitchell proposal had constructed a detailed chart to display what they considered to be both the cost and complexity of the legislation. Senator Daschle, a Democratic ally of Mitchell, went to great lengths to directly refute the conclusions being drawn by those using the chart. This instance demonstrates that evidence might not only serve as an individual discursive feature of the floor debate, but also as a discursive means to display clash and fit the overall debate into a larger framework.

One can also fit the use of evidence into a larger framework. As with crisis discourse, proponents of comprehensive health care reform employed evidence descriptively, to point to flaws that exist in the present health care system. Senator Mitchell offered this particular bit of evidence early in the debate:

The General Accounting Office found that 63 percent of women on Medicaid, or without insurance, do not get proper prenatal care. About 1 in 8 has a low-birthweight baby as a result. (S11007)

Here again, Mitchell was stating what the nature of the current health care system was like and was describing its direct health-related consequences. The discourse of those advocating comprehensive health care reform was once again present-oriented, this time in the use of evidence. It was also clearly confined to the parameters of health care. Proponents of reform did not say what the nature of the economy or the nation was like evidentially. They only said what the current health care system was like and what the effects or consequences would be within that specific realm.

Opponents of the Mitchell proposal used evidence more broadly. They used numerical instances, opinion-centered testimony, and other forms to construct a discursive image of the larger, negative consequences that would follow passage of the Mitchell proposal. Senator Dole offers one illustration of this discursive practice in the form of a question:

Will countless small businesses be forced to close their doors and countless more working Americans lose their jobs because of government mandates? . . . And if you are in a state like Kansas where 90 percent of our employers have 10 or fewer employees, it is a serious question. (S11009)

This example is very illuminating. Dole not only employed numerical evidence with all of the appeal that it potentially contained, but he also broadened the nature of the issue to the economy and not just the more narrow segment that dealt with health care. "Small businesses," "employers," "employees" and the overall economy were at risk if the Mitchell proposal passed, such statements made clear. Thus, when deciding whether to embrace the Health Security Act or not, it became necessary to look beyond the current status of health care in America, to the future status of the larger economy.

Other examples of evidence usage confirmed this contrast in overall discursive behavior. Senator Kennedy's opening remarks were typical of those advocating passage of the Health Security Act to ensure comprehensive health care:

We stand here today with the health of 260 million Americans at stake. We must decide whether we will guarantee health insurance for every citizen—or whether we will continue to let millions of fellow citizens suffer every year from conditions they can't afford to treat, while millions more worry about losing their insurance. (S11025)

Kennedy's comments and use of numerical data were confined to health care and to a description of the current system. Contrast Kennedy's remarks and evidence usage with those of Senator Kassebaum:

We had an opportunity to focus on the root of the public's concern, namely, rising costs. Instead, the bill before us, like the Clinton plan that preceded it, has been constructed almost as if cost were no object. Far from streamlining the costly promises in the Clinton proposal, the Mitchell bill would create at least four new entitlements and cost taxpayers a projected $1.1 trillion over the next decade. (S11028)

Kassebaum did not restrict her use of evidence to an account of the present health care system, but rather pointed to concerns of "the public" and the future impact for "taxpayers." There might be some flaws or problems with the present health care system, noted opponents of the Mitchell proposal, but enactment of the Health Security Act would have consequences—negative consequences—that went beyond the confines of that system and the relatively few individuals who were clearly tested by it.

NARRATIVES

According to the typology employed here, a relatively small number of narratives seemed to be used during the August 1994 Senate floor debate on comprehensive health care reform. This was probably due to the nature of the narratives examined. Personal narratives, other-person narratives, and social narratives were examined as specific discursive features. That was obviously a much more limited perspective regarding narratives than what had been articulated by Fisher in his overall narrative paradigm as a means of constructing all communicative behavior. A relatively small number of narratives here did not suggest that narrative was of lesser importance in this particular discourse; rather, it merely reflected the methodological approach employed.

The value of narrative was certainly not lost on the advocates who engaged in the August 1994 floor debate. A great many of them explicitly pointed to both the use of narratives or stories, and to their value. Senator Cohen's statement was not atypical: "I have listened to the debate and I must tell you I have been moved by the recitation of the tragic stories that have affected so many thousands and perhaps millions of Americans who lack adequate health insurance coverage under the current system" (S11663). In fact, Senator Hutchison suggested that it was the very telling of such stories that brought about the debates on comprehensive health care reform and a need for action:

Do these stories sound familiar? They are all true, and they are all tragic. And they have all been told by the President of the United States in an attempt to incite a revolution that would cause a radical change in American life. These stories are a legitimate cause of action. They call for responsible actions, not impetuous experimental upheaval. (S11778-11779)

Many Senators also suggested that the stories presented should be considered carefully in making a decision regarding comprehensive health care reform. Senator Warner, for example, noted: "These are the stories we have before us here. These are the stories that we take into consideration as we confront this problem" (S12175). There certainly appeared to be a perception that stories would play an important role in the debate.

The smallest number of narratives employed as discursive features during the Senate floor debate were those in the category of personal narratives. Very few Senators offered personal narratives regarding the issue of health care, but this is not to say that they lacked value. Senator Dole, for example, offered personal narratives regarding his own war-related health care problems and this seemed to help establish credibility on the issue. Many other Senators probably depended more heavily upon other-person narratives and social narratives because those forms might be better perceived as proof, deriving their strength from a source external to the individual speaker.

Many of the other-person narratives, stories about individuals other than the speaker, were used by advocates of comprehensive health care reform to help make the need for action appear real and personal. Senator Mitchell, for instance, employed a number of other-person narratives in constructing his opening case for passage of the Health Security Act. One example is illustrative:

Senator Boxer told of a Californian, a young 19-year-old boy who had been a high school football star in Sonoma County, stricken with cancer, a terrible disease that every American fears. His only chance of overcoming the cancer was a bone-marrow transplant, but his health insurance did not cover it. (S11005)

Such stories or other-person narratives seemed to be a discursive device that helped make a situation vivid and put a face on it in a way that many other forms of proof would be unable to accomplish.

Social narratives were often used in much the same way as other-person narratives in order to construct a case by making it appear more vivid and realistic. The statement of Senator Kennedy offers a good example:

So when I hear the Republican pundits, Bill Kristol to name one, say there is no health care crisis, well . . . maybe there is not one for him and his friends who may well be wealthy, but for ordinary citizens in our country—and that is most of the citizens in our country—they have troubles, they have problems, they are worried that their own health insurance could be canceled at a moment's notice when they need it the most. (S11235)

Kennedy and the other advocates of comprehensive health care reform thus employed social narratives to construct the health care crisis as both something real and as something significant and widespread.

Opponents of the Mitchell proposal for comprehensive health care reform were also adept at using other-person and social narratives to promote their case. For instance, Senator Hutchison offered this narrative to highlight the evil of government mandates in the area of health care:

A nurse here in Washington said that when a little boy asked her to sit with him during a chemotherapy session she had to leave that little boy alone to go to a mandatory class on how to fill out a form that had no direct bearing on the health of the children she was treating. (S11778)

Numerous other narratives were employed by opponents of Senator Mitchell's Health Security Act to cast the potential growth in the involvement of the federal government in the area of health care in a negative light.

Opponents of comprehensive health care reform seemed to have a sense of the role of narrative rationality in the evaluation of stories, particularly narrative fidelity as developed by Fisher (1987). As Fisher argued that a listener could employ narrative fidelity as a means to evaluate communication based upon past experience and whether a story seems to ring true or not, the opponents of comprehensive health care reform similarly noted that such elements might play an important role in judging the consequences of passage of the Mitchell proposal. Senator Grassley, for example, emphasized that most Americans were satisfied with their care under the present system and that the Mitchell proposal would actually worsen care for them. He challenged everyone to write about the status of their health care in their diaries:

Describe your view of the American health care system and everything that is associated with it, including insurance, your doctor, your hospital, because you may look back in your diary and compare what you wrote in 1994 to what you have in 2000 or 2010 and find that in the future, you do not have anything of the quality or the quantity and the satisfaction that you had in 1994. (S11922)

Grassley seemed to be suggesting that an application of narrative fidelity would work against the Mitchell proposal. Senator Markowski also pointed to narrative fidelity with regard to the potential risk of expanded bureaucracy: "That does not ring very well with the American people because they are also concerned about the expanded bureaucracy. They do not want to see any more agencies" (S11885). Narrative fidelity may have played an even larger role than what these references suggest, as will be argued in the rhetorical analysis of the floor debate.

There are interesting contrasts that can be made with regard to the various types of narratives used during the floor debate. It is possible to distinguish between narratives that tend to be positive and those that tend to be negative. In earlier research, Gronbeck (1992) identified negative political campaign narratives as those that create unattractive or undesirable images of one's political opponent. A slightly different perspective was employed to examine the various types of narratives used during the August 1994 floor debate. Positive narratives were simply those that offered a positive outcome—someone overcomes adversity, some individual talent is displayed, a form of success is reached, and so on. Negative narratives were, on the other hand, those that offered a negative outcome—increased taxes, higher prices for health care, limited access to medical resources, and so forth. These operationalizations of positive and negative reflected a common-sense understanding of outcomes that are desirable and those that are undesirable.

Positive and negative narratives tend to be used in differing numbers and in different instances by proponents and opponents of comprehensive health care reform. The use of personal narratives is, however, an exception. Most personal narratives used by both proponents and opponents of reform tend to be positive. It would only make sense that an individual would prefer to point to positive outcomes when he or she is telling a story about him- or herself. Most of the personal narratives employed during the floor debate are accounts of individual effort and work. Many Senators offer narratives that detail their efforts to interact with their constituents and to carry out tasks for the states which they represent. The other-person narratives employed by reform proponents tend to be negative, whereas those of opponents tend to be positive. Reform proponents typically provide accounts of individuals who lack sufficient health care coverage and must suffer the consequences. Alternatively, opponents often speak of the individual success of a small business owner or the accomplishments of a state official in improving delivery of health care. There is also a clear contrast in terms of social narratives. The social narratives offered by reform proponents tend to discuss the failure of the present system to provide adequate care for such groups as children and older adults. The social narratives of reform opponents are also largely negative, but they focus on future outcomes such as the necessary increase in taxes and establishment of mandates on business that would follow passage of the Mitchell proposal. These narratives are summarized in Tables 8.1 and 8.2.

Table 8.1
Pro-reform Narratives

Type of Narrative	Positive	Negative
Personal	More than 90%	Less than 10%
Other-Person	Less than 20%	More than 80%
Social	Less than 20%	More than 80%

Table 8.2
Anti-reform Narratives

Type of Narrative	Positive	Negative
Personal	More than 90%	Less than 10%
Other-Person	More than 70%	Less than 30%
Social	Less than 20%	More than 80%

An examination of the use of narratives during the Senate floor debate on comprehensive health care reform was also reflective of the general discursive pattern developed during the debate. As the illustrations above suggest, the narratives employed by proponents of the Health Security Act focused around a description of the present health care system. Other examples confirm such usage, consider Senator Wellstone's use of narratives:

I hear voices and I see faces as I speak on the floor of the U.S. Senate tonight in this historic debate: "Senator, my mother has Alzheimer's disease, and if you don't pass a reform bill, it's going to bankrupt our family. . . . Senator, I lost my job and now I've lost my health care coverage. What am I going to do?" . . . These are the voices that I hear as we debate this reform bill. (S11031)

The "voices" or narratives Wellstone recounted may be compelling, but they were descriptive of the current health care system and only pointed to serious ill for individuals who are failed by that system. The discourse was again, narrow and present-oriented. These narratives did serve to illustrate present conditions, but they failed to impact the issue beyond the scope of those specific individuals who had been deprived by the existing health care system.

Earlier illustrations also suggest that opponents of the Health Security Act employed narratives as a specific discursive practice. The opponents of the Mitchell proposal did not, however, restrict their use of narratives to a characterization of the limits that the present health care system poses for some individuals. Senator Boren employed a personal narrative to illustrate the risks associated with the political process of "nationalizing" something as basic as health care:

When I had the opportunity to study in Great Britain, I saw what happened in that country. They nationalized some of the basic industries when one of the parties got in power. When the other party got into power the next election, they denationalized the industries. When the other party won they renationalized the industries. Then they denationalized it again. By the time it was all over, there was precious little left of the basic industries . . . of that country. (S11238)

Senator Boren was doing more than merely offering an account of his travels abroad, he was pointing to the potential devastation of a vital portion of the national economy that could follow passage of the Health Security Act. Passage of the proposal might mean health care relief for certain individuals, but it might also mean economic devastation that could potentially impact everyone.

LANGUAGE STRATEGIES

The three specific categories of language strategies examined here—naming, blaming, and categorizing—were, as noted, developed by Schuetz (1986). The present investigation confirms her claim that such language strategies are frequently employed as a part of political discourse. Examples of naming, blaming, and categorizing were all found in examination of the August 1994 Senate floor debate on comprehensive health care reform and a total of nearly 600 overall instances of use of such strategies was identified.

The naming strategy appeared to be the most popular of the three specific language strategies examined here. Both proponents and opponents of the Mitchell proposal employed naming. Many opponents of the Mitchell proposal named it the *Trial Lawyers Protection Act*, due to the potential risk of increased litigation associated with the bill. On the other hand, Senator Dole's far more limited health care reform proposal was tagged by advocates of the Mitchell bill with the name the *Insurance Industry and Tobacco Industry Protection Act*, due to its very limited effect on the current insurance system and its failure to secure funding through an increased tobacco tax. Both sides also used naming in a way that centered on a play on words. The Mitchell proposal was, for example, named "health scare legislation" and the tactics of opponents of comprehensive health care reform were named "a thousand points of fright."

Several other examples of naming can be found in the August 1994 floor debate. Naming was often used, for example, to label the health care issue as a particular type of problem. One Senator named health care in this way:

I finally believe . . . that this is a moral issue, it is an economic issue, and it is inexcusable for us to allow millions of our children to go without the medical care that they need. But this is also, as I said a moment ago, an economic issue. (S11450)

Many opponents of comprehensive health care reform also named the issue in a particular way. Many, for example, labeled the nature of the debate a "philosophical issue." In addition, some Senators appeared to recognize that labeling or naming was being employed as a strategic device. Senator Sarbanes noted, "I do not think we ought to engage in this kind of labeling, a lot of which has happened over the last couple of weeks. . . ." (S12201)

Naming was probably used so frequently as a language strategy during the August 1994 floor debate on comprehensive health care reform because it can be both a powerful force and a relatively simple tactic. Dewey and Bentley (1960) have argued that naming can be seen "as itself directly a form of knowing" (p. 147). This suggests that naming may have an epistemic function; it can help instruct an audience in how they should think about something. Edelman (1965) has extended this view by noting:

The terms in which we name or speak of anything do more than designate it; they place it in a class of objects, thereby suggest with what it is to be judged and compared, and define the perspective from which it will be viewed and evaluated. (p. 131)

Thus, naming something a "health care catastrophe" or a "government nightmare" points to how we should think about those things. Further, naming is a relatively simple language strategy. It is both quick and easy to place the label of "Clinton-style health care reform" on a piece of legislation. It also works to provide a convenient way to view something; everyone knows what President Clinton's reform entailed.

Blame was also used fairly frequently as a language strategy during the debate regarding comprehensive health care reform. Blame was often employed to point to the consequences of the passage of particular legislation. Many opponents of the Mitchell proposal, for instance, would blame it for a greatly expanded role for the federal government if passed. The far more limited proposal of Senator Dole was often blamed for allowing too many of the flaws and problems of the current health care system to exist and potentially escalate. Senator Wofford's comparison of the Mitchell and Dole proposals is a good illustration of the use of blame in this way. He noted, for example, that "unlike the Mitchell bill, the Dole bill will not guarantee choice of doctor and health plan" (S11773). Senator McConnell offered a particularly clear illustration of opponents of comprehensive health care reform placing blame on the government: "[A] government-run health care system would be more expensive, more bureaucratic, and less responsive to each individual's medical needs than the system we have today" (S11861).

Categorizing was employed less frequently than naming or blame as a language strategy. Categorizing did, however, often serve a useful function during the floor debate. Senator Mitchell offered one example of the use of categorizing: "The keys to health care reform are access, affordability, and universal coverage. Those who say the problem is access and not price are mistaken. It is both access and price" (S11007). Senator Packwood also used categorizing in his description of managed care: "Managed care is a system of health delivery that tries to gather patients and doctors and bring them together in more or less of a collective manner" (S11021). This may point to one reason that categorizing seemed to occur less frequently than other language strategies. The use of categorizing in this particular debate appeared to largely be descriptive, while naming and blaming were more explicitly suasory in nature.

Many Senators seemed to recognize that particular language strategies were being employed during the floor debate over Senator Mitchell's Health Security Act. In fact, a number of them suggested that "language games" and "semantic tactics" were being employed. Senator Daschle suggested that such strategies were being employed when he, apparently, touched a desk and said, "We can call this a horse if we want to and we can continue to refer to it as a horse, but it is a desk, regardless of how many times we say it is a horse" (S12068). Senator Daschle's comment is typical of the generally negative view of language strategies by those who explicitly acknowledge their use. This is not to say that such usage was, in fact, always negative. It merely demonstrates that one speaker may label another speaker's language strategies in a negative way, even if that speaker also employs language strategies.

Proponents of Mitchell's Health Security Act tended to use language strategies to describe the current health care system and to create a characterization of that system and its consequences for individuals who are not served well by it. For example, Senator Dodd named or labeled health care a "basic right." He noted: "[S]omething as basic as health . . . is not a privilege, that is a right: basic health care" (S11453). Senator Dodd also used categorizing when he attempted to distinguish between "benefits" and "subsidies." Advocates for adoption of comprehensive health care reform also used blame as a language strategy. Senator Wofford, for instance, pointed to blame for inaction and its consequences: "It should hurt every one of us if we failed to act because it sure is going to hurt the American people" (S11200).

Opponents of the Health Security Act were very effective in their use of language strategies. They employed naming, blaming, and categorizing to point to the broad, negative impact of passage of the Mitchell proposal. Senator Gramm, for example, used categorizing to define the nature of the debate when he noted, "This issue is about the role of government in a free society" (S11196). Gramm made it clear that the nature of the debate extended beyond the narrow parameters of health care. He also effectively used blame: "[W]hen fully implemented, the average American family with two children is going to be sending $1 out of every $3 it earns to Washington, DC"

(S11196). Here, Gramm extended the debate to include "the average American family" and he cited the consequence of passage of the Health Security Act by suggesting that it would deprive the public of fully one-third of its income. Senator Dominici was also effective in his use of language strategies. He named portions of the Mitchell proposal as "job destroying employer mandates" (S11099). He also used blame to point to the broad economic risks associated with passage of comprehensive reform legislation: "And so the Clinton-Mitchell bill would penalize small businesses, in low income states with a mandate which will only make matters worse" (S11099).

MEDICAL METAPHORS

Given the great power and pervasiveness of metaphor in language, the single most significant finding in this investigation may well be how few medical metaphors were employed in the Senate floor debate. Less than three dozen medical metaphors were used throughout the several days of debate. This may be due, in part, to the fact that overuse of a particular metaphor can render it ineffective. Fairhurst and Sarr (1996) noted "that the heavy use of particular metaphors results in their losing the novelty and surprise they once held" (p. 107). If everything is compared to a medical procedure, a patient, or some other medical practice or concept then such comparisons become stale and unsurprising. In fact, Thomas (1969) has argued that an overused metaphor soon becomes a cliché. Speakers want their metaphors to be thought of as new, innovative, and creative. Listeners typically think of clichés as tired, old, and unoriginal. An innate sense of this possibility may well have been at work for those using medical metaphors during the Senate floor debate on health care reform.

Many of the medical metaphors that were used in the floor debate were creative and colorful. For example, Senator Wofford spoke at length about the need to perform an "annual checkup" on the nation's health care system as a way to make it clear that there was a need for ongoing review and evaluation of that system (S11683). Senator Gramm, in assessing the progress of health care reform legislation as proposed by President Clinton and Majority Leader Mitchell, suggested that "national health care reform was moving from the intensive care ward to the morgue" (S11882). Senator Mosey-Braun spoke of the importance of the issue of health care reform and the need to "cure" a "sick" health care system (S11242). Similarly, a number of other Senators spoke of the need to "treat" the "ills" of the present health care system with some form of "prescription." Senator Hatch's remarks are illustrative: "The bill's prescription for health care reform includes massive doses of new taxes as well as new levels of spending and government intrusion" (S11836). Senator McConnell relied more heavily upon such medical metaphors than any other single speaker during the floor debate. McConnell referred to the need to restrict "diagnose" the Mitchell proposal, to examine what "treatment" was proposed, and to restrict "doses of mandates" contained within the bill, all within a few passages. In fact, he characterized the Mitchell proposal as an "ailing piece of legislation" (S11866).

Several Senators, like McConnell, mixed different types of medical metaphors within their discourse. McConnell, for example, used medical metaphors that related to diagnosis, treatment, and specific procedures. Senator Gramm employed a similar mixed medical metaphor when he explained an alternative to Mitchell's proposal as "a nonpartisan prescription for the widely acknowledged ills of America's health care system" (S11882). There can be a danger of confusion in the use of mixed or varied metaphors in a single discourse (Fairhurst & Sarr, 1996). Listeners may focus on the wrong comparison or confuse comparisons in such cases. This was not likely to be a problem with the use of multiple medical metaphors, sometimes in a single instance, as they all had what Lakoff and Johnson (1980) call "shared entailments." Entailments, according to Lakoff and Johnson, are the relationships and conceptualizations constructed by use of metaphors. In the case of these medical metaphors, all of the entailments made an implicit comparison of the health care system or health care reform to some medical element. Some of the metaphors directly related to a "diagnosis," others to "treatments," and still others to "physicians" or "patients," yet they were all attempting to evoke a comparison to something within the medical system. The use of the varied medical metaphors, unlike a speaker's reference to a "tide" of change for a "team" in a "battle," pointed to the same general relationship.

Dealing with the medical system or medical procedures is something with which most people have some common-sense familiarity or at least a general level of understanding. This may well have been part of the purpose of the use of the medical metaphors to facilitate understanding. Metaphors help us to understand and experience one thing in terms of another (Lakoff & Johnson, 1980). In a discussion of popular business metaphors, Clancy (1989) notes that "these are ideas that ground our experience and determine our actions. We take a very concrete concept, with all of its implications, and apply it to something else that may resemble the original concept in some ways but surely is not identical with it" (p. 27). Thus, when Senator McConnell says that a "Do Not Resuscitate" sign should be placed on the Mitchell proposal, many will readily recognize the comparison and understand it to mean that the Majority Leader's measure was beyond help.

Metaphors clearly play a role in making discourse compelling. They can take a fairly dry subject and make it vivid, colorful, and dramatic. Fairhurst and Sarr (1996) note: "Through the comparisons they draw, metaphors help us to think in new ways and, often, with more vividness and clarity" (p. 103). Anyone who has read any work of great literature can probably recall an event or scene that seemed extremely compelling because it was developed metaphorically. When the Mitchell proposal was characterized as a "prescription" that contained heavy "doses" of taxes and mandates, the images conjured up were more vivid and compelling than if the bill had merely been understood to levy some fee and include some regulation.

Metaphors can also help to give others a clue as to how a speaker's conceptual system works. Lakoff and Johnson (1980) and many others contend that thinking and understanding tend to be metaphorical—people conceptualize issues, events, and problems in terms of other things with which they are familiar. Perrin (1987) argues that when faced with new issues and complex problems, people generate metaphors that help them understand present events in terms of their past experiences. The medical metaphors employed by opponents of the Mitchell proposal were rather telling in a similar way. The medical metaphors that cast Mitchell's proposal in a negative light reflected both the vividness of medical encounters and, more importantly, a conceptual framework that viewed broad federal responses to problems as

problematic and unnecessary extensions of federal power. McConnell's characterization of the Majority Leader's bill, for example, clearly articulated a belief that federal
spending and authority should be held in check. For McConnell, a "dose" of taxes and
mandates was the last thing that the nation needed.

The use of medical metaphors was consistent with the general discursive pattern
of proponent remarks being both narrowly focused on health care and present-
oriented, whereas the remarks of reform opponents were broader in nature and much
more future-oriented. Virtually every proponent of the Mitchell proposal who
employed a medical metaphor stuck to those that concerned "ills" or "diagnosis"—the
present health care system was sick and in need of a good check-up. Opponents of the
Majority Leader's bill once again extended the discourse to include such things as
future economic consequences. For example, Senator McConnell spoke repeatedly
of the heavy "doses" of taxes and mandates associated with the Mitchell proposal and
stated that such "treatment" had "predictable side effects of impaired automony and
severe economic contractions" (S11866). For McConnell and other opponents, the
reform proposal would do nothing to "cure" the "ills" of the *present* system, and it
would produce broad negative consequences in the *future*.

SUMMARY

The data reported here suggest that many discursive features were employed
during the August 1994 Senate floor debate on comprehensive health care reform.
Further, each of these discursive features—crisis discourse, evidence, narratives,
language strategies, and medical metaphors—played a role in the process of
conducting the floor debate. In fact, these language strategies could be thought of as
the very means by which the debate over comprehensive health care reform was
constructed. Writing specifically about political communication, Edelman (1988) has
confirmed a view held by many who study language generally, when he noted that
"language is the key creator of the social worlds people experience, not a tool for
describing an objective reality" (p. 103). The language or discursive features
employed in the Senate floor debate on comprehensive health care reform certainly
went beyond "describing an objective reality." Indeed, a particular discursive pattern
emerged that warrants additional assessment.

As displayed through the examination of each specific discursive feature, a clear
pattern developed: The proponents of comprehensive health care reform spoke in a
manner narrowly fashioned around that subject, whereas their opponents spoke in a
manner that more broadly pointed to the role of government and the larger (and
negative) economic impacts that would occur as a consequence of passage of the
Mitchell reform proposal. Throughout the debate, the specific discursive features of
crisis discourse, evidence, narratives, language strategies, and medical metaphors all
worked in a similar manner to define the nature and character of that debate. It is
possible to provide some further explication of why the discourse of the floor debate
followed such a pattern.

First, the opponents of comprehensive health care reform seemed to be more
adept at connecting to the core concerns of the voting public. Despite a general level
of interest in health care reform, the economy always loomed as a larger issue. During

the 1992 presidential campaign, for example, the phrase "It's the economy, stupid" stood as the defining feature of the election. In addition, Miller's (1993) survey assessment of voter attitudes tends to confirm this view. Miller found that "economic" issues such as inflation, unemployment, and taxes were viewed as substantially more important to voters than health care reform and other "social" issues. The Democratic party may have successfully latched onto the economic bandwagon to win the presidency in 1992, but in the 1994 Senate floor debate on comprehensive health care reform it was largely their Republican opponents who capitalized on the issue. Health care was of direct and immediate importance to some individuals, but "pocketbook" issues like tax increases, regulatory controls, and price increases were more directly and immediately felt by members of the public.

Tied to this general concern, Republican opponents of comprehensive health care reform more directly connected to the overriding idea of "political economy." The notion of political economy is by no means a new one. Aristotle conceived of the total community as political and many others have implicitly embraced a view that links the political process and the larger economic system together in some manner. Many political observers view politics, economic matters, and the society at large as an integrated whole. Dolbeare and Edelman (1985) have provided a detailed operationalization of political economy that typifies the view held by a great many political scientists:

We use the term, *political economy*, to refer to the web of political and social institutions and human activity that are interwoven with the contemporary economy. We include society and culture as well as government and politics in this conceptual approach. However, we do not mean to suggest that all areas are merely reflective of economic conditions or forces; each area has independent characteristics and causes of change that affect all the others. Rather than seeing the "areas" as either reflections or causes, we want to stress their continuing relationship and interdependence, as well as the centrality of economics to each. (p. 7)

Republican foes of the Health Security Act also clearly recognized these interconnections and "the centrality of economics." As noted, their discourse always pointed to larger or broader economic consequences associated with the health care "area" and they made it clear, as American voters have tended to do, that it really is "the economy, stupid" that is at the heart of decision making.

Opponents of comprehensive health care reform also employed a discourse focused around broader economic issues to reshape or to redefine the nature of the debate itself. While proponents of comprehensive health care reform stuck closely to a discourse that defined that issue—examples of the health care "crisis," statistics on the number of uninsured citizens, and the like—the opponents of comprehensive reform employed a discourse that essentially argued that the debate was about something different. The opponents of comprehensive health care reform were not forced into the untenable position of suggesting that all was right with health care in the United States. Rather, they said the debate was not about health care alone. It was really about expanding the role of government to provide yet another social service that would raise taxes, strengthen regulatory powers, and generally impose additional burdens on the economy that all taxpayers would be forced to pay. This strategy also enabled opponents of comprehensive health care reform to define their role not as obstructionists to reform and "cure," but as protectors of the health of the economy and saviors from the "curse" of expanded government with its inherently negative economic consequences. (The rhetorical analysis featured in the next two chapters extends this line of reasoning in a number of regards.)

The discursive behavior of opponents of comprehensive health care reform permitted them to do even more than define the nature of the debate. They were also able to discursively shape a "geography" of the debate; they could define the place of health care reform in comparison with the larger role of government and the even larger nature of the economy. As Figure 8.1 indicates, the discourse employed by opponents of comprehensive health care reform framed the role of government and the nature of the economy as larger elements that encompassed the more narrow issue of health care. Health care was discursively identified as a smaller, component part of other issues and thus as an element that was subsumed by those issues and one that directly impacted a smaller number of individuals. This discourse worked in a way similar to the use of a map to explain a geographic location: x is located within the state of y, which is a component part of the nation of z. In this case, x would always then be subsumed by y and z. This is also important in the comprehensive health care debate. Not only was health care subsumed by governmental and economic forces, it was also subservient to them—it was a minor feature *controlled by* the other two, not to be *controlling of* the others.

Figure 8.1
The Geography of Health Care

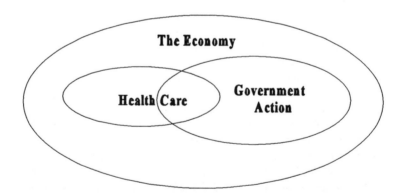

A few additional examples from the floor debate further illustrate this geographical representation of how arguments were constructed. Senator Cohen's remarks are particularly illuminating: "It is almost certain that the spending associated with the new entitlements and subsidies in the bill are going to exceed all expectations and further fuel the deficit that threatens to cripple the economy right now" (S11664). Cohen is clearly stating that the Mitchell proposal is crafted to deal with health care, yet its consequences expand to capture other elements of the government (entitlements, subsidies, the deficit) and ultimately to impact or "cripple" the whole economy. Senator Lott took a similar position when he stated that "It is high time to tell the truth about the so-called health reform bills that have the Government taking over 14.5 percent of our economy" (S11460). Lott again has the scope of this bill broadening and "creeping out of the lab" like some creature from a 1950s science fiction film to have *the Government* take over a huge chunk of *our economy*. Lott also makes it clear that the Clinton and Mitchell proposals are only "so-called" reform bills that are really designed to expand the size and scope of the federal government.

Several other Senators similarly developed this broad geography of the issue. Senator Gramm's remarks offer another good example:

Here is my concluding point: Why is this so important? This is so important because, if we adopt anything like the Clinton health care plan, we cannot fix it. If we adopt anything like the Clinton health care plan, we are not going to be able to back all these promises. Once we make all these promises, we will never be able to take them back. We will never be able to pay for them. We will go back and forth between bankrupting the Government and rationing health care. In the end, we will destroy both the economy and the greatest health care system in history. (S11198)

Gramm's claims seem fairly obvious: Passage of the reform proposal does not remain limited to repairing the problems with the present health care system, it will also destroy that system and expand outward to destroy the economy as well. Indeed, Gramm's claims are also explicit in their future orientation: Attempting to treat the ills of the present system will put *us* in the position of *never* paying for those actions, *never* restricting the expansion of federal power, and *never* having health care as good as what is currently available.

As Gramm's remarks and earlier analysis indicate, the discursive features employed by proponents and opponents of comprehensive health care reform also contrast in their respective present and future orientations. Proponents of comprehensive health care reform employ all of the specific discursive features to describe the present nature of the health care system in the United States. Opponents employ these discourse features to construct an image of the future negative consequences that would flow from passage of the Mitchell reform proposal. This discursive pattern enables opponents of reform to both "build" or shape the debate for their own purposes and to contrast the relatively satisfactory "here and now" with a bleak and dark "there and then." They are able to shape the debate by casting it in economic terms that loom larger than individual health care concerns. "Health" may still be a central theme, but it is the health of the entire economic nation-state, not merely the health of those few individuals who are unfortunate enough to have failed to obtain adequate health care. This discursive behavior functioned in the form of a cost-benefit calculus. Opponents of reform characterized the costs of comprehensive reform as far outweighing the benefits—comprehensive care would provide an incremental quantitative improvement for a small segment of the population (those not currently covered by some care options), whereas it would entail qualitative costs (taxes, regulation, etc.) for the whole of the population. Further, most people are covered by relatively satisfactory health insurance in the present. By contrast, a future characterized by passage of the Mitchell proposal would be one where everyone pays more and gets less. All of this allows opponents of comprehensive health care reform to make a simple discursive choice available: you can say "yes" to the relative good of the present system and say "no" to the clear and present danger of a future rendered unattractive by passage of the Mitchell proposal.

A fundamental epistemological difference also seemed to be at work in the discursive behavior of proponents and opponents of comprehensive health care reform during the August 1994 Senate floor debate. The discursive examples offered here tend to illustrate the single-minded focus of proponents of the Mitchell proposal: They were squarely focused on the specific issue of health care reform. By contrast, the discursive behavior of opponents tends to suggest that they thought beyond the realm of the specific social issue at hand to a more general way of looking at the world. Proponents seemed to be thinking directly about the individual in a health care "crisis" and the stories of lack of affordability and care. Opponents of comprehensive health care reform seemed to think in terms of examining the appropriate role of government and the potential long-term impacts of action upon the economy. As noted, the thinking of opponents of comprehensive health care reform may have been more in line with the thinking of the general public.

Opponents of reform were also more effective in their approach to policy discourse. The discussion of policies is an inherently future-oriented enterprise. The reason to change or replace a policy is grounded in the desire to get something different in the future. The discourse of opponents focused around undesirable future consequences of reform. Such a focus places policy in perspective—it suggests that the nature of the present system alone is insufficient warrant for change; it is also important to examine what one will end up with. Discussion of a health care crisis simply said "Here's what is wrong," whereas the discourse of opponents said "Here's what you will get."

The emergence and examination of these discursive patterns during the Senate floor debate clearly work to confirm my general thesis that talk is power. Opponents of comprehensive health care reform employed several features of talk—crisis discourse, evidence, narratives, language strategies, and medical metaphors—to define the very nature of the debate and to cast the issue in broader, future-oriented terms. Let there be no mistake: This process was a utilization of talk as power. The talk thus far examined demonstrated enormous powers—it could change the direction and, ultimately, the outcome of the debate regarding comprehensive health care reform. Examination of this individual discursive features and the patterns that emerge from their use is, however, only one step in illuminating the discourse of the debate and building my argument that talk is power. As Fisher (1985) aptly noted, "any instance of discourse is always more than the individualized forms that may comprise it" (p. 347). That is certainly the case here. Even more can be revealed about the power of talk as one looks to a more general rhetorical analysis and both the overall flow of the deliberation and the final triumph of the "big government" argument. The next two chapters play out that process, grounded in a focus upon the centrality of "crisis" in this particular dispute.

Chapter 9

The Deliberation

" [T]he Clinton plan was deader than Elvis."

—Senator Phil Gramm

By now, everyone knows that Senator Gramm was right. The Clinton plan was dead. The Mitchell bill was dead. In fact, unlike the pop icon Gramm invoked, it is unlikely that you will see any version of comprehensive national health care reform popping into a Dairy Queen in your neighborhood any time soon. There is a general consensus that the issue of comprehensive health care reform was once again derailed and displaced from the national agenda in 1994. Various interpretations of the defeat of the proposals by President Clinton and Senator Mitchell have been posited by political pundits and observers of the political process in Washington. Rovner (1995b) has argued that structural features of policy making in Congress played a central role in the 1994 defeat of comprehensive health care reform. Schick (1995) contends that health care reform failed primarily because of a misreading of the public mood by proponents of reform. And, Starr (1994) has argued that a mix of political forces tended to work in favor of the Republican opposition and cost the advocates of comprehensive reform their best chance for action in decades. In fact, Starr proclaimed "The collapse of health care reform in the first two years of the Clinton administration will go down as one of the great lost political opportunities in American history. It is a story of compromises that never happened, of deals that were never closed, of Republicans, moderate Democrats, and key interest groups that backpedaled from proposals they themselves had earlier co-sponsored or endorsed" (p. 21). Despite Starr's allusion to narrative, all of these explanations failed to address the centrality of discourse and the power that was played out through talk. This chapter will continue to address the actual discourse of the 1994 health care reform debate by focusing upon the deliberation that shapes the debate itself.

The earlier discussion of discourse patterns confirms that talk played a major role in the August 1994 Senate floor debate on comprehensive health care reform. The present discussion of the deliberation will extend that position by arguing that an overall assessment of the discourse in that floor debate reveals much about the power of talk in the political process. Specifically, I will argue that the Senate floor debate is best examined as a case of crisis rhetoric. I will further argue that, although the health care debate can be viewed as part of the genre of crisis rhetoric, it is also a unique type of crisis rhetoric and that analysis of its component elements extends the boundaries of that genre.

THE GENRE OF CRISIS RHETORIC

Many genres of rhetorical criticism have evolved over the years. Some scholars have focused their critical examination on the discourse of dissent and unrest. Others have turned a critical eye to the rhetoric of the Presidents of the United States. Still others have evaluated the discursive attempts at oppression and empowerment as displayed in the rhetoric of the contemporary civil rights and women's movements. All of these scholars have examined, evaluated, and criticized rhetorical acts through the framework of a particular genre due to the potentially revealing power that each genre offered. Indeed, Karlyn Kohrs Campbell and Kathleen Hall Jamieson (1990) have argued that the purpose of a rhetorical genre should rest not in its quick and simple classification system, but rather in its ability to illuminate how and why discourse operated as it did in a particular case. The genre of crisis rhetoric offers great illumination potential for the August 1994 Senate floor debate on comprehensive health care reform.

As will be explained at some length later, the Senate floor debate on comprehensive health care reform was replete with the development of crises. This should not be surprising given that many rhetorical scholars argue that crises are rhetorical events crafted through creative use of language rather than true events that require attention or action. As previously noted, language plays an important role in politics, and language can be used to construct a crisis or give meaning to a particular event. Edelman (1971) has explained how language works with regard to political events:

Political events can become infused with strong affect stemming from psychic tension, from perceptions of economic, military, or other threats or opportunities and from interactions between social and psychological responses. These political "events" are largely creations of the language used to describe them. (p. 67)

Cherwitz (1978) has further explained that language is a cause, not an effect, of meaning. It is used to construct meaning. And Edelman (1965) contends that "language is a necessary catalyst of politics" (p. 117).

Language is used to help construct a perception of crisis for the public. It has been argued that this has often been the case with regard to international or foreign policy crises. Cherwitz and Zagacki (1986) note that "it is widely held that international crises are rhetorical artifacts: Events become crises, not because of unique sets of situational exigencies, but by virtue of discourse used to describe them"

(p. 307). Vatz (1973) contends that it is this descriptive discourse that gives meaning to an event. He writes, "When political communicators talk about issues they are talking about situations made salient; not something that became important because of its intrinsic importance" (p. 160). Cherwitz (1978) has stated more simply that "the rhetoric employed to describe an event gives that event its significance" (p. 100). Political events, particularly political crises are often clearly crafted rhetorical products. "Political crises are primarily rhetorical. The President announces to the people that a situation critical to the United States exists. Situations do not create crises. Rather, the President's perception of the situation and the rhetoric he uses to describe it mark an event as a crisis" (Windt, 1973, p. 7). Similarly, Cherwitz (1987) contends, "It is often the president's rhetoric that draws attention to the situation and defines it in such a way that the nation's response is clearly implied" (p. 188).

Critical attention to crisis rhetoric has been offered by many scholars. Pratt (1970), for instance, examined three crisis speeches that centered around foreign policy issues. In fact, the bulk of rhetorical scholarship in the area has focused upon foreign policy or international crises. Cherwitz (1978), for example, examined the Gulf of Tonkin crisis and President Lyndon Johnson's persuasive promotion of U.S. engagement in Vietnam. Hahn (1980) explored President Gerald Ford's appeals for action with regard to the Mayaguez Affair. Hersey (1986) has compared and contrasted the rhetoric of America's Ronald Reagan and France's François Mitterand in various international crises. And Klope (1986) focused on the examination of President Reagan's crisis rhetoric regarding foreign policy actions in both Lebanon and Grenada.

Many of the critical investigations of presidential rhetoric in times of international crisis paid particular attention to the construction of a drama for public consumption, with heavy reliance upon the conflict between villains and heroes. Cherwitz and Zagacki (1986), for example, offered a rather critical look at how consummatory rhetoric often functions to clearly define an adversary as an enemy. Klope (1986) similarly relied upon pointing to Reagan's appeal to freedom, progress, and other American myths in order to aid the development of victimage. In fact, in an introduction to a collection of essays concerned with international affairs and its rhetorical treatment, Ivie (1986) noted that much of the crisis rhetoric examined pointed to values, myths, and beliefs "which intensify the motive for victimage, i.e., for vilifying the enemy" (p. 305).

As will be demonstrated, the rhetorical construction of crises during the August 1994 Senate floor debate on comprehensive health care reform also suggested that villains were at work and that important American beliefs and values were threatened. Also, much like the international crises examined by rhetorical scholars, it was the power of discourse that was central to the construction of events that would warrant some public or audience response. The final response in the August 1994 floor debate was the rejection of the Mitchell proposal for comprehensive health care reform. The development of the discourse that led to rejecting any response to the health care crisis and embracing a crisis of big government was unique in several ways. In fact, examination of the crisis rhetoric in the Senate floor debate functions to extend the critical power and potential of the genre of crisis rhetoric.

EXTENDING THE CRITICAL GENRE

Whether it was the Gulf of Tonkin crisis, the Mayaguez Affair, the invasion of Grenada, or the situation in Lebanon, all of these international crises had one striking similarity: They each involved only one crisis at a time. For example, in the Gulf of Tonkin the only crisis at hand—as developed by President Johnson—was the crisis of a foreign power attacking a U.S. vessel abroad. There was no competition for the claim to crisis. The August 1994 Senate floor debate on comprehensive health care reform was most unlike these international crises. Instead of a single event or set of circumstances that would be rhetorically crafted into a crisis, there was the appearance of two competing crises. Proponents of the Mitchell bill and comprehensive reform rhetorically pointed to the existence of a health care crisis. The opponents of the Mitchell proposal, alternatively, constructed a potential crisis of the expansion of the federal government—a crisis of big government—if the comprehensive health care reform measure were enacted. Many of the other unique features of this particular case of crisis rhetoric derived, at least in part, from this apparent competition between two crises. The characteristics of these competing crises will be more fully illuminated as the rhetorical construction of each crisis is examined, but a brief preview is worthwhile.

The health care crisis was largely descriptive of those who had failed to garner adequate coverage and protection from the present system. The health care crisis was grounded in both the logic of the statistical implications associated with millions of uninsured and underinsured individuals, and the emotional appeal associated with the physical and other consequences of health care that is not obtained. The health care crisis was an account of a situation that existed, objectively, in the present system.

The crisis of big government was grounded principally in the notion that extension of universal or comprehensive health care amounted to an expansion of the federal government. The crisis of big government featured a vision of what the potential consequences would be if the Mitchell proposal were passed. The crisis of big government was also an account, but it was a very subjective interpretation of what would follow passage of the Majority Leader's bill.

The two competing crises drew much of their respective "raw materials" from the specific discursive features examined in the previous chapter. The analysis of the rhetoric employed to construct these crises pointed to the role of narratives, evidence, language strategies, and metaphors. For example, those who described the present health care crisis relied very heavily upon use of numerical instances and other-person narratives. Many elements of the health care crisis were easy to describe statistically —millions who lacked adequate coverage, for example. In addition, the health care crisis involved narratives that described the personal tragedies that individuals had suffered due to a pre-existing illness or a canceled insurance policy. The construction of the crisis of big government, however, relied very heavily upon the language strategy of blame and social narratives. Blame was used to attach responsibility for undesirable future social and economic consequences to the Mitchell proposal. Social narratives were utilized to point to the threats that loomed large for significant social groups, particularly "the taxpaying public."

Much like President Clinton before them, Senator Mitchell and his allies invoked the image of a health care crisis as the underlying rationale for crafting a comprehensive reform proposal and overhauling the existing health care system. Health care reform proponents pointed to a crisis that involved personal stories of medical tragedy, statistical data proclaiming enormous numbers of uninsured and underinsured Americans, and illustrations of "real people" who "did everything right" suffering because of the failure of the United States to ensure universal health care coverage and access.

A number of health care reform advocates pointed to the high costs associated with the existing health care system as an indicator of a crisis condition. Numerous Senators promoting reform action noted that some 14 to 15 percent of Gross National Product was devoted to health care on an annual basis, and yet there were still millions of U.S. citizens who lacked medical coverage. The remarks of Senator Sarbanes were typical of this appeal to the financial nature of a crisis:

The current system in the United States spends significantly more as a percent of our national income on health than other advanced industrial nations and yet provides less comprehensive coverage for a substantial portion of the population. (S12199)

Senator Sarbanes's point was fairly clear: The United States pays heavily in financial costs for health care yet reaps relatively few benefits.

Many reform advocates went beyond an appeal to the costs of the present system to a potentially more compelling issue: the impact on the lives of individual citizens. This process did not always progress in a clear step-by-step manner. Some Senators spent the bulk of their time dealing with accounts of these individual citizens, and little time on the cost issue. Individual Senators tend to select a mix of organizational or dispositional patterns to construct or describe the health care crisis. However, virtually every Senator, who spoke of a health care crisis gave considerable attention to the personal tragedies that had befallen so many people who either were underinsured or had limited access to needed medical care. Indeed, many pro–Mitchell proposal speakers sought to link all of their listeners to the type of personal health care crisis that so often occurred under the existing system. Senator Mosely-Braun, for example, noted, "Well the answers are too clear to everybody who is paying attention or knows somebody, and I think there is not a person around who does not know somebody who has not had a health care crisis" (S12188). Senator Mitchell also hit at this notion of personal tragedy when he called for action by stating: "The difference between secure coverage and an unaffordable policy can be as heartbreaking as one sick child. That is not fair or right. That is why we need reform" (S11006). These cases of personal tragedy were, according to reform advocates, indicators of a health care crisis that warranted significant, comprehensive action.

Those who favored the Mitchell proposal for comprehensive health care reform did not want their auditors to assume that the cases of personal health care tragedy were isolated or atypical. The health care crisis was, by their account, a significant and widespread situation. Many reform advocates noted that 35 million, 37 million, or perhaps as many as 45 million Americans lacked insurance coverage for protection against some grave medical emergency. Indeed, a number of speakers argued that several thousand Americans lost their insurance coverage every minute. Those who lost their insurance were, proponents noted, not personally at fault for their loss of insurance. Many of those who lost insurance had developed a catastrophic illness, suffered a serious injury, or, in many cases, had simply switched jobs. Several days into the floor debate, Senator Daschle attempted to put all of this into perspective as he noted that "500,000, half a million people have lost their health insurance since this debate began. About 48 a minute now lose their health insurance" (S11888). The suggestion was that the drama of the situation was intense and that the numbers were staggering.

Reform advocates also attempted to paint the health care crisis as one affecting ordinary Americans. They argued that this was not a crisis isolated to remote pockets of the poor. Indeed, it was often noted that the very poor typically receive some health care benefits through Medicare and other assistance programs. This was a crisis of middle class America. Ordinary people with ordinary lives and, unfortunately, ordinary problems were the victims in the current health care crisis. The stories that detailed the terrible circumstances of such individuals were read into the record, they were often accompanied by the phrase that these were "people who did everything right." They were not welfare cheats, gang members, or other social outcasts. They were people who had worked hard and had "followed the rules of the game." Senator Lautenberg's statement is typical of this account of the health care crisis: "We have created a system which provides health security to the rich and the poor, but not for the middle class, not for ordinary working Americans" (S11081).

The nature of the health care crisis, advocates argued, also imposed heavy burdens upon American families. Senator Lautenberg expressed the type of "tough" choices that the health care crisis posed for millions of Americans:

No family should be forced to choose between putting food on the table and taking care of their children's health, or choosing between helping with a college education or health care or jeopardizing their own retirement to take care of parents stricken with Alzheimer's disease. But that happens in New Jersey and in our country every day of the week. (S11891)

To Lautenberg, then, it was the very nature of the current health care crisis and the health care system as it exists that were the villains in this case; they could force an ordinary family to make potentially crippling decisions.

Some characterized the health care crisis as a "nightmare." Others argued that the present health care system was "perverse." Many of the advocates for reform attempted to characterize the issue of health care reform as a matter of social justice. Senator Mitchell put it this way:

Health care reform is a matter of simple justice. Human beings are born unequal in ability and in strength. None of us chooses our family circumstances. None of us is immune to bad luck. We are all susceptible to accident and illness. We all grow old. (S11005)

Thus, according to Mitchell, we are all at risk due to the vagaries of health and wellness. We need the government to step in with a comprehensive package of reforms that will extend the safety net and protect us all in a just manner.

The dimensions of the health care crisis had been laid out by Senator Mitchell and others who advocated action on a comprehensive health care reform proposal. The current costs were great, both financially and in terms of countless personal tragedies. Millions, perhaps tens of millions, of Americans were victims of the health care crisis and everyone was potentially at risk of suffering a personal health care tragedy. Social justice was at stake along with the lives and health of ordinary, hard-working Americans. Senator Mitchell suggested that these were not the characteristics of a "civilized society." The remarks of Senator Dodd typified the portrayal of the health care crisis as constructed by reform advocates:

We all lose, obviously, when the worker or the person of tomorrow is crippled for life by untreated illness. That occurs today. We all lose when a completely preventable disease—let me emphasize that it is a completely preventable disease—like measles ripple through the child population. We all lose when parents cannot change jobs for fear of losing coverage for their children. (S11450)

Senator Dodd's message and the message of all health care reform advocates was clear: The health care crisis makes everyone a loser; everyone is a victim.

Opponents of the comprehensive health care reform proposal embodied in Senator Mitchell's bill did not spend much time or effort attempting to directly refute the details of the status of the current health care system. Opponents of the Mitchell proposal, instead, constructed their own crisis. The opponents of the Mitchell proposal feared that it would ultimately lead to an unprecedented growth in the size and scope of the federal government. These fears were crafted into a crisis of big government. Enactment of the Mitchell bill, the Clinton plan, or any such federal overhaul of the health care system would produce staggering economic costs to the economy and to taxpayers and generate a growth in bureaucracy unmatched by any other legislative proposal, with a corresponding decline in the high quality of care that most Americans had become accustomed to.

A number of Republican opponents of the Mitchell proposal offered much more limited legislative proposals of their own. These alternatives were often used to help characterize the Mitchell proposal as a big government scheme and to point to the type of risks it entailed. Senator Dole's remarks regarding his limited measure are typical of this strategy:

We are not a bit defensive about our proposal . . . maybe it can be changed. It certainly can be made better. But if better means more government, more bureaucracy, more mandates, more price controls, or more taxes, then we do not want to make it better. That is not better for most Americans. I think that is the bottom line. (S11246)

Senator Dole seemed to offer the bottom line for the crisis of big government as well: More government, more bureaucracy, more mandates, more regulation, and more taxes were the real villains for most Americans.

Opponents of the Mitchell proposal constantly characterized it as a measure that would produce a government-run health care system. They argued that the mix of regulations, mandates, and powers embodied in the proposal were, in effect, an attempt at a government takeover of the system. And, the risk of government-run health care was enormous. Senator Lott expressed this view clearly:

Government-run health care will not save money, but it will cost jobs. And guess whose jobs? Some of them will be low-income jobs, but a lot of middle-income jobs are really going to get lost. The middle class after government-run health care are going to find their wallets a lot thinner and in far too many instances pink slips in their wallets. (S11461)

Government-run health care and big government would, therefore, hit many people where it really hurts—in the pocketbook. Senator Lott, like so many of his like-minded colleagues, was often very intense in this display of anti–big government rhetoric. Indeed, Senator Lott continued by noting:

We do not need government-run health care. We do not need new bureaucracy. We do not need mandates. Government-run health care is like giving a lobotomy when they only have a headache. It is overkill. Middle-class Americans know this. (S11462)

And, this was part of the rhetorical appeal that Lott and others hoped to play upon, that "most Americans" know that more government is not a good thing.

Senator Lott's remarks and those of others who made claims regarding the evils of big government raised the specter of hypocrisy. Lott and his fellow Republican colleagues were, obviously, *members of* the federal government, not somehow apart from it. They were, in effect, "biting the hand that feeds them"—attacking the very agent which made their positions and power possible. This apparent hypocrisy was not lost on Majority Leader Mitchell. After discussing Republican support for Medicare, Veterans Administration health services, and other government programs, he noted:

So while they stand here and say they are against "Government-run programs," when they go back home to their constituents, they spend a lot of time and effort and money telling their constituents how they are going to protect those very Government health insurance programs. (S11877)

Mitchell also may have found an explanation for the existence of this apparent hypocrisy as he stated: "I know the mood in our country today is that a popular way to attack anything is to say it is 'Government-run' and to suggest somehow that it is therefore inefficient" (S11877). Thus, attacks upon the government provide popular political ammunition. Such attacks or claims allow a rhetor to position himself or herself as the "voice of the average person" who has been compelled to take a role in the "enemy camp" in order to expose its true motivations and to put some constraint on its unwarranted expansion. This is a rhetorical tactic that was popularized by Ronald Reagan in the 1980s (Wills, 1987). Despite being the chief executive of the federal system, Reagan successfully latched onto public discontent and argued heartily and repeatedly for constraint of the federal government.

Senator Danforth made the general negative view of the Mitchell proposal clear when he stated, "We think it is too big, that it goes too far . . . it is just too much. It is too extreme" (S11766). The Mitchell bill was characterized as a measure that would vastly expand the role that the federal government played in health care. The new powers and authority that the Mitchell bill would assign to the Department of Health and Human Services were, for example, attacked as grants of authority to an "omnipresent" Secretary of Health and Human Services. In fact, Senator Lott concluded that the Mitchell proposal "is just too much for us as a country to choke down" (S11768).

Senator Gorton characterized big government as threatening "due to its often unaccountable, expensive, arrogant, and sometimes oppressive nature" (S11774). This was not a pretty picture. The threat seemed to loom large. Big government held great power—power to tax, power to regulate, power to penalize and enforce actions. Employer mandates were labeled as "oppressive" and price controls were called "undemocratic." Indeed, the image of the coming crisis of big government was very threatening: It would require Senator Hutchison, for example, "to sell my constituents into a world of long lines, new taxes, and bureaucrats rationing treatment" (S11781). She further argued that the Mitchell proposal would involve government deeply in personal, private decisions: "The Clinton and Mitchell bills insert the cold hand of government into this private discussion and tell doctors and patients what sort of care will be covered and what sorts will not" (S11780).

The rhetorical development of a crisis of big government points to an interesting "before" and "after" or "problem" and "remedy" contrast. As explained in the previous chapter, the discourse of reform proponents was grounded in the present tense—here are the problems and ills that we must currently deal with. The discourse of reform opponents was more future-oriented—here are the tragic consequences that will follow passage of the Mitchell proposal. Put another way, advocates of reform were developing a crisis that caused problems that could not be solved *before* passage of comprehensive health care reform. The opponents of such reform proposals were developing a future crisis that would occur *after* passage of the measures. This contrast is even more important when considering the comparative "visions" that these rhetors held; it is addressed in the assessment of why the "crisis of big government" argument was successful.

The opponents of the Mitchell comprehensive health care reform package wanted their auditors to see that the Mitchell bill would expand the power and scope of the federal government and that such expansion would be inherently dangerous. Further, the proponents of comprehensive health care reform were characterized as agents of this expansion and "true believers" in big government. Senator Wallop put it like this:

There are, unfortunately, those in Congress who subscribe to a "big nanny" philosophy and they are the same people who have crafted the health plan now being debated. That we Americans have not the ability to choose what is good for our families, what is good for our employers, what is good for our country. We must have this group here in this Senate and in those bureaucracies doing it for us because we are not to be trusted. Only inside the Beltway resides wisdom—so those people would think. (S11821)

To Wallop, not only was there a potential crisis in the consequences of acting on the Mitchell proposal, but there was a crisis in the way that some people think about the role of government.

The Mitchell bill was not merely another ingredient in the mix that created a risk of the crisis of big government, it was central to the crisis. Many opponents of the Mitchell proposal viewed it as a vehicle for the unprecedented expansion of federal power. The remarks of Senator Coats are typical: "If you read this bill, you will see it as the single greatest expansion of government in the history of this nation. You will see it as government control run amok" (S11945). This expansion was not only viewed as the most significant of its type, but it was also viewed as something far from benign. It posed a real destructive potential. Senator Craig noted:

Governments do not create communities. They destroy communities. They destroy volunteerism. They destroy individuals coming together to provide for themselves and their community. We all know that. (S12071)

The government was a killer—it killed communities, it killed volunteerism, it killed individual initiative, Craig maintained. And, the Mitchell bill turned that killer into a giant.

The crisis of big government was laid out in great detail and the potential threat was portrayed as one that could not be ignored. The Mitchell bill would, according to opponents of the comprehensive reform legislation, expand the federal government and in doing so pose serious risks to everything Americans held near and dear, from individual freedom to a hefty pocketbook. The opponents of the Mitchell proposal characterized it as radical, even as an attempt at the "socialization" of health care. This was a crisis that most Americans knew all too well—long lines, delays, high costs, low quality. Images of the DMV or IRS handling serious health problems readily came to mind. In fact, many opponents of comprehensive health care reform saw the Mitchell bill as transforming health care into the image of the U.S. Postal Service.

This appearance of two competing crises—a health care crisis and a crisis of big government—was not the sole feature that distinguished the August 1994 Senate floor debate on comprehensive health care reform from other cases of crisis rhetoric. As noted, studies that fit under the rubric of crisis rhetoric have tended to focus on foreign policy or international affairs. Rhetorical scholars have examined the Gulf of Tonkin crisis, the invasion of Grenada, the bombing in Lebanon, and a number of other international policy situations. Cherwitz and Zagacki (1986) have summarized: "The subject of international crises is the focus of significant scholarly investigation . . . [R]hetorical critics scrutinize the wealth of discursive features constituting the genre of crisis rhetoric" (p. 307). The present investigation on the Senate floor debate regarding health care reform was squarely focused on domestic crisis situations. The health care issue, as characterized by reform advocates, was clearly a domestic crisis of great proportions. Similarly, the expansion of the power and scope of the federal government posed a crisis of big government for the domestic population.

Previous scholarly attention to crisis rhetoric had also focused upon the discursive behavior of a single rhetor—the President. Cherwitz (1978) focused upon the rhetoric of Lyndon Johnson. Hahn (1980) attempted to illuminate the discursive behavior of Gerald Ford. And, Cherwitz and Zagacki (1986) and Hersey (1986) were concentrating on the persuasive strategies of Ronald Reagan in a time of crisis. In addition, most of these investigations focused not only upon a single rhetor, but upon a single address. The most recent edited volume on the subject, Kiewe's (1994) *The Modern Presidency and Crisis Rhetoric*, focuses, for example, upon several addresses made by American Presidents since Harry Truman. The Kiewe volume includes an account of John F. Kennedy's rhetorical construction of the Berlin controversy, examination of Ford's pardon of Vietnam Era draft resisters, analysis of Jimmy Carter's reaction to the Iran hostage situation, and an appraisal of Reagan's management of the Iran-Contra affair. The present investigation extends both the number of rhetors examined and the number of speeches. The floor debate regarding comprehensive health care reform hinged on the construction of two crises by two competing elements within the Senate chamber. Schuetz (1986) has argued that the Senate represents a specialized argument field and Kane (1995) and many others have argued that the Senate is a unique public forum for the examination of argumentative discourse. The present investigation recognizes that uniqueness and extends that very unique rhetorical context as an arena for examination of crisis rhetoric.

Another substantive difference derives from this departure from examining crisis rhetoric in times of foreign policy or international affairs problems by the President. In those international crisis situations, internal value conflicts arise for the President. He must choose to embrace diplomacy or intervention; to relish freedom and power or to cherish compromise and peaceful survival. David Zarefsky (1983) has explained:

When a president must choose between peace and freedom, ideology and self-interest, as diplomatic and energy goals, two values—both of them desirable—are pitted against each other, one cannot maximize both. These conflicts are seen most starkly, perhaps, in times of crisis. Not only do values conflict, but decisions must be made under severe constraints of time and information. (p. 59)

Thus, crisis rhetoric has tended to examine situations where an individual policy maker suffers an internal value conflict. A value conflict also took place during the crisis rhetoric of the Senate floor debate on comprehensive health care reform, but it was very different in nature. It was an external, overt conflict of values. At center stage was a question of what was most important—taking whatever action necessary to extend the protections of health care, or to draw the line and stop the expansion in the size and scope of the federal government. In fact, as will be seen later, many opponents of the Mitchell proposal made conflicting values a central theme in the August 1994 floor debate. Further, it was not an internal value conflict for one actor.

It was an open conflict for all the parties in the Senate and the larger public audience as well.

Perhaps the most striking feature of the crisis rhetoric employed in the Senate floor debate was that it represented the success of a rhetorically constructed crisis over a crisis that could be argued to have intrinsic quality and exist on a more objective level. An abundance of evidence speaks to the actual condition of the United States health care system in the early 1990s. As previously noted, a great many sources confirmed that large numbers of people were uninsured, that even more were underinsured, that medical costs were skyrocketing, and that serious health problems had befallen a good many individuals due to limitations in coverage, access, and affordability. On the other hand, the crisis of big government was virtual, all threat and potential—the expansion of the size of government could cost trillions of dollars, government-run health care could deny individual decision making and choice, and an expanded federal government could pose a danger to values that Americans hold near and dear. Even though some objective evidence spoke to the existence of a health care crisis, the rhetorically crafted virtual crisis of big government prevailed in the debate. This seemingly remarkable outcome leads to an important question: How could the rhetorically constructed *virtual* crisis of big government outweigh the *actual* health care crisis? That question will receive my attention in Chapter Ten as I discuss the triumph of the big government virtual crisis or argument.

Chapter 10

The Triumph of the
Big Government Argument

Examination of the actual talk that shaped the 1994 health care reform debate will reveal that the debate hinged upon the success of the "big government" virtual crisis. I contend that not only did the rhetorically crafted crisis of big government succeed during the August 1994 Senate floor debate, but that it is possible to identify specific discursive reasons for its success. It is possible to extend from the discussion of discourse patterns and to offer an overall rhetorical interpretation suggesting that opponents of the Mitchell proposal were simply successful in "pushing all of the right buttons" rhetorically. Further, it is possible to embrace the concept of narrative rationality developed by Fisher (1984) and argue that the crisis of big government passed the test of narrative fidelity, that it seemed to "ring true" for auditors of the debate. In addition, opponents of the Mitchell proposal were more successful, rhetorically, at connecting to the inherent political tension between reassurance and threat, and in capitalizing on the bimodal nature of values on the subject. I will also argue that the rhetorical construction of the crisis of big government was uniquely successful in the use of what I term an "implicit metaphor." Finally, I will contend that opponents of the Mitchell proposal were able to subsume the health care issue and recast it not as a crisis itself, but merely as a symptom of the crisis of big government. I will also explain how that process can be expressed as an exercise in framing and reframing. I will proceed to construct each argument in turn.

PUSHING THE RIGHT BUTTONS

As the discussion of discourse patterns indicates, the August 1994 Senate floor debate was characterized by the use of language strategies—naming, blaming, categorizing, plus a recounting of narratives such as personal, other-person, social narratives—and was rich with evidence of many types and some "peppering" of medical metaphors. Both proponents and opponents of the Mitchell proposal employed these various discursive devices, but those who constructed the crisis of big government were far more successful at rhetorically "pushing every button." They hit appeals that connected to many different auditors and worked in a very clear suasory sense to help derail passage of a comprehensive reform proposal. Appeals were grounded in financial issues and costs, in risks to the quality of care, and in threats to traditional American values. Opponents of the Mitchell proposal basically found something for everyone to hate, or at least to fear.

Appeals to the pocketbook were an important part of the rhetorical onslaught by opponents of the Mitchell proposal. Many opponents of reform consistently and clearly raised the issue of "Who would pay the price for the bill?" They labeled reform advocates the agents of a "taxoholic" Congress that would strap the American public with billions, perhaps trillions of dollars worth of new costs. Opponents also characterized the federal guarantee of health care coverage as a new "entitlement"— something the government assures and that cannot be taken away. Senator Danforth summarized the sort of cost-benefit calculus that typified Republican opposition to the Mitchell bill: "We cannot afford $1.2 trillion in new entitlement programs, no matter how wonderful they are" (S11766). Senator Gorton extended this equation by stressing who would actually pay: "Difficult choices are ahead, but the option of having the American taxpayer forking over more hard-earned pay is not an appropriate one. Everywhere but on Capitol Hill it is obvious that this option is not affordable" (S11775). The appeal to "pocketbook issues" was clear: The Mitchell proposal would cost taxpayers too much, it threatened wages, income, and general financial well-being.

Opponents of the Mitchell proposal also appealed directly to the perception that most Americans held about the quality of health care under the existing system, and how that quality might be negatively impacted by an expanded government role in the funding and delivery of health care. For example, Senator Gramm offered many accounts of the evils of government-run health care in Canada and in Europe, which he characterized as the failures of socialized medicine. In fact, he noted that "people who have had an opportunity to look socialized medicine in the face . . . have found that face to be an ugly, uncaring face" (S11195). Many other Senate opponents of the Mitchell proposal for comprehensive health care reform evoked fear by suggesting that Americans would end up standing in long lines waiting for rationed care. Senator Shields, for example, noted that "The high-growth plan tax is not only a tax on quality health benefits, but . . . would result in rationing of health care services offered by health plans" (S11685).

Much of this collection of appeals offered in opposition to the Mitchell proposal was made compelling through the use of specific discursive techniques. Two of these—specific terminology and metaphors—have already been discussed at length. As was noted with regard to crisis discourse, specific terms—such as those items Weaver (1953) labeled "god" and "devil" words—can have almost immediate effects upon an audience. For example, when Senator Gramm describes the "ugly, uncaring face" of government-run health care, the immediate response is a desire to shun something so unattractive and to find it repulsive. The use of medical metaphors also added vividness and color to the rhetoric. When Senator McConnell advised his colleagues to place a "Do Not Resuscitate" sign on the Mitchell proposal, it was clear that he viewed the bill as beyond help and one that should be left to a peaceful demise.

Two additional discursive strategies helped to make the rhetoric of reform opponents compelling. Both repetition and the use of what are called "intensifiers" (Erickson et al., 1978) operated to make the rhetorical construction of an alternative, larger crisis more dramatic. In his analysis of the Mitchell proposal, Senator McConnell repeatedly labeled its provisions "radical." He drew upon the reactionary power of the term and employed it several times to add emphasis and to stress his characterization. Senator Wallop also used repetition to stress the cost of the Mitchell proposal, which he said "will cost $1.4 trillion between the years 1995 and 2004—in that decade, $1.4 trillion" (S11820). Senator Wallop's repetition of the specific cost figure—$1.4 trillion—helped to make it clear that this was simply a price too high to pay. Opponents of reform also used intensifiers—words that increase or emphasize the force of an assertion, such as "very," "definitely," and "surely." For example, Senator Wallop described the Mitchell plan as "the most massive explosion of Government—maybe in this half century" (S11820). The Mitchell plan was not, according to Wallop, another growth in government, it was "the most massive" increase in the size and scope of the federal government. Senator Brown attempted to draw a parallel between the earlier enactment of the Hill-Burton bill and Majority Leader Mitchell's proposal and noted "It was a very large program, and between 1946 and 1974, $4 billion was spent on it" (S11878). Brown made it clear that such proposals do not offer moderate advances or minor repairs, they become "very large" programs. These discursive strategies added emphasis and attention to many of the rhetorical appeals made by reform opponents. Their other strategies and appeals were also of interest.

VALUE CLAIMS

Appeals were made by opponents of comprehensive health care reform to the traditional American belief in "rugged" individualism. Bellah (1985) has explained at some length that Americans place a great deal of pride in the ability of individuals to accomplish goals and to account for themselves. The Mitchell bill would, opponents contended, replace individual choice with government decision making. Senator Hutchison made the point clearly and simply when she proclaimed that "The American people are sick and tired of having decisions made for them by the Federal Government" (S11779). This appeal to individual choice and the traditional belief in individualism was also grounded in a slippery slope argument—that given the chance, government would tend to seek more and more power, and ultimately take control. Senator Wallop described the nature of this trend toward government takeover:

Government slowly, slowly, slowly has been overtaking our lives. In one generation, Government has doubled the amount of money that it takes from Americans and it has increasingly used that money to deprive us of control over our own lives. (S11821)

Senator Wallop went on to note how this trend is directly linked to the proposal for comprehensive health care reform:

If we embark on the course that President Clinton and Majority Leader Mitchell set for us, we will vastly increase both the scope and the power of the Federal Government and the ability to wield influence in each of our individual lives. (S11826)

The growing threat to individualism was made clear.

Other important American values were also utilized as appeals by opponents of comprehensive health care reform during the August 1994 Senate floor debate. Senator Wallop, for example, suggested that more government control was inherently "undemocratic" as it removed direct power from the people. He characterized the Mitchell proposal as a direct threat to both liberty and freedom:

Freedom and liberty will be lost through the imposition of 50 new bureaucratic regimes that will impose so many rules and regulations that bureaucrats, not individuals, will tighten the existing controls that they have over our lives. (S11822)

If the Mitchell proposal threatened both freedom and liberty, only apple pie and motherhood would be left. In other words, opponents of the Mitchell bill wanted the public to feel that no traditional American value would be safe.

Appeals were also clearly directed to elements or groups within the broader public audience that placed high priority on particular issues. For example, Senator Helms was fond of noting that the Mitchell proposal would pay for elective abortions as part of its benefits package. This would obviously be something that pro-life advocates could latch onto and therefore join the opposition to comprehensive health care reform. Senator Wallop even suggested that the growth of government associated with the Mitchell proposal posed a potential threat to religion: "I have said more than once that the more secular this country becomes, the more we pray to Government to do that which we used to pray for our Maker to do or to provide" (S11829). The implication was that an expanding role for government—such as that associated with the Mitchell bill—would increasingly replace worship of a supreme being with worship of a supreme bureaucrat!

JUDGING THE STORY

The simple rhetorical ability to make appeals that were attractive to many auditors was one way to characterize the success of the construction of the crisis of big government. Another answer for this rhetorical success might be found in the narrative perspective or paradigm as articulated by Fisher (1984, 1985, 1987). Application of the standards or tests associated with narrative rationality suggest that the crisis of big government possessed great narrative fidelity; that is, it seemed to "ring true" for the audience. It is worthy of note prior to proceeding along these lines, to mention that Fisher implicitly endorsed application of his narrative paradigm to the genre of crisis rhetoric. In his 1985 elaboration of the narrative paradigm, Fisher suggested that one application of the tests of narrative rationality that might be illuminating would be to the United States invasion of Grenada. As noted, this military intervention has attracted the attention of scholars interested in crisis rhetoric.

As Fisher (1984) originally explained the concept of narrative rationality, it consists of both narrative probability or coherence and narrative fidelity. Narrative coherence fundamentally deals with how a story seems to fit together; whether it is consistent, lacks contradictions, and whether it plays out logically. Although I do not intend to treat the narrative coherence of the crisis of big government at length here, a few comments are in order. The crisis of big government as a narrative or story had what may be called "plot coherence." The story line in this crisis was always consistent and developed in the same manner: The federal government passes major social legislation, that legislation establishes new power (regulatory, taxing, etc.) for the federal government, those powers tend to grow along a slippery slope to total government control, and the consequences are grave for individuals, the economy, and the nation as a whole. This somewhat standardized plot played out logically for audience members who had seen the size of the federal government expand as their discretionary incomes and individual choice declined. Narrative fidelity, on the other hand, is basically a test of whether a story "rings true" for an auditor, whether it is consistent with the beliefs and experiences of the audience. Narrative fidelity is, according to Fisher, inherently grounded in "good reasons." Good reasons are more than the logic of a particular argument; they relate ultimately to appeals to how one would characterize the "good life." Narrative fidelity is an important test for a story because it will often determine whether or not someone will 'buy into' a particular story. Application of narrative fidelity to the rhetorical construction of a crisis of big government suggests that the crisis was one that tended to "ring true" for listeners.

The most obvious attempt to relate the potential experience of a big government crisis to the beliefs held by average Americans was made with regard to references about the Post Office. For example, Senator Gramm noted, "I am not going to support tearing down the greatest medical care system in the history of the world to rebuild it in the image of the Post Office" (S11195). Senator Murkowski elaborated on the point:

The public is concerned, of course, about the Government going into the health care business. The point has been made sometime in this body that if you like the Post Office system in Washington, DC, you will love the Government once it takes over health care. (S11885)

Senator Helms posed the issue as a simple question: "Do you want . . . the Government that operates your Postal System, to decide whether you should have an operation or not?" (S12167). Typically, we can conclude that the answer would be no. Despite whatever objective success the U.S. Postal Service may claim, most Americans have a negative view of it or at least can recall a negative experience—standing in a long line, losing a package, receiving a letter or package several months late, or having their favorite magazine arrive nearly shredded. This is clearly the image of the federal government that reform opponents wished to construct for the public. They wanted to represent the government as an enormous, inefficient bureaucracy that could not do something as simple as get a letter or package from point A to point B, no less something as complex and important as providing citizens with health care. Such a representation was conveyed throughout the rhetorical construction of a crisis of big government—that entire crisis, in many respects, depended on *making it really seem like a crisis for the public.*

Beyond the specific case of the Post Office, most Americans have either suffered some negative experience in their interactions with the federal government or they have developed a generally negative view of how the government operates. Senator Dole suggested that a general distrust of government extended to the various proposals for comprehensive health care reform:

And plain and simple, the American people did not trust the Clinton plan. They did not trust the secrecy in which it was written. They did not trust the principle that "government knows best." And they did not trust the endless maze of new government boards and bureaucracies that would have been created. (S12083)

Senator Dole and his Republican colleagues also cited poll after poll that tended to confirm that general distrust of the comprehensive reform proposals. In addition, a number of individuals seem to display an innate distrust of some specific segment of the federal government—the IRS, the military, the CIA, and, of course, the Post Office.

Indeed, a number of Senators spoke to the general distrust of government and the overall disillusionment with government that tended to be so pervasive at the time of the floor debate on comprehensive health care reform. Senator Dorgan summarized this sense of disillusionment and hostility:

There is, I know, great rancor, anger, cynicism by some about this health care debate, about Congress generally, about the Government, about Washington. All of us see it and hear it. We feel it every day from the phone calls we get and contacts when we are back home. (S11943)

Even proponents of health care reform recognized the pervasiveness of such negative attitudes toward government. Senator Mitchell, for example, commented:

That has become the dominant theme of the statements made by our Republican colleagues seeking to capitalize on a public sentiment of disillusionment with Government and even hostility to Government. (S11937)

It was, therefore, no secret that the public had a generally fearful, untrusting view of government.

Although Fisher proposed his narrative paradigm as an alternative way to conceptualize public discourse, narrative fidelity shares much in common with the more traditional rational concept of presumption. From the time of Whateley, argumentation scholars have suggested that locating presumption is often key in evaluating the disposition of an argument. The most traditional view of presumption holds that it rests with those things that currently exist—current attitudes, current values, and so on. Ehninger and Brockriede's (1963) view is typical: "Natural presumption reflects things as they are viewed in the world about us. If an argument involves a belief concerning existing institutions, practices, customs, mores, values, or interpretations, the presumption is automatically in favor of that belief simply because the institutions, etc., are thought to exist" (p. 83). The parallel with narrative fidelity should be apparent: Both views are grounded in the present values, beliefs, experiences, and so forth held by an audience. Hollihan, Riley, and Baaske (1985) have suggested that narrative fidelity warrants a reconceptualization of presumption: "The new perspective . . . also requires a different understanding of the concept of presumption . . . [C]ritics seeking to develop a narrative will . . . be determining whether arguments hang together as stories and evaluating them in terms of their own cultural beliefs, values, and experiences" (p. 818). Although Hollihan and his colleagues were speaking of changes required of judges in competitive academic debate, their point extends the position here; narrative fidelity may be appropriately reconceptualized as a form of presumption. In the present case, presumption seemed to rest squarely against expanding the role of government in health care.

CAPITALIZING DISCURSIVELY
Whether characterized as a test of narrative fidelity or more traditionally as a case of locating presumption, the crisis of big government did seem to carry appeal—or, perhaps more accurately, revulsion—for some auditors. Opponents of comprehensive health care reform were also very effective at capitalizing on the nature of the political dispute surrounding health care. The health care debate might be viewed as a classic illustration of what Murray Edelman (1965) has characterized as an inherent and enduring tension between reassurance and threat:

For the spectators of the political scene every act contributes to a pattern of ongoing events that spells threat or reassurance. This is the basic dichotomy for the mass public. The very fact that the same acts which are grouping favors looms ominously for another reinforce each side in its perceptions for it seems to make it all the more clear that the enemy is really there fighting against the good life or against life itself. (p. 13)

In other words, a single political act can be seen simultaneously as a step toward reassurance by one group and as a threat by another.

This tension between reassurance and threat should be apparent with regard to the Senate floor debate on comprehensive health care reform. Mitchell and the other proponents of health care reform were explicitly offering reassurance to the public—that comprehensive health care reform would extend medical coverage, improve access, enhance affordability, and put an end to denial of insurance coverage for pre-existing illnesses. Opponents of comprehensive health care reform crafted the crisis, or threat of big government—taxes would increase, individual choice would decline, freedom and liberty would be lost, and our health care system would be modeled on the Postal Service. As noted, opponents of reform employed many rhetorical appeals and other discursive strategies to make big government the common enemy, around which the masses could rally. Finlay and his colleagues (1967) have argued that the construction of an enemy in this manner is a typically successful political strategy. In addition, Edelman (1965) has noted that "the threatening trends naturally loom larger than the reassuring ones" (p. 13).

Opponents of comprehensive health care reform were also successful in crafting the development of a crisis of big government because of the unique nature of public values on the issue of health care. Although a society may well seek what Lane and Sears (1964) have termed "unimodal" values—values that reflect a relatively unified mass responding to fairly enduring features of life—the controversial issues of the time tended to render that impossible. Lane and Sears offered this explanation:

We can determine which position is modal within the population; i.e., which opinion is held by the most people. . . . If there is only one mode, as in the case of opinion toward universal suffrage, the issue cannot be described as highly controversial. However, sometimes public opinion is bimodal, that is there are two very popular, and opposed positions. (pp. 7–8)

Health care might, thus, be characterized as a case of bimodal values; there are two very different, competing views on the subject.

Bimodal value conflicts offer unique opportunities for the construction of an enemy and a chance to capitalize on the fear inherent in such a case. Edelman (1965) has noted: "When on the issues that arouse men emotionally, there is bimodal value structuring, threat and insecurity are maximized. Those who hold the other value are the enemy . . . [and] responses are chiefly to threat perceptions" (p. 175). In a discussion relating bimodal values to the process of events in a debate, Thomas (1992) similarly noted: "When a group feels threatened and it sees those who disagree as the enemy, then the weapons it uses in its struggle are no-holds-barred" (p. 235). The opponents of the Mitchell proposal saw the rise of big government as the enemy and they unleashed every rhetorical weapon in their arsenal.

IMPLICIT METAPHOR

In addition to the ability to capitalize on the unique tension between reassurance and threat and the bimodal nature of public values on the question of health care reform, opponents of the Mitchell proposal were also successful at the use of what I would term as "implicit metaphor." In rhetorically constructing a crisis of big government, the opponents of comprehensive health care reform evoked an implicit metaphor to fit the meaning that they had established. That is the nature of an implicit metaphor. Rather than explicitly using a figure of speech to characterize an event or situation, an implicit metaphor fixes a meaning and allows the auditor to affix an appropriate label to that meaning. An implicit metaphor derives much of its appeal from the features of explicit or natural metaphor, yet its suasory appeal extends beyond that.

As noted earlier, rhetorical scholars have recognized the power and appeal of the concept of metaphor. Scholars and commentators such as I. A. Richards (1936) and Kenneth Burke (1952) have attested to the utility of metaphor as a component of rhetoric. Metaphors help to facilitate understanding. When a businessperson tells a new CEO that she is the "quarterback of the team and must call the right plays," it is not meant as instruction in the rules of football. Such an expression is employed to tell someone how he should view something. Burke (1952) explained how metaphor works by writing, "Any metaphor is . . . reductive, as it enables us to see one thing in terms of something else" (p. 97).

Additionally, a great many scholars hold that metaphor possesses epistemic value. Sadock (1979) has described metaphor as a "tendency of thought" (p. 49). Metaphors help us see things, in light of other things and to also think of things in light of other things. Schwartzman (1995) has expressed this epistemic nature of metaphor very clearly: "Metaphor is more than a vehicle for expressing knowledge; it is a way of arriving at knowledge" (p. 43). Indeed, Lakoff and Johnson (1980) contend that metaphor is the principal means for knowing. They contend that the conceptual system is essentially metaphorical.

The implicit metaphor also functions in an epistemic fashion. It provides a way of thinking, a way to understand something. When Senator Wallop states, "The Clinton-Mitchell bill will transform one-seventh of our economy, by creating 50 new bureaucracies . . . that will cost $1.4 trillion" (S11820), he is providing a way to think about the reform proposal, a way to understand it. The specific implicit metaphor may vary for auditors—a threat, a catastrophe, a nightmare, a crisis—but the way of seeing it or of understanding it is very clear.

An implicit metaphor is potentially more powerful than its explicit counterpart. The implicit metaphor works to involve the audience in much the same way that has been attributed to the enthymeme. An enthymeme is, in effect, an incomplete syllogism—it has a premise or its conclusion missing when it is constructed, and the audience is left to fill in the missing material. Bitzer (1959) contends that the enthymeme principally derives its power from involving the audience. The implicit metaphor also requires audience participation; the auditor must assign a metaphorical label to the definition constructed by the rhetor. Although Black (1965) argued that enthymemes cannot work effectively when values are in dispute this is not the case for the implicit metaphor. The implicit metaphor tends to capitalize on value conflict by offering a "quick and easy" way for auditors to reference and classify an event or issue.

The implicit metaphor also offers more than the advantage of audience participation. Unlike an explicitly expressed metaphor, the implicit metaphor subverts the process of internal evaluation and questioning. When someone expressly called the situation with health care a "crisis," for example, it raised the possibility that the auditor would question the "fit" of the metaphor. Was it really a crisis? Did it resemble other crises with which I was familiar? Was "crisis" the label I would attach to the situation? When an implicit metaphor is employed, by contrast, the process is reversed; rather than offering a name or label and letting the audience seek out their own meanings, the implicit metaphor establishes a fixed meaning and lets the audience select its own label. The label, the frame, the reduction, or whatever may vary, but the meaning remains constant. The implicit metaphor capitalizes on the ambiguity of the process by pointing in a particular direction—to good or evil, for example—and letting the audience know that direction and its potential consequences without placing a particular title on it. In addition, an implicit metaphor cannot be misperceived as a "mere figure of speech." Unlike an expressly stated metaphor, it derives its power from meaning, not from naming.

The entire rhetorical construction of a crisis of big government operates through the use of the implicit metaphor. Opponents of health care reform construct very clear meanings—more government is costly, taxes will increase, individual choice and freedom will suffer, rationing and price controls will proliferate—and the audience is left to assign their own labels to what has been crafted for them. The crisis of big government told listeners how to think about and how to understand what would happen if the Mitchell proposal for comprehensive health care reform were enacted.

THE FINAL OUTCOME

At this point, one might still be able to argue that the success of an implicit metaphor, the narrative fidelity of the big government story, the political features that were capitalized upon, and the other rhetorical strategies thus far discussed do not fully account for the success of the construction of a crisis of big government, particularly in light of the competing crisis of health care. To finish the answer one must look to how the opponents of the Mitchell proposal characterized the health care situation. The debate, these opponents of reform argued, was not about health care. It was about the role of government. Health care was not, in and of itself, a crisis. It was, as pursued by the Mitchell proposal, merely a symptom of the crisis of big government. The crisis of big government was thus used to subsume the health care crisis and make the philosophical question of the appropriate role of government the central issue.

"The Clinton plan isn't about health care," proclaimed Senator Hutchison with more than a touch of hyperbole. "It is about the lifeblood of America—Freedom" (S11781). That was, in essence, the viewpoint that Hutchison and her like-minded colleagues hoped to convey. Americans were not being asked, so this view goes, to help solve problems in health care, but rather to give license to an unprecedented increase in the size and scope of the federal government. The advocates of comprehensive health care reform were clearly the enemy here as they were using health care as a vehicle to secure greater government control: "The focus on insurance is merely a device, not to provide health care, but to control this portion of our economy. That is what this is all about, a sincere and honest belief that this country would have better health care if indeed we had more Government control" (Senator Brown, S11878).

Opponents of the Mitchell proposal for comprehensive health care reform acknowledged that the focus of their opposition was grounded in philosophical differences. Senator Wallop commented:

The debate on health care reform is a philosophical debate. It is a debate which clearly delineates the differences between Republicans and Democrats over the role of Government in our individual lives. Republicans are unwilling to risk this debate, not because we do not want to have health care reform, as the Democrats cry, but because we are unwilling to vote for a health reform proposal that is philosophically opposed by our constituents. (S11820)

The debate was bigger than the question of health care. It was, according to this view, about what philosophy of government we and the public will support. In fact, Senator Wallop went on to lay out the choices very clearly:

The fundamental issue . . . that we must decide, is whether we believe in a bigger Government, or in a wiser and more empowered people; whether we will be ruled by an anonymous bureaucracy which has the power to levy taxes or assign them, which has the power to limit choice—or whether democracy will continue to be our form of Government. (S11821)

Opponents of the Mitchell proposal were not, therefore, asking people to choose between health care and no health care, but instead to choose between government control and real democracy. The potential threat of big government appeared to loom very large.

The Mitchell proposal was not to be viewed as a response to a heath care crisis, but instead as a symptom of a crisis of big government. Senator Wallop characterized the Mitchell proposal as yet another illustration of "the expanding entitlement society" (S11822). The Mitchell proposal for comprehensive health care coverage and access simply fueled the fires raging over big government. Senator McConnell characterized the Mitchell proposal as just another step in the process of building big government responses to issues: "The Great Society is over. Welcome to the Great Bureaucracy" (S11862). In fact, a number of Republicans argued that just as America was beginning to tear down some of the big government programs of the 1960s, along came the Democrats with a health care proposal that would not merely replace them, but would dwarf them in size and scope.

Opponents of comprehensive health care reform argued that the key question was, "What role should the government play in peoples' lives?" This question permitted the Republicans to redefine the very nature of the debate. It was not about two competing crises, it was about the real crisis of big government that would simply expand and explode if the Mitchell proposal were enacted. The words of Senator Smith cut to the heart of the opposition's ability to define the nature of the crisis:

So now we stand . . . at a fork in the road—and it is a fork in the road. We can go to the left, as the Senate considers a massive restructuring of one-seventh of our economy, which will probably make it one-fifth Government involved. We can take that path toward a health care system controlled by an inefficient, uncompassionate, expensive government bureaucracy. . . . Or we can go this way, to the right, which will lead us to a more efficient marketplace that can meet the needs of all Americans. The left fork gives us bureaucracy, more taxes, job-killing mandates, rationed care, diminished quality. (S11936)

Smith laid out the choice in vivid detail: Americans could embrace the perils of big government or they could accept the alternative that protected individual choice and promoted freedom and liberty.

It is worth noting that proponents of comprehensive health care reform recognized that the potential threat of big government was key to the success of the opposition. Senator Mitchell and many of his pro-reform colleagues noted that Republican opponents were playing on the emotionally charged distrust and disillusionment with government that was so pervasive at the time. Senator Feingold, for example, noted:

The other side has a tremendous skill. The other side knows how to keep it simple. They weigh a bill. They say it is Big Government. They bring out a chart that looks complex but is actually less complicated than the current system. They are darned good at that. (S11872)

Senator Feingold was right. The opponents of comprehensive health care reform were "darned good" at what they did. They successfully crafted a crisis of big government and defined the Mitchell bill as a symptom of that crisis. They captured the health care issue and reconceptualized it in a manner that facilitated their political ends.

This process whereby the opponents of reform redefined the nature of the debate might be expressed as an exercise in *framing* and *reframing*. Entman (1993) has explained that frames relate to how problems are seen. More specifically, he notes: "To frame is to select some aspects of a perceived reality and make them salient in a communicating text, in such a way as to promote a particular problem definition, causal interpretation, moral evaluation, and/or treatment recommendation for the item described" (p. 52). In the political context, especially, framing "plays a major role in the exertion of power and the frame in a news text is really the imprint of power—it registers the identity of actors or interests that competed to dominate the text" (p. 55). Entman generally defines framing and links it to political discourse, but his analysis is largely focused on examination of mediated news coverage. The present work will rely more upon the recent work of Fairhurst and Sarr (1996).

Fairhurst and Sarr are writing explicitly for managers and leaders in an organizational context, but their treatment of the issue is germane to any analysis of the purposeful use of language. In fact, they characterize framing as the management of meaning through language. They define framing this way: "When we share our frames with others (the process of framing), we manage meaning because we assert that our interpretations should be taken as real over other possible interpretations" (p. 3). In a manner similar to Entman, Fairhurst and Sarr also explain that when we frame something, we choose specific aspects or elements to emphasize for an audience. They go on to note, "For this reason, frames determine whether people notice problems, how they understand and remember problems, and how they evaluate and act upon them" (p. 4). This is critically important in the Senate floor debate: The opponents of the Mitchell proposal framed, or reframed, the debate in a manner that facilitated their goal of defeating the proposed legislation.

Fairhurst and Sarr contend that a successful frame requires the existence of a clearly constructed message. As discussed earlier, the Senate opponents of comprehensive health care reform had a very clear message—that passage of the Mitchell proposal would lead to a disastrous growth in the size and scope of the federal government. This message became the theme that opposition forces employed to reframe the nature of the debate. Proponents of reform had constructed a frame that essentially argued that the current health care system was flawed and that it was in need of comprehensive change. The opposition reframed the nature of the debate as an excuse for the expansion of the federal government, rather than a solution to a serious problem.

This process of reframing the debate was apparent in the rhetoric employed by Senators opposing the Mitchell proposal. Senator Hutchison's remarks are illustrative:

Universal coverage essentially means that the Government will run our health care system. Everyone may have coverage, but at what price? Some of the looming prices include less quality, less access to needed services, less freedom, more government, and more taxes. (S11868)

Hutchison made it clear that the debate was not simply about improving present conditions, it was about government control and the inherently negative consequences that follow. Indeed, she reframed the issue clearly as she said that "universal coverage *means* that the Government will run our health care systems"—a rather obvious attempt to manage meaning. Senator Brown essentially argued that the pro-reform forces were only offering a frame of the situation and that a true interpretation was far more disturbing:

The focus on insurance is merely a device, not to provide health care, but to control this portion of our economy. That is what this is all about, a sincere and honest belief that this country would have better health care if indeed we had more Government control. (S11878)

Senator Brown's reframing is also rather explicit. He says the debate is not about health insurance, it is about government control.

Other Senators who opposed the Mitchell proposal also framed or reframed the debate as an attempt to further federal control with its naturally negative consequences. For example, Senator Burns went to some length to show that the proposed solution (the Mitchell bill) would be much worse than the problem (the health care crisis). Senator Shelby was particularly adept at the management of meaning which, according to Fairhurst and Sarr, is so essential to framing. Shelby made it clear that the Mitchell proposal was not merely a reform measure, but rather a tax plan that would place burdens on the "backs of middle-class" Americans (S11685). Shelby redefined or reframed a health care growth provision in the Mitchell plan by claiming that "The high-growth plan tax is not only a tax on quality health benefits, but is also intended as a form of price control" (S11685). Near the end of his remarks, Shelby made the reframe very clear: "A vote for a bad health care bill is not a vote for reform. Health care reform should not be an excuse for expanding the size and power of the Federal Government" (S11685). Shelby exemplified the rhetorical ability of reform opponents. They made the case very clear that the debate was not a noble crusade to improve the nation's health, it was actually an effort to expand "the size and power of the Federal Government."

Fairhurst and Sarr contend that certain ingredients are necessary for a communicator to successfully frame or reframe an issue. One of these ingredients is the skillful use of language. Fairhurst and Sarr explain, simply, that "language choices are critical to the management of meaning through framing" (p. 7). The focus of the present analysis and the categorical investigation are squarely concerned with such language choices. Fairhurst and Sarr, however, identify another ingredient that they contend is equally important to successful framing. They argue that it is necessary to have a well-developed *mental model* in order to frame or reframe with success. This is essentially an epistemological perspective, as Fairhurst and Sarr explain:

Leaders who understand their world can explain their world. That is the principle that makes mental models important to communication. Mental models of how the world works (or is supposed to work) help us to size up situations and formulate our goals for communicating. This enables us to decide what and how we choose to frame. (p. 23)

Fairhurst and Sarr explain that speakers need to have a vision of their world, and only when that vision is clearly developed can they successfully frame a situation. Opponents of the Mitchell proposal were, in part, successful at reframing the debate because they held well-developed mental models.

As noted throughout both the categorical investigation and this rhetorical analysis, opponents of the Mitchell proposal held a very rigid view that characterized the government as an agent of harm rather than a means to deal with contemporary social issues. This was a highly defined mental model. Senator Hatch said that the view that government can do good is "plain loco" (S11838). Similarly, Senator Brown said that government control is "just plain goofy" (S11880). Both Hatch and Brown held a mental model of the role of government—it should be limited and kept in check; to do otherwise is either "goofy" or "loco." Senator Gramm expressed the manifestation of his mental model: "People cannot seem to understand why there is so much passion on our side of the aisle about this. Well, my passion comes from the fact that I believe in freedom" (S11197). The future vision expressed by the opposition was equally clear. As many of the examples throughout this work demonstrate, the opponents of the Mitchell proposal saw it as a path to disaster. After recounting the serious perils associated with expanding the federal government, Senator Gramm cut directly to the "vision thing": "The future of America is going to depend on the outcome of this debate. And we are going to debate it and we are going to fight it out as if the future of America depends on it. It does" (S11198).

The opposition to the Mitchell proposal met both of the essential prerequisites that Fairhurst and Sarr establish for successful framing and reframing. They successfully and skillfully managed meaning through language and they held clearly developed mental models that helped them interpret the nature of the situation and fit it with their general views. This is another way of defining the nature of the debate and capturing health care reform in a manner that characterizes it as the path to a crisis of big government.

When Senator Gramm described proposals for comprehensive health care reform as being "deader than Elvis," he could have gone on to explain that it was the crisis of big government that killed them. The crisis of big government was an excellent case for study in the genre of crisis rhetoric. Language, words, discourse were used to construct the crisis, to lay out its dimensions, and to craft villains or enemies. Big government was rhetorically cast as the ultimate threat to all that Americans hold near and dear. This case also extended the boundaries of the genre of crisis rhetoric. It examined what appeared to be competing cases of crisis, with a clearly domestic focus grounded in the unique public policy forum of the U.S. Senate. It was also a case of external or social value conflict, where a rhetorically crafted crisis prevailed over a crisis that might be said to exist at some objective intrinsic level. That rhetorical success was grounded in the ability to make all of the right suasory appeals, the narrative fidelity exemplified in feelings regarding the Postal Service, the ability to capitalize on unique political value conditions, and the use of the implicit metaphor. Further, the crisis of big government subsumed the health care issue and redefined it as a symptom of the true crisis. And that process of redefining the nature of the debate could be effectively expressed as an exercise in framing. Late in the floor debate, Senator Mitchell assessed what was going on in terms of opposition claims and concluded by stating, "And so I hope that people will look beyond the rhetoric" (S11877). They obviously did not. It is possible at this point, however, to "look beyond the rhetoric" to explore broader implications of the power of talk that one can surmise from examination of the 1994 health care reform debate.

Part IV

The Implications

Chapter 11

An Ethical Assessment

Late in the Senate floor debate on comprehensive health care reform, Senator Kerrey offered an important perspective on the nature of that discursive dispute: "I really, as a member of Congress, do not have the ability to make detailed decisions that very often are not economic decisions. They are moral decisions. They are ethical decisions, about life and death" (S11104). Senator Kerrey was in the unusual position of being both very right and very wrong. Much about the comprehensive health care reform debate was moral or ethical in nature. In fact, a special 1994 issue of *The Journal of Medicine and Philosophy* was devoted to an explanation of ethical and moral issues on the subject of health care reform. However, decisions about life and death are often the cornerstone of legislative practice. Members of Congress are often asked to explicitly vote on the life or death decision to engage in a particular military action or not. Much more often they must make less explicit or indirect life and death decisions in connection to legal sanctions, food and nutrition programs, educational benefits, and, of course, health care. In each of these cases, the decisions made by members of Congress may well determine whether people waste away in a punitive justice effort, fail to provide their young children with ample dietary supplements, lack the educational skills to pursue a career outside the "underground" economy, or have the ability to pay for a heart bypass operation.

Kerrey's comments further suggested that ethical assessments of the 1994 comprehensive health care reform debate would be appropriate due to the serious "life and death" consequences associated with the outcome. As noted, special journal issues and other formalized medical discussions have made some such efforts. In addition, Aday (1993) has suggested that simple issues of cost and accessability might well have been the "wrong" questions to raise if one were to examine the need for health care reform through an ethical lens. None of these assessments, however, have focused on the discursive behavior that actually shapes or frames the ethical issues surrounding comprehensive health care reform. As talk is power generally, it is also the vehicle for the deliberation and resolution of ethical issues. Indeed, an issue replete with ethical considerations, such as health care reform, is best examined through a discursive perspective. A focus on discourse reveals how participants in an ethical dispute come to label and determine their competing views and it also goes a long way toward shedding light on how they have come to think in this way, as language often reflects intrinsic judgment.

In this chapter, I will attempt to provide an ethical assessment of the 1994 health care reform debate that is guided by my general argument that talk is power, and is therefore a discursive perspective. In addition to the value of assessing this particular case study, though, an ethical judgment provides the first of several important implications that reach well beyond the specific instance of that August 1994 floor debate. I will first offer a brief explication of the general values associated with understanding such an ethical assessment. Next, I will point to the richness of communication ethics scholarship that is germane to the present discussion. I will then provide a specialized framework for assessment grounded generally in argumentation, and specifically in the use of argument fields. I close this chapter by examining some of those implications that may be gleaned from this ethical assessment and applied to broader realms.

VALUE

Most people would agree at some intuitive level that there is some intrinsic value to carrying out ethical assessments or judgments. Everyone has some sense of right and wrong or good and bad, and those innate feelings explain a great deal about what we call ethics. People have sort of a "moral sense," and there are some in both ethics and psychology who feel that people are "hardwired" for ethics; that ethical assessments are built into that most complicated of all machinery, the human brain. Such intuitive or instinctive feelings regarding ethics extends to our understanding of the use of discourse. Bostrom et al. (1997) recently observed:

Deep down, we all have feelings of right and wrong about the way people communicate. We all recognize that civil discourse and behavior in our society are guided by the ethical choices that citizens make. The inherent belief in the value of resolving conflicts without violence and making decisions based upon sound reasoning underscores our fundamental faith in ethics as a guide for socially acceptable behavior. (p. 34)

Such comments are harbingers of the rich relationship thât exists between and ties together communication and ethics, but they also stress the more general point that ethics is somewhat of a naturally occurring human concern. Given that, it would seem most appropriate to raise that natural concern with regard to something as important and complex as health care reform.

Consideration of ethical issues has long fascinated thinking individuals. Ethics, along with metaphysics and epistemology, has traditionally been one of the principal focal points of all philosophy. Philosophers, scholars, and other thinkers have long pondered the goodness of human conduct. Classical Greek and Roman scholars were, for example, often drawn to the examination of appropriate and inappropriate human behavior. Plato's *Phadreus*, which has extensive and important discursive connections and implications, suggested that people can be classified as noble lovers, base lovers, and neutral lovers in regard to their daily practices. Kant, Rawls, and many of the other most often cited and studied philosophers have been centrally concerned with ethics. Ethics has therefore been a study of longstanding importance, especially to the world of philosophy.

The more general world of education has also long stressed the importance of ethics and ethical assessment. "Sunday schools" and other theologically driven educational settings offer explicit indoctrination into particular moral codes and rules. The secular education community is no stranger to ethics either. In addition to courses on the subject of ethics in such diverse disciplines as philosophy, political science, physics, journalism, and communication, the subject of ethics is addressed more indirectly and yet more thoroughly across the entire realm of education in other ways. Education itself teaches students certain ethical standards for inquiry and problem solving. Each society and community stresses certain rules or norms as conveyed through instructional practice in schools and colleges. In fact, Oliver (1962) noted that "The whole educational process . . . has as a central purpose the inculcation of ethical standards" (p. 27). Thus, the instructional implications of an ethical assessment of the 1994 health care reform debate serve to further display the value of such an undertaking.

Perhaps the single greatest value of conducting an ethical assessment of the 1994 health care reform debate and drawing out the broader implications of that assessment rests in the linkage between such assessments and public confidence in American government. There is general agreement that an overall malaise, if not outright distrust, drives contemporary public feelings toward the operation of government in the United States. Such a state of mind has been growing over the past three decades as concerns with executive branch practices ranging from engagement and escalation in the Vietnam conflict, to the Watergate break-in and subsequent attempted cover-up, to Iran-Contra and Savings and Loan debacles of the 1980s, to questions regarding the sexual practices of the President in the 1990s. Indeed, Johannesen (1990) has cited a great deal of literature that stresses the lack of confidence that many Americans have in the IRS, the CIA, and many other elements of the executive branch of government.

Issues regarding public confidence in government extend beyond the confines of the Oval Office. For many Americans, "the government"—in all its manifestations—is corrupt and cannot be trusted, or at least not given full faith and respect by all its citizenry. Joseph Nye, Jr. (1998), dean of the John F. Kennedy School of Government at Harvard University, recently reported that overall confidence in the government had declined sharply since the 1960s. Such declines in public confidence are not merely benign consequences of improved polling techniques, for real consequences can be ascribed to a lack of public confidence in government. Jaksa and Pritchard (1994) noted the general result of declining confidence by stating that, "Public trust in, and respect for elected officials is fundamental to the effective functioning of a democratic government and its institutions" (p. 39).

In addition to a generally problematic condition for democratic government, lack of public confidence in government can have far more practical and direct consequences. For example, Jaksa and Pritchard (1994) refer to Bennett who has pointed to the importance of public trust or interest to resolving important policy issues:

Restoring public interest in government, trust in leadership and commitment to a liveable society for all are essential steps toward real solutions for problems like crime, homelessness, drug abuse, education, economic revitalization, and other obstacles to the good life. (p. 34)

Thus, Bennett sees the restoration of confidence in government as a central pillar of dealing with the most significant issues that plague American society heading into the twenty-first century. More recently, Nye (1998) has spoken of a number of changes in public-government relations and has observed that:

If these changes weaken people's trust in government, citizens may become less likely to comply with the laws, to support government programs through taxes, and to enter government service. Without those critical resources, government will be unable to perform well, and people will become even more disaffected—a dangerous downward spiral that can weaken democratic institutions. (p. 136)

For Nye the lack of public confidence in government represents an evil that slowly creeps through the body politic, like a creature ravishing each healthy element it encounters. I think that Nye is correct and his concerns also play an important starting point in my later discussion of contemporary currents connected to the 1994 health care reform debate that do not bode well for the well-being of society as a whole. It suffices for now, however, to conclude that an ethical assessment of the 1994 debate is in order for both important scholarly or philosophical reasons and practical values associated with such a task.

COMMUNICATION AND ETHICS

As the earlier reference to Bostrom and his colleagues (1997) suggests, most people seem to have some innate sense of ethical concerns related to discursive behavior. Indeed, the relationship between discursive and ethical concerns is even more integral than that. Johannesen (1990) argues that all communicative behavior is replete with ethical considerations:

Potential ethical issues are inherent in any instance of communication between humans to the degree that the communication can be judged on a right-wrong dimension, involves possible significant influence on other humans, and to the degree that the communicator consciously chooses specific ends sought and communicative means to achieve those ends. (p. 2)

There are certainly few instances of human behavior where Johannesen's criteria for communication ethics would not be met.

Not only have philosophers and scholars been generally concerned with ethics since the days of antiquity, but some of those same thinkers have focused specifically upon communicative ethics. Plato's tri-level assessment of noble, base, and neutral lovers as an ethical perspective essentially identifies the various roles that may be embraced by public speakers. Aristotle is renowned for writing eloquently about both ethics and rhetoric, and Quintillian defined the orator as "a good man speaking well," stressing the need for an ethical or moral stance for discourse. This interest has continued into modern times as characterized by the works of Johannesen (1990), Jaksa and Pritchard (1994), and many others.

A great many of the common ethical standards one can glean from an examination of speech and communication textbooks would fall under the rubric of what Johannesen (1990) has labeled "political perspectives." Johannesen explains his use of the political perspective heading in this way:

> As used here, the scope of the label "political perspective" ranges far beyond just the communication of presidents, politicians, political campaigns, or a particular political party. Any communication on public issues and public policy broadly defined, whether military, economic, social or political, whether national, state, or local, could be assessed by one or more of the . . . political perspectives. (p. 21)

This rather broad definition is important to the present discussion in two significant ways. First, this labeling process indicates that assessment of an important public policy issue like health care reform is appropriately examined through some form of political perspective on communication ethics. And, second, Johannesen's standard on political perspectives goes a long way toward punctuation of the centrality of the political in any assessment of discursive ethics.

One can extend Johannesen's explanation of the connection between the political and the discursive by turning more directly to his summary of textbook standards on communication ethics. Johannesen suggests that most communication textbooks, especially those focusing upon persuasion or argumentation, either explicitly or implicitly embrace elements that represent a political perspective on the ethicality of discourse. In summary, eleven common standards tend to emerge:

1. Do not use false or fabricated evidence to back an argument.
2. Do not intentionally use poor reasoning.
3. Do not misrepresent yourself as an "expert" on a subject, if you actually are not.
4. Do not use irrelevant appeals to divert attention from the issue(s) at hand.
5. Do not ask your audience to draw false emotional relationships to a subject.
6. Do not mislead your audience by concealing your true purpose.
7. Do not distort, in any way, the potential consequences of your advocacy.
8. Do not use poorly reasoned or unsupported emotional appeals.
9. Do not reduce complex issues into overly simplistic polar disagreements.
10. Do not pretend certainty when uncertainty or tentativeness exists.
11. Do not advocate something in which you do not believe yourself. (pp. 31–32)

Unfortunately, such a listing of standards or guidelines is often the sole bit of advice offered in some communication textbooks. Some other communication scholars have, however, explained and elaborated on these perspectives and have offered much more.

As I summarize some of the most important works in communication ethics, I will rely heavily upon Johannesen's (1990) review of various ethical approaches in the field that best represent the political perspective on the ethicality of public discourse. His review of these approaches suggests that several specific elements tend to emerge as the most salient features of such political perspectives. These elements or features include an evaluation of the degree of rationality represented by an instance of discourse, the availability of significant alternative choices offered by that discourse, and an overall embrace of *reasoned* claims as being critical in the judgment of the ethicality of discursive behavior. Several specific scholarly viewpoints illuminate these central elements and link them to the maintenance of a healthy context for deliberation and debate on significant public policy issues.

Karl Wallace (1955) who expressed many of his most significant thoughts on rhetoric at the height of the Cold War, felt that certain core values could be identified as being essential to the welfare of our democratic system of government. In addition, Wallace argued that citizens of democratic states must work to implement such core values through the communicative behavior they employ, and he went on to identify four "moralities" that correspond to the core values and that serve as ethical guidelines that citizens should pursue. The first of the core values was *respect*, or a belief in the dignity and worth of the individual corresponding to respect, meaning that Speakers should work to develop the *habit of search* or a commitment to thorough research and preparation for the process of imparting knowledge to others. The second core value was *fairness*, the belief in the equality of opportunity. Wallace felt that to implement fairness, it was important to cultivate the *habit of justice* by selecting and presenting fact and opinion fairly. Third among the core values was *freedom*, coupled with adherence to the responsible exercise of such freedom. The communicative and ethical collary to freedom was the notion that speakers should habitually prefer public to private motivations; that the public good should take precedence over the pursuit of personal goals. The final of the four core values was identified as a belief in each person's ability to *understand* the nature of democracy, which could also be actuated through cultivation of the *habit of respect for dissent* and challenges to accepted norms.

A somewhat different view of central democratic values and the means to implement them was offered by Franklin Haiman (1952). Haiman's overall perspective has come to be characterized as one of the leading statements on the degree of rationality as a controlling force for ethical assessment of public discourse in a democratic society. Haiman's degree of rationality perspective was grounded squarely in a recognition of the value of the human ability to reason logically. Further, Haiman felt that encouraging such rational capacity was critical to the adequate functioning of our political system. Specifically, the degree of rationality perspective focuses upon a determination of the degree of conscious free choice reflected in and promoted by any specific discursive technique or appeal. Most notably condemned under this perspective were discursive techniques designed to short-circuit conscious thought processes and intended to promote automatic, non-reflective behavior. For Haiman, speakers would be in violation of important democratic ideals if they promoted uncritical acceptance of their stance.

One other illustration of the rich literature on communication ethics that is grounded in a political perspective was developed by Thomas Nilsen (1974). Nilsen was particularly well known for his embrace of and explanation of the concept of significant choice. This view very much paralleled Haiman's view in the emphasis it placed upon providing reasonable alternatives to the public hearers of messages. In addition, Nilsen felt that reason was a value essential to the functioning of American democracy. In the way that it served as an instrument of individual and societal development, Nilsen viewed healthy public debate as the natural and appropriate manifestation of this perspective:

We have come to value highly the process of public debate wherein there is confrontation of case with case, where advocates challenge each other's information and conclusions. Such confrontation produces the kind of information and criticism of conclusions that makes possible more intelligent choices on the part of the listeners. (p. 74)

The generation of "more intelligent choices" was embraced by Nilsen and, as will be noted, a number of others in association with the practice of public debate. In fact, a faith in public debate helps to provide the foundation for development of a specialized argumentative perspective on the ethicality of public discourse.

AN ARGUMENTATIVE PERSPECTIVE

Argumentation scholars, much like their colleagues in the broader rhetorical studies and communication discipline, have long been concerned about the ethicality of discursive behavior. I share that concern and will offer a particular argumentation perspective on the ethics of discourse that is framed by employment of argument fields as an assessment approach. My utilization of argument fields as a framework for ethical judgments of public discourse is grounded in the importance of two benefits or values associated with such a framework. First, a natural parallel of my general argument that talk is power is an emphasis upon argument construction and evaluation. Talk that asserts and in some way supports claims is inherently argumentative. To pursue the ends of power, individuals must be capable of both constructing such claims and critically assessing the claims presented by other advocates. The centrality of argumentation is of even greater significance when examining public policy discourse. As I have explained at some length earlier, the discourse employed during the August 1994 Senate floor debate on comprehensive health care reform—much like the discourse surrounding any critical question of policy action by a public body—is best understood as a form of argumentation and should therefore be assessed through a lens appropriate to such discourse. Second, argument fields provide a unique framework for the assessment of discursive behavior that is both more flexible and broader in scope than any of the alternative perspectives that are available. The argument fields perspective, despite its specialized values, does not stand entirely apart from other approaches to the assessment of ethicality. In fact, some preliminary attention to the overall argumentative view of ethics and discourse reveals much about the pillars upon which argument fields rest.

Even casual observers might recognize that argumentative perspectives on the ethicality of discourse are unique in their underlying *self ethics*. By self ethics, I am suggesting that the selection of argumentative discourse in contrast to alternatives is inherently ethical.   Argumentative discourse naturally embraces the values of significant choice, rationality, and reason as articulated by many scholars and summarized as political perspectives by Johannesen (1990). In addition, selection of argumentative discourse is obviously more generally accepted as ethical than the selection of either violence or discursive means that are uncritical or nonreflective in nature.

Perhaps the most eloquent of spokespeople who tout the self ethics of argumentation was the argument and debate scholar Douglas Ehninger (1974). Ehninger voiced the position that the selection of argument as a strategy or process was inherently ethical and humanizing in the way that it capitalizes upon qualities unique to humans. To Ehninger, the qualities of reason, understanding, and reflection were noted as features that best define people as human. In a nearly idealistic way, Ehninger expressed the humanizing nature of argument in this way:

[B]y resorting to such humanizing instruments as argument, we gradually create a society in which peace, tolerance, and mutual appreciation flourish, a society in which the maximum development of each person and of the group as a whole becomes possible—the sort of society, in short, in which we all wish to live. (p. 7)

Although idealistic, Ehninger's belief in the inherent ethicality and humanity of argument was not meant as some utopian concept that merely generates healthy conversation. He felt that speakers should strive toward the ideal this suggests and embrace the process standards that it demands. Ehninger said that advocates who choose argument as an instrument of persuasion have also chosen to treat their listeners as humans to be reasoned with rather than as things to be manipulated.

The practice of argumentation does not always reflect the ideally humanizing quality discussed by Ehninger, but the utilization of public debate as a means to facilitate governance has been endorsed as an ethical approach when dealing with significant public policy issues. Nilsen's (1974) earlier remarks are representative of the value that many communication ethics scholars have attributed to public debate. Argumentation and debate scholars have similarly acknowledged the value of public debate. Branham (1991) has argued that debate as a means of decision making confirms a society's commitment to participatory democracy. "The ability to argue," notes Hollihan and Baaske (1994), "is a fundamental survival skill for life in a democracy" (p. 6). Dennis Day (1966) has observed that, in a democracy, debate is generally recognized as a procedurally acceptable means to the accomplishment of specific ends, especially decision making. Day was somewhat unique in the way that he expressed the true value of public debate. Day felt that it was the flash of competing claims that rendered debate valuable, even more so than the use of reason. He stated:

The ethics of democratic discourse requires a commitment to debate, not a commitment to reason. In practice, the appeal to reason often proves to be the most effective technique in debate, and thus we tend to think of debate as "reasoned discourse." But the essential feature of debate is the confrontation of ideas. We may have appeals to reason without having debate, and we may have debate without appeals to reason. (pp. 8–10)

Despite his differing orientation to the subject, Day did make it clear that debate is valuable as a practical exercise of ethical discursive behavior in a democratic society.

Another important argumentation standard for the ethicality of discursive behavior was posited by Wayne Brockriede (1972). Brockriede embraced the discursive power of metaphor as a mechanism for the enlightenment of ethical speaking practices. He described "arguers as lovers" categorically as "rapists," "seducers," and "lovers." The arguer who is labeled a rapist is one who will employ any and every means available, no matter how discursively unfair—lies, manipulation, propaganda, and more—to force her audience to accept a particular end. Seducer arguers are not as openly unethical in that they utilize a great deal of "glitz and glamour" to tell half-truths, instead, and to oversimplify claims. Ideally, the arguer as lover is one who fairly represents his claims and permits the audience to exercise the greatest degree of choice with regard to the argument being presented. This perspective latches onto the compelling connotations generated by the metaphorical characterizations of arguers, and it has been embraced as a framework of ethical standards for all speakers who must negotiate some common ground with a public audience (Bostrom et al., 1997).

All of the argumentation-specific discussions of the ethicality of discourse noted here are valuable individually and collectively. Individually, each points to a particular perspective that might better guide one's assessment of discursive ethics. Collectively, they demonstrate the importance of argument as a specialized conceptualization of discourse that warrants specialized treatment with regard to ethical practices. Each is also, however, lacking. None of the argumentation standards for ethicality possesses a robust enough framework for actual practice. To suggest that development of such a framework is desirable does not simultaneously dismiss all previous perspectives out of hand. Rather, it does indicate that some broader, overarching design may be important as a means to facilitate use of these perspectives and to extend beyond them. Employment of argument fields as an ethical framework does just that.

At its broadest, the argument fields perspective provides a means to contextualize the understanding of ethical assessments of discourse. As noted, argument fields are traced to the work of Stephen Toulmin and the value of the concept for argumentation more generally has been embraced by countless scholars, instructors, and researchers. Argument fields represent the metaphorical boundaries within which arguers reside and arguments take place. Disciplines, rational enterprises, and other particularized notions have been employed to explain the function of argument fields and the bounds of specialized fields. I have identified four features common to most of the sometimes conflicting literature on argument fields: (1) existence of some commodity of discourse usage, (2) some sense of shared purpose or goals among the members of such communities, (3) a common-sensical or metaphorical resemblance to actual fields, and (4) an understanding that fields help make up the matrix of power associated with discursive practice. It is that characterization of argument fields that serves also as a framework for ethical assessment of discursive practice.

Argument fields may be employed to overlay discursive practice and to provide a specialized viewpoint for the assessment of ethicality. Just as all argument fields can be thought of as operating in a layered fashion (see Figure 5.1), so too can all discursive patterns be examined for ethicality through such a lens or perspective. Critics may assess the ethicality of discursive practice as it exists within a particular layer of an argument field, as it relates between layers within larger field views, and as it impacts the broadest, public field.

Application of argument fields as an ethical perspective for discourse to the case study of the August 1994 Senate floor debate on comprehensive health care reform both further illustrates the significance of that debate and also sheds light on use of such a framework to assess the power of talk as governed by moral or ethical standards. One may start dissection of the layers of the health care reform argument field at any particular level, but the political party membership level makes for an interesting starting point to guide the present discussion. The political makeup of the health care reform argument field is split into a liberal camp, which is singularly guided by the health care reform debate, and a conservative camp that works endlessly to extend beyond the narrow confines of health care to touch the larger economy and, ultimately, to criminalize big government.

At the political level of the debate, the assessment of ethicality for discourse is guided primarily by an examination of the particularized intentions of participants in the debate. For example, the liberal camp is considered ethical by members of a particular collective that would view the discursive behaviors of Senators as consistent with the good intentions of expanding access to needed health care and improving overall health care coverage. In other words, an ethical assessment *within* the political level looks to see whether participants have effectively "towed the party line" or if they have betrayed the intentions of their camp. This is not to say that such standards have been expressly articulated as guidance for discursive behavior. Indeed, the discussion of discourse guiding the present illustration is drawn from the patterns associated with earlier discussion of individualized discursive features such as narratives and medical metaphors, and the larger discourse patterns that emerged. Looking back through that particular lens would also confirm that the conservative camp would also characterize its own behavior as ethical in that it consistently waged a discursive onslaught against expansion of the federal government.

Some readers may contend that application of argument fields to the political discussion level of ethical assessment adds little illumination. On the contrary, application of argument fields at this stage confirms that differing groups or collectives must necessarily embrace differing standards for ethical practice of discourse to permit their respective ideological viewpoints to continue to exist in their current manifestations. If the conservative camp were, for example, to embrace other standards for the assessment of discursive practice, they may be forced to accept the untenable position of "being opposed to health care reform." Continued embrace of the particularized standards regarding intentions noted above permits them, rather, to be "opposed to big government," a villain far more dangerous than health care reform.

The Senate, as a specialized forum or institutional setting, represents another argument field layer worthy of examination. As noted, the Senate has long been a place with specialized rules or norms for operations and behavior. Those rules have long influenced discursive practice in the Senate. No Senator would openly label an opponent's argument as unethical, nor would she take kindly to an opponent labeling her own stance as stupid. The same rules were largely operative during the 1994 health care reform debate. As noted, there was some discussion of the apparent hypocracy of conservative Senators demeaning government health care and at the same time being participants in its actual practice and benefits. Nonetheless, even this was done within the traditional institutionalized norms of the Senate. No liberal proponent of health care reform called an opponent a liar in this regard, nor did any conservative Senator say that health care reform was inherently evil or unnatural.

Although explicitly unacceptable outbursts did not characterize the August 1994 floor debate on comprehensive health care reform, there was a difference when one looks more closely at what was said during the debate. As proponents of comprehensive health care reform advocated for their proposal, they often suggested that support of health care reform was necessarily and normally the right thing to do. For example, Senator Mitchell characterized health care reform as a matter of justice. He stated:

Health care reform is a matter of simple justice. Human beings are born unequal in ability and in strength. None of us chooses our family circumstances. We are all susceptible to bad luck. We are all susceptible to accident and illness. We all grow old. (S11005)

Mitchell's remarks are reflective of the nature of pro–health care reform advocacy. That advocacy strove to place health care reform on an agenda equal with racial and sexual discrimination and other moral and ethical "crises" that have garnered the attention of the Senate. On a somewhat idealistic level, such advocacy appeared to work toward achievement of the goal implicitly embraced by Senate norms: to promote the Senate as the greatest deliberative body on the planet.

The conservative opposition seemed less concerned about working toward the ideals of the Senate, but much more concerned with defeat of the specific proposal, what they viewed as the specific threat, at hand. In fact, the Republican opposition painted the health care reform advocates as liars without having to resort to use of that connotatively negative label. The opposition clearly suggested that the debate was not *really* about health care reform—even if it was a matter of justice or moral righteousness—it was *really* about big government expansion. The remarks of Senator Wallop get right to this point:

The debate on health care reform is a philosophical debate. It is a debate which clearly delineates the differences between Republicans and Democrats over the role of Government in our individual lives. Republicans are unwilling to risk this debate, not because we do not want health care reform, as the Democrats say, but because we are unwilling to vote for a health care reform proposal that is philosophically opposed by our constituents. (S11820)

That philosophical opposition, according to Wallop, was an opposition to expanding the scope and power of the federal government. Here, Wallop was saying that the Democrats were liars when they claimed they were interested in real health care reform, and that it was the Republican opposition that occupied the moral high ground by opposing the hated expansion of government control. Defeat of comprehensive health care reform was clearly facilitated by such remarks, but how such a spin on the "liar issue", was promoting the ideals of the Senate was much less obvious.

Extending beyond the Senate layer in a multifaceted argument field assessment of the ethicality of health care reform discourse reveals an even greater difference between the more liberal proponents of reform and their conservative opposition. If one moves up the layers of this particular argument field to the public "supra field" level, it becomes quite apparent that opposition advocacy was less than ethical on at least two accounts. First, the opponents of health care reform failed to debate the substance of health care reform itself. There was virtually no conservative challenge to the fact that millions of Americans lacked adequate health care coverage or that the consequences of such a lack of coverage could be devastating. Rather, the opposition rallied round their "big government is bad" position. If liberals had challenged President Ronald Reagan's attempts to purge Latin America of communist influences in the 1980s solely by framing it as an international matter better left to some global authority rather than challenging the estimates of the strength and consequences of such influence, the Republicans would have been quick to call foul. Much the same is true in reverse on the health care reform debate. Few removed from the opposition political layer of the argument field would embrace the avoidance of substance as the pinnacle of ethicality.

In addition, virtually all ethicists both inside and outside communication would agree that looking to the effects in the broader public sphere of some institutionalized discourse is a legitimate means to assess the ethicality of what occurred within the institutional arena. Although I will devote the entirety of Chapter Thirteen to discussion of the contemporary currents and effects of the 1994 health care reform debate, it is important to offer a glimpse at that discussion as it informs this ethical assessment. The effects of Democratic discourse to promote comprehensive health care reform were largely found in the way that it spurred greater discussion of important health care–related issues, including the appropriate role of managed care and HMOs, the harmful consequences of cigarette smoking, and the safety of food products. On the other hand, the effects of conservative opposition discourse to comprehensive health care reform were largely tied indirectly to escalating hatred of and challenges to the federal government. Senator Wallop described the comprehensive health care reform proposal by stating, "The proposal now in front of us represents a reversal of recent successes against Government centralization and control" (S11821). Wallop was making it clear that so-called mainstream conservatives feel that there should be "success against Government," *against Government*. It was only a very small step along the path of conservative ideology from successes *against Government*, to like the defeat of health care blowing up federal office buildings and assassinating ATF agents. It is not ethical to promote unwarranted physical assaults, either directly or indirectly.

EXTENSIONS

It is possible to extend the influence of the present ethical assessment beyond the boundaries of the specific case study of the 1994 comprehensive health care reform debate. The most obvious extension would be to merely endorse use of an argument fields perspective to contextualize assessments of the ethicality of discourse. Great illumination and informative power may be garnered from the application of textbook standards for the ethicality of discourse, use of "significant choice" perspectives or Brockriede's arguers as lovers categorization, or any number of other standards and guidelines in existence that turn a critical eye to assessment of discursive ethics. All such perspectives, however, become more robust in their effects when contextualized in a manner that provides a more focused framework for examination of the ethicality of discourse. The layered argument fields perspective suggests that a critic might attempt to identify the "rapist," "seducer," and "lover" advocates in the obvious segments of the abortion debate, for example. Such a contextualizing frame better ensures that the critic's ethical microscope is clearly focused.

It would also be relatively simple to "lift" the present argument fields layers designed to facilitate assessment of the Senate floor debate regarding comprehensive health care reform and to employ them to examine other Senate floor debates. Critics could examine the political, the Senate, the public, and other layers or levels of the Senate field in connection with debate on any subject that has been raised on the floor of that institution. The "Protection of Marriage Act" might, for example, warrant assessment in such a layered approach in order to reveal nuances of advocacy and opposition in that particular debate.

Chapter Thirteen of the present work will draw connections that reflect back upon the ethical discussion of the effects of discursive practice, and such efforts would be in order for other cases as well. Tracing the longer-term consequences of a specific case of discursive practice would help place it in a broader social perspective and identify critical agents in the development of present and future actions that may well seem at first unrelated to the specific case at hand. As noted, health care reform opponents made it clear that it was desirable to be *against Government* and, as we all know, some have taken being against Government to deadly extremes. The connection between the two is not rock solid and direct, but exposing the potential linkage sheds light on significant consequences of public policy practice that have largely been unexplored. Consideration of the longer-term ethical effects of public policy discourse on other significant issues might offer equally illuminating possibilities.

On a more general and broader level, it is important to stress the centrality of assessments of the ethicality of public policy discourse. All too often, rhetorical, argumentation, and other communication critics examine significant public policy discourse in both theory and practice without taking the step of making any sort of ethical judgment. Such criticism is rich in a great many other ways, but it would add to the overall confluence of discussion germane to the proposition that talk is power by also assessing ethicality. The real power of particular discourse might not reside merely in what happens within the practice of a discursive exchange or the development of a pattern of talk. It may be much more subtle, grounded in nuances of morality and examination of future practices. Thus, making specific ethical assessments of discursive cases—whether one employs an argument fields approach or not—would be a healthy reminder of why we are bothering to go to the trouble to look at any discourse in the first place. There are a number of other ways that future scholars can extend the limits of the present discussion well beyond the bounds of the

1994 debate on comprehensive health care reform, and those extensions warrant additional attention. In fact, the next chapter is devoted entirely to the discussion of theoretical and research horizons connected to both the present case study and the general proposition that talk is power.

Chapter 12

Scholarly Horizons

Quite often many of the implications of an academic work are most closely tied to the academy itself. Aristotle's *Rhetoric* not only provided practical advice on the exercise of oral public discourse, but it served as the cornerstone of rhetorical theory for thousands of years and continues today to influence instruction and research. Certainly, Aristotle's *Rhetoric* is atypical among the works of scholars, and very few works can even attempt to share its lofty status in academe. It is, however, also archetypical in a sense. The *Rhetoric* demonstrates that the importance of any work is often measured differently by scholars who seek heuristic assistance in framing instructional and research practices. Much like other contemporary academic works that examine practices in the so-called real world, this book will attempt to spell out some of the contributions that it can add to that pursuit. Also much like other contemporary academic works, its scope and implications will surely be dwarfed by classical works like the *Rhetoric* and many others, but it was my goal to add something to the scholarly community's understanding and examination of public policy discourse. This chapter will work to point out some of those contributions and perhaps spur the indirect development of others by some of its readers.

There are three interrelated areas that I will address in this chapter: (1) a preliminary assessment of the scholarly contributions made by this work, (2) a discussion of numerous research potentials generated by this work, and (3) identification of several theoretical advances associated with the understanding of the practice of public policy discourse. These three areas are interrelated in that they all share common foundations grounded in the understanding of talk as power and in the examination of the August 1994 Senate floor debate on comprehensive health care reform as a particular case study in support of that general argument. In addition to their own interrelationship, these scholarly horizons also have potential implications connected to several disciplines and to the employment of several methods of scholarly investigation. In addition to rhetorical studies scholars and others in the broader communication discipline, many who specialize in political science, sociology, public policy and administration, and several other academic disciplines may find some portion of this work heuristic for their own specialized efforts, and the combination of categorical examination of discursive features and overall rhetorical analysis employed here demonstrates that scholars who embrace any particular methodological preference for the investigation of discursive practice may be able to make connections to this work.

PRELIMINARY ASSESSMENT

Several preliminary contributions are made to our understanding of talk as power through examination of the comprehensive health care reform case study. An important critical context for examination of the 1994 floor debate on health care reform is clearly established. Several components of the U.S. health care system are identified and examined. The historical development of health care reform efforts in this century has been outlined, and the tendency of policy makers to respond through incremental action has been explained. A large body of literature has been examined in order to provide a critical appraisal of the broad public debate on the health care issue in the early 1990s. Further, the Senate has been identified as an important public policy forum and as a unique argument field. As will be noted, such context offers future researchers an important starting point.

As public address scholars have attempted to do for decades, this work focuses the attention of the discipline on a very important instance of public discourse. The historical context helps to establish that the August 1994 Senate floor debate was special. It was the first congressional floor debate on comprehensive health care reform in this nation's history, and this work is the first to focus on the discourse of that remarkable event. Both the categorical examination of specific discursive features and the rhetorical analysis presented serve to underscore that this debate was not only an important historical occurrence, but also an impressive exercise of communicative behavior in the public policy realm.

The value of the *Congressional Record* as a textual database has been reinforced and extended by the present work. The comprehensive review of the history of the *Record* and examination of critical concerns for accuracy confirm that it is an appropriate source for the investigation of discursive behavior in the U.S. Congress. More important, this study moves beyond the traditional emphasis taken by earlier investigators. Rather than examining slavery, the League of Nations, or other relatively distant historical events, this work demonstrates that the *Record* is a valuable source for investigation of contemporary social and public policy issues. Future researchers interested in the welfare reform debate, controversy over late-term abortion legislation, passage of the "Protection of Marriage Act," and numerous other contemporary issues should take advantage of the *Congressional Record* as a textual database.

The role of discursive behavior in the public policy context has been examined at length. Indeed, the centrality of discourse to the political and public policy process has been illuminated in many ways. Each of the categories of discursive behavior—crisis discourse, evidence, narratives, language strategies, and medical metaphors—has been interpreted in a way that demonstrates that there is unique value for the use of each in a public policy debate. Examination of those discursive elements also reveal that larger patterns can be observed in discursive exchanges, and that such patterns can have an effect on the outcome of a debate or controversy. The discursive behavior of opponents of the Mitchell proposal was both more future-oriented and broader in nature than that of proponents of the legislation. As noted earlier, those patterns were revealed in terms of each specific discourse feature, and functioned to shape the outcome of the debate. Indeed, this is one of the most significant findings revealed by this project: Discourse that is future-oriented tends to overwhelm policy discourse that is present-oriented. Such a revelation also adds credence to my general argument that talk is power. In this particular case, one mode of talk or discursive pattern was much more powerful than another and resulted in the abandonment of comprehensive health care reform as a critical public policy goal of the Clinton administration.

The genre of crisis rhetoric has received considerable attention here. Examination of the health care debate demonstrates that the genre need not be limited to examination of the public speeches of U.S. Presidents. A crisis can be constructed rhetorically in other public policy forums by other actors—in this case the proponents and opponents of comprehensive health care reform in the U.S. Senate. This work also demonstrates that the rhetorically crafted crisis of big government had pragmatic appeal as a means to guide the outcome of legislation. The discussion of narrative fidelity proves that Fisher's narrative paradigm is applicable to crisis rhetoric situations. The discussion of framing extends that concept beyond the news media and management situations to demonstrate that it operates rhetorically in public policy debate. This rhetorical analysis also proves that public policy debaters can be successful if they can subsume their opponents' issue and redefine it as one of their own. This offers guidance for strategic use in future public policy debates.

The examination of a critical public policy issue presented here did not rely upon a single research approach. The categorical investigation of specific discourse features functioned through an eclectic blend of content analysis, discourse analysis, qualitative interpretation, and other procedural measures. The rhetorical analysis, as noted, extended the generic approach associated with crisis rhetoric. This mix of investigatory devices demonstrates that public policy debates may be fruitfully assessed through a variety of research strategies. This study also demonstrates that modified social science tools can be combined with rhetorical analysis to offer a robust evaluation of critical public discourse. Many years ago, Black (1965) put forth the contention that rhetorical criticism can be said to be "scientific" because it must build a defensible case. The same is true here: The claims made are arguments that can be defended based on a mix of data.

Many of the disciplinary specialties within communication should find this work to be of interest. Certainly, public address and rhetorical scholars can look to this study for a critical appraisal of an important, recent, public policy debate. Argumentation scholars should also find appeal in the assessment of such a heated debate. Those interested in language and discourse can look to the data regarding the specific discursive features and the patterns of discourse that are identified and interpreted in the present study. Political communication scholars will find that political outcomes, such as the defeat of the Mitchell proposal, can be clearly linked to the overall development of communicative behavior.

Health communication scholars might also find examination of the Senate floor debate on comprehensive health care reform illuminating and insightful. The "real world" development of policy that shapes the nature of the health care system in the United States should be of interest to all of those engaged in the study of health communication. Investigations such as the present project and many of those suggested here offer the potential of revealing rather directly how communication shapes the actual health care system that every person must use at some point. A number of scholars in the field have also recently pointed to the potential that such practical activities might offer. In a passage concerning the need to coordinate research efforts across disciplines, Becker (1995) suggested that multidisciplinary investigations could help by offering "many essential perspectives that only scholars from a variety of relevant disciplines can provide—from medicine . . . perhaps even political science and law—in addition to communication studies" (p. 1). Becker's point helps to inform this project, which is squarely grounded in a blend of communication studies approaches or methods and political science content, and it further points to some of the benefits that efforts of this sort could offer. Similarly, Ratzan (1994) contends that it is essential for health communication researchers to "evaluate health policy," and the present effort is clearly an important step in that direction. Further, Sharf (1999) has more recently urged health communication scholars to focus greater attention on examination of health care activism and advocacy. She notes that, "Recent advocacy activities for AIDS, breast cancer, and physical disabilities provide paradigmatic case studies for analyses of the impact of grassroots rhetoric on health care issues" (p. 198). Perhaps this work can similarly serve as a "paradigmatic case study," for analysis of public policy and political discourse on health care issues, particularly reform proposals. Such guidance for health communication scholars, like much of this preliminary assessment of contributions, suggests a number of implicit research opportunities. In the next section of this chapter, I will attempt to explicate several more explicit research potentials associated with this work.

RESEARCH POTENTIALS

Some extended discussion regarding the *Congressional Record* has previously been presented. Although concerns about accuracy will persist until some procedure for verbatim transcription is put in place, previous research does suggest that the *Record* can serve as a valuable database for a textual examination of discursive behavior. The bulk of previous research, particularly the procedures employed by Quadro (1977), tends to confirm both the accuracy and the utility of the *Record* as a database for communication investigations. Suffice it to say that the *Congressional Record* offers the most readily available, the most frequently employed, and the most accurate textual account of the sessions of Congress that scholars have available today. A few specific features do, however, warrant further attention.

As with any printed document, the *Congressional Record* could suffer shortcomings associated with the recording process. Such shortcomings may often reflect simple errors that would not confound a scholarly investigation. In the current project, for example, "interest rates" were recorded in the *Record* as "interest rats" on one occasion. Such errors do not risk skewing a textual investigation and, generally, pose little hazard to scholars. On the other hand, however, if a percentage figure, a proper name, or many other discursive elements that might inform an investigation were to be recorded improperly, the costs to scholars could be much higher.

Although complete letters, CBO reports, and other documents are often printed in the *Congressional Record*, it still does not and cannot capture every element that could be of value in a discursive examination. Visual aids employed by legislators are not, for example, available for examination in the pages of the *Record*. Consider the remarks of Senator Domenici: "On this chart, the President's promise is reflected in the red or orange area. Here we are. Here is where we were going to be on the green line if we left everything the same" (S11096). In the pages of the *Congressional Record* you will find no green line. No red or orange area. No chart. These visual elements are simply not available. One cannot examine fully how they aid or distract from oral behavior or whether they offer an important supplement to a rhetorical strategy.

Documents and graphic materials are not the only items that cannot be examined in the pages of the *Congressional Record* despite their use (and potential effect upon) the floor debate. Actual objects cannot be taken into full consideration. A number of Senators apparently touched or pointed to a desk in order to make some reference. The potential force of such a directive or referential effort cannot be measured from the text of the *Record*. Several advocates of health care reform also, apparently, were holding pens and making reference to President Clinton's veto pen (as when he threatened to use a pen to veto any health care reform legislation that was not comprehensive in nature). Handling the pens may well influence the overall presentation, yet that cannot be determined from the simple textual accounts offered of speeches in the *Congressional Record*.

One interesting and potentially promising database alternative does exist in our video-driven culture. For the past several years, sessions of Congress have been aired over the C-SPAN cable system. C-SPAN is a nonprofit channel created by the cable television industry that offers televised proceedings of both the House and Senate and material from other policy-making forums (Green, 1991). The availability of such a video option offers many possibilities for extending research and scholarship. One could, of course, actually see a chart or pen if such objects were being used by a particular speaker. This would provide a more robust view of the entire discursive or rhetorical act. Further, any nonverbal feature of communication—gestures, eye movement, facial expression, and so forth—become available for examination when such a video source exists. There is, however, a risk associated with use of video material from C-SPAN. For some investigations, scholars would also need to produce a transcript and their own recording procedures would be potentially less accurate than the *Congressional Record*. It would be possible, however, to extend the work of Hendrix (1965) and others who have compared the *Record* to other printed sources by making a similar comparison with C-SPAN video.

The floor debate was not the only forum available to members of the Senate for discussion and examination of the issue of health care and potential reform proposals.

Schuetz (1986) has argued that committee hearings, constituent letters, and floor debates can all capture elements of the argumentation that takes place in the Senate. In addition to the floor debate examined here, the other communicative means discussed by Schuetz were also available with regard to the health care issue. In fact, during the floor debate many Senators made reference to the large number of constituent letters that they had received on the issue. And, Evans (1995) has argued that virtually every committee in both the House and Senate had some "piece of the action" on the issue of health care reform. Textual investigations and assessments such as those offered here or elsewhere could be applied to both of these other forums for discursive behavior. One could potentially make arrangements to examine constituent mail from members of Congress and all committee hearings are readily available in print from the U.S. Government Printing Office. Such investigations of alternative forums might offer interesting opportunities to mark and to compare and contrast similarities and differences with the discursive behavior in the floor debate.

In addition to materials available in other forums, the potential exists to more fully harvest the resources that do appear in the *Congressional Record*. The present investigation examined the full floor debate, but inserted material was not coded for the specific discursive features identified here nor was it treated to any separate qualitative or rhetorical examination. Many extended letters, dozens of complete newspaper articles, and other documents were inserted into the record of the debate by participating Senators. It would be possible, for example, to apply the coding for discursive features used in the present investigation to such documents. Such an application would have the potential to point to differences in evidence use, the role of narratives, and numerous other specific discursive features. These documents could also be treated to other forms of textual analysis that might reveal other valuable information hidden from the present investigation.

It would also be possible to extend the overall discursive examination of the comprehensive health care reform debate that raged in the early 1990s. Although the *Congressional Record* is the most significant of textual sources for examination of public policy discourse in the U.S. Congress, it is merely one outlet or source on the issue of comprehensive health care reform. In addition to the constituent letters and committee hearings that are all employed in the same forum or argument field—the U.S. Senate—as the floor debate, investigators could turn to a variety of other sources. The *New York Times*, the *Washington Post*, and most other major news outlets of note contained some form of coverage regarding the issue of comprehensive health care reform. An investigator could examine these news outlets for specific discursive elements, overall rhetorical effect, and other features. It might also help illuminate the full debate by turning to sources that are representative of specific argument fields, audiences, or political elements. For example, one could look to the professional health care or medical community and examine such sources as the *New England Journal of Medicine* and the *Journal of the American Medical Association*. Given the power and influence that Starr (1982) and others attribute to the medical profession, examination of such textual resources might help reveal discursive features used to exercise or reflect that power and influence.

Discourse features such as analogies also hold promise as potential points for examination and investigation in the Senate floor debate. A number of Senators, for example, cited analogies to make a point. Senator Feingold's statement offers an illustration:

Guaranteed coverage is like good mosquito netting. Anything less than 100 percent is not much good. It does not matter if the hole is an 8 percent hole or 10 percent hole, unless the mosquito net gives you 100 percent coverage, it is not very pleasant camping in Wisconsin at night. (S11876)

Senator Feingold appeared to be stressing the importance of comprehensive health care coverage. Investigators might track the use of all analogies in the floor debate and attempt to offer an explanation and assessment of their use.

Both qualitative investigators and rhetorical scholars might be interested in taking a more narrow view of discourse that occurred during the floor debate on comprehensive health care reform. A researcher might, for example, focus upon examining the specific discursive features or overall rhetorical approach of an individual Senator. As noted, a number of authorities point to the election of Senator Wofford of Pennsylvania as a critical point in bringing the issue of health care to the top of the national agenda. An investigator may focus upon the discourse of Senator Wofford. Such an investigation might help explain why he was successful in sparking the debate and highlighting the issue. Other policy makers may also be appropriate figures for research. Many people associate the issue of health care with President Clinton and an examination of his discursive behavior might be informative on many levels.

Discourse analysts and other scholars who focus their attention on types of "talk" might wish to explore the institutional talk employed during the Senate floor debate on comprehensive health care reform. Silverman (1994) has suggested that it is often possible to characterize a particular institution, such as a courtroom, by the talk used in the institution. Heritage (1984) has examined institutional talk at length and has suggested that it derives much from ordinary conversation but also contains features unique to the procedural or formal nature of the talk. Such talk can be found in the Senate floor debate. There was, for example, extended procedural discussion regarding Senator Dodd's amendment to the Mitchell proposal to cover children at an earlier time. Senator Specter made explicit reference to the unique procedural process in the Senate: "[T]he American people do not understand all of our procedural rules, one being that any Senator can offer an amendment to any bill at any time" (S11202). Investigators might wish to examine such procedures to see if they were consistent with other institutional talk, how they function, and how they work to define a particular organization or institution.

Other potential options for future investigations and examinations might be illuminating to rhetorical scholars. Rhetorical scholars might be interested in applying a variety of critical methods and in making interpretations of the rhetoric that constructed the floor debate. Such further investigations might be of great interest to argumentation scholars trained in the rhetorical tradition who might wish to explore the use of enthymemes and similar strategies. And there are a good many ways in which rhetorical scholars could extend analysis of the genre of crisis rhetoric.

As previously noted, the focus of crisis rhetoric scholars has long been upon the individual speaking behavior of the President of the U.S. Such a traditional focus obviously could be applied to the overall debate on comprehensive health care reform in the early 1990s. President Clinton is very often identified with the issue of comprehensive health care reform. Rhetorical scholars might wish to examine specific speeches, such as his address on the issue to Congress, or his overall construction of the health care crisis. It might be highly informative to explore Clinton's construction of crisis rhetorically and to offer assessments as to the effectiveness of that construction. Another approach would be to compare and contrast the rhetorical construction of a health care crisis in the Senate with that of the President. One could further extend the boundaries of the genre by offering similar attention to the rhetorical construction of a health care crisis by the First Lady, Hillary Rodham Clinton. A comparison and contrast of the two Clinton approaches might be highly illuminating.

Another relatively direct extension of examination and commentary in the genre of crisis rhetoric that one could draw from the present enterprise would be to make further application of Fisher's (1984, 1985, 1987) narrative paradigm. Here, specific narratives are examined as discursive features and the role of narrative rationality, specifically fidelity, in the Senate floor debate is considered. It would be possible to carry out similar operations with regard to other crisis rhetoric situations. In addition, previously examined crises might warrant treatment via the narrative paradigm. As noted, Fisher (1985) by making reference to the Grenada invasion has implicitly suggested such an approach. In addition, when Ivie (1986) noted that several crisis rhetoric essays pointed to the role of traditional American myths and values which a president could evoke, he was pointing to a constellation of features that could easily be associated with narrative fidelity. Scholarship that would offer a robust treatment of both narrative coherence (probability) and narrative fidelity in specific case study form offers the potential of further illuminating the role of narrative and the full range of rhetorical powers and strategies used to construct crises.

This book notes the success of a triumph of the big government argument during the August 1994 Senate floor debate on comprehensive health care reform. Current implications associated with the exercise of that argument will consume the closing chapter of this book, but several research potentials connected to it will be addressed here. Indeed, this is a concept pregnant with potential in the political arena of the 1990s. Many campaigns, debates, individual speeches, and other discursive events tend to focus on the evils of big government and the need to decentralize and downsize government. All such discursive events pose the potential of serving as cases or illustrations for the rhetorical construction of a crisis similar to what was discovered here. The Congressional floor debates that ultimately led to passage of a major welfare overhaul bill in 1996 exemplify such a case. The general election campaign of 1994 that resulted in a tidal wave of Republican elections also offers an opportunity for such examinations. Clearly, rhetorical critics could examine such situations to determine (1) if a crisis was constructed, (2) if so, how it functioned, and (3) the effect it had.

The present rhetorical analysis also suggests that one element that contributed to the success of the crisis of big government was the employment of an implicit metaphor. The concept of the implicit metaphor in crisis rhetoric seems to hold great potential. As Cherwitz and Zagacki (1986) and others have noted, most crisis rhetoric focuses on international or foreign policy crises. It may well be that those crisis situations have employed implicit metaphors that construct images of good and bad and right and wrong. In fact, such cases may well represent "archetypical implicit metaphors." Osborn (1967) has offered a well-developed explanation of what he terms "archetypical metaphors" such as the contrast between light and dark. A similar operation may well exist with regard to the implicit metaphor. If one thinks of most international crisis situations, it would not be difficult to suggest that the archetypical implicit metaphor of war and peace is at work. In international crisis situations, the President is often constructing a choice between war—combat with an enemy, potential casualties, inherent dangers—and the restoration or maintenance of peace—with the security and comfort that it entails. There are also other war and peace elements in these situations; roles for generals (leaders) and for troops (followers), a clear and present danger, potential costs. In fact, such archetypical implicit metaphors may operate in a more abstract sense in the Senate floor debate examined here. There are enemies—villains who advocate the extension of federal power. There are potential casualties—the loss of individual choice and liberty. And there are paths to victory—the defeat of particular legislative provisions. Extension of the implicit metaphor to archetypical implicit metaphors and the examination of crisis rhetoric in that light seems to bode favorably as a task for future scholarship.

Classification schemes similar to those employed in the categorical portion of the present investigation might be useful to rhetorical scholars who wish to extend the examination of the August 1994 Senate floor debate on comprehensive health care reform. It would be possible, for example, to examine the use of the classic modes of proof—logos, pathos, and ethos—in the floor debate. Some or all of the categories of evidence examined here might, for example, be reinterpreted as elements of logos or appeals grounded in logical proof. Examples of pathos or proof stemming from passions and emotions could also be identified and examined. When a pro-reform Senator says that "real lives are at stake," that would seem to be a form of pathos. Attempts at building credibility through qualifications and experience might be conceptualized as elements of ethos. Pointing to the usage of these features and exploring their effectiveness would appear to be a means to extend the rhetorical analysis of the August 1994 floor debate and to reveal even more about the power of rhetoric as displayed through a classical or traditional frame. This might be an excellent opportunity for neo-Aristotelian scholars who are fond of examining such rhetorical features.

THEORETICAL HORIZONS

Much of the explication of the preliminary assessment and identification of research potentials thus far offered suggests a number of "indirect" theoretical horizons. I call them "indirect" in that they are points connected to the development of theoretic constructs, yet they are not derived directly from the discussion or application of theoretical constructs. For example, the conclusion drawn from the examination of discourse patterns that emerged from the Senate floor debate speaks squarely about how one might better understand policy discourse. As noted, the future orientation of opposition discourse may well be an archetypical illustration of the nature of policy discourse. Theoretically, this implies that a "temporal theory" of policy discourse might provide the single most constructive, arching over perspective regarding such practice.

Another important "indirect" theoretical horizon is associated with the applications and extension of the genre of crisis rhetoric. If crisis rhetoric is viewed as a guiding perspective for some rhetorical criticism efforts in addition to simply a genre or collection of similar works, the research potentials discussed here point to what might be significant theoretical insights. Identification and understanding of the implicit metaphor concept may well help to provide a general knowledge base for our understanding of how policy makers talk about crisis situations. In addition, application of the crisis rhetoric genre to a collective policy making body—in this case the U.S. Senate, rather than to the individual decision making of the U.S. President—suggests that we might understand a body of policy discourse situations better by framing them as crises. Such a perspective could help theorists and researchers draw clear parameters around contemporary problem situations. And examine the development and consideration of various crises that would better inform many regarding hotly contested foreign and domestic issues.

At least two important theoretical horizons might be gleaned from the employ-ment of Stephen Toulmin's argument fields theory offered in the critical assessment of the August 1994 floor debate. The "layering" notion regarding argument fields (as illustrated in Figure 5.1) developed in this work offers helpful advice for those seeking a better understanding of Toulmin's concept. The argumentation community has been plagued by enormous disagreement as to the exact boundaries or units of any given argument field (Prosier, Miller, & Mills, 1996). Viewing argument fields more as systems or layers helps to resolve that disagreement. Fields might not always have precisely defined limits; rather, they may well be more fluid or dynamic in the way in which they function in the real world of day-to-day practice. Further, such a perspective advises us to be more conscious of the relational nature of fields. By "relational," I am once again indicating that the system-like nature of argument fields is important. As there is somewhat of a natural relationship between a suprasystem, a system, subsystems, and component parts, so too is there a relationship between the layers of an argument field. One or another layer may represent an ultimate audience—similar to the larger public and body politic in this case—a pivotal location dictating the nature of discursive behavior—much like the two political fields represented in the comprehensive health care reform debate. Application to other argument fields of the layering concept might help to generate illumination similar to what has been shed upon the health care reform debate. In addition, Wenzel (1982) argues that "the upshot of recognizing" the nature of significant social issues in the contemporary world "is to call for amendment to our theory, practice and pedagogy of argumentation" (p. 5). The notion of layering can serve as one small step in that amendment process.

A second step toward amendment of argumentation theory, specifically argument fields theory, is drawn from the employment of fields as a framework for the ethical assessment of the August 1994 Senate floor debate. The step offered here also helps those who study communication ethics to advance their various assessment and evaluative perspectives. An overlaying of argument fields may provide the most robust context or framework for ethical assessments of argumentative disputes. The layering construction of argument fields just discussed helps demonstrate that such assessments of the ethicality of discursive behavior might best be conducted in an incremental manner, examining such behavior at the different layers of the field in which it occurs. Such application might also facilitate a better understanding of how particular agents reason through their own ethical decision making and why assessments of ethicality so often appear to disagree.

The most significant theoretical horizon to emerge from the case study of the comprehensive health care reform debate clearly relates to my general proposition that talk is power. As noted, this is not a brand new theoretical or applied construct. Cold War–period scholars found such a view most compelling. Weaver, Borcherds, and Smith's (1952) comments offer another typical illustration: "[A] society which does not concern itself with the ways in which its members speak and the purposes for which they speak is neglecting a process which will either strengthen and develop that society, or weaken and destroy it" (p. 16). The comprehensive health care reform debate certainly did not "destroy" American society, but examination of the debate points to contemporary reasons to continue and enhance our embrace of the notion that talk equals power. At the very least, this work renews consideration of the theoretical understanding of talk as power and thus opens the floodgates to other case studies, to assessment of other debates, and to more extensive examination of the discursive behavior that actually does determine the outcomes of the policy process in contemporary American society.

Renewed discussion of talk as power also points to the need for greater attention to examination of some of the specific talk employed by policy makers and others who exercise agency over day-to-day life in the postmodern community. As Weaver (1953), Edelman (1965), and others have pointed to the power of specific terms or words, it might be worthwhile to code the floor debate for expressions other than that of "crisis." A number of opponents of comprehensive health care reform during the floor debate, for example, refer to it as "socialization" of medicine. It might be informative to code the number of times that particular term is employed to see whether opponents of reform hope to have it function as a "devil" term or to evoke some specific audience reaction. Other terms like "radical" and "extreme" offer similar investigatory potential. Such terms as "socialization" and "socialism" might be coded to offer some extension of Starr's (1982) argument that the "red card" was played effectively in earlier health care reform debates. Such applied actions point to another form of theoretical renewal: a greater understanding of the individualized power of specific words. Again, this too is a renewal grounded in a rich history, but it is also one that can help us to better understand the overall nature of talk as power and how it works in specific contexts and situations.

Another theoretical implication associated with those just outlined relates to instructors regarding both communication and political theory. Far too often, instructional discussions in both disciplines seem divorced from consequences in the real world and more directly focused upon abstract concepts seem very difficult to apply. An embrace of talk as power as a theoretical construct that underlies all discourse and most certainly public policy discourse would add a greater "practical" dimension to theory instruction in communication and politics. Although not speaking directly to this point, rhetorical critic Marie Hochmuth's (1948) promotion of speech education half a century ago does help to shed light on the potential value of such instruction:

Speech is a means to an end. It must be cultivated as a means for bringing stability in human relations and as a tool for helping to secure peace in our time. . . . It must be done by people who recognize the psychological, sociological, and political implications of talk. . . . [U]ntil the schools give more attention to the development of social competence that has even been given in the history of our country, there can be little hope for finding these personal disciplines that are necessary for cooperative behavior in an industrial society, a democratic nation and a world order. (p. 33)

Theoretical instruction centered around talk as power might not "secure peace in our time," but it will place proper emphasis upon the nature of discourse and how it factors into the outcome of virtually every important social and public policy decision confronting contemporary society.

The general embrace of talk as power offers a more general understanding for everyone of how discursive behavior dictates serious and significant issues in day-to-day practice. Examination of the August 1994 U.S. Senate floor debate on comprehensive health care reform vividly illustrates how discursive behavior determined the outcome of what was the first Senate floor debate of its type and the fourth major incarnation of health care reform during the twentieth century. As we turn to Chapter Thirteen of this book, the focus will be placed upon illustration of contemporary currents connected to that particular discursive dispute. That discussion should further reveal the practical significance of talk as power and therefore do even more to stress its worth as a theoretic construct.

Chapter 13

Contemporary Currents

Talk is most certainly power, but that power is not always manifested in a particular way. Much like any other force or path to power, talk may generate effects or consequences both directly and indirectly. Everyone recognizes, in a practical sense, that a truck is a *powerful* vehicle. Its power is exercised directly as it functions as a means of conveyance for a heavy payload of concrete blocks, timber, or other bulky material. Its power is also exercised indirectly as it bumps the rear end of a car ahead of it and skids and scrapes occur for miles along the highway. The same holds true for talk. A representative from the Red Cross may directly exercise power by making a speech at a local industrial complex that compels dozens of workers to sign up for the weekend blood drive. She may also exercise power indirectly by instilling a sense of commitment among some of her listeners that, perhaps many months or even years later, results in organ donations, assistance at soup kitchens for the homeless, and a host of other social goods.

The paths to power are, indeed, often manifested in a manner that may vary temporally or effectually. Some of the power of talk is very obvious and very direct. That was certainly the case with regard to the 1994 comprehensive health care reform debate, where opposition rhetoric derailed the fourth attempt at such reform this century. Other power connected to talk is more indirect. (These two paths to power are illustrated in Figure 13.1.) The second path to the power of talk is often mediated by interpretations made by various audiences, modifications, or adjustments in the messages and other forms of changes that ultimately produce differing consequences, but can nonetheless still be tied to some "original" instance of talk, such as the 1994 health care reform debate.

The 1994 comprehensive health care reform debate is illustrative of the indirect path of talk to power, much as it has been illuminated regarding its connection to the direct route. The 1994 debate has generated three principal "contemporary currents"

Figure 13.1
Talk's Paths to Power

Direct   Talk = Effect

Indirect   Talk = Immediate Effect = Interpretations
                    = Modifications = Changes = Indirect Effects

or indirect paths to power. They can easily be thought of as currents in that they are analogous to the currents a stone might make in a body of water. The failure of comprehensive health care reform was the big splash from the rhetorical stone tossed by reform advocates in 1994, and the features discussed in this closing chapter are the currents made on the body politic by those same rhetorical stones. Three principal contemporary currents seem to emerge from the 1994 debate. Incrementalism, particularly with regard to health care reform, is one dominant current tied to the 1994 debate. A second current is the triumph of the "big government" argument. A final current that is in some ways the most direct of the three is what can best be identified as "retrospective closure," an attempt to better assess the full potential of the comprehensive health care reform debate in 1994. We will first turn to incrementalism.

INCREMENTALISM
       Historical trend data clearly demonstrate that incremental, small, step-by-step, reform measures are a natural result of major political or social crisis, certainly health care crises. Starr (1982) aptly noted that efforts undertaken to identify a point of health care crisis and to campaign for comprehensive reform of the American health care system in the early 1900s, during the postwar Truman administration, and again in the 1970s were not marked by total inaction with regard to health care reform, but rather by incremental measures to adjust the existing system. Such incremental measures have included Medicare and Medicaid, policies tied to Social Security, and a number of other more modest and limited health care reform proposals. Senator Wofford recalled the earlier health care reform debates by noting, "I thought we were further along. We seem to be at this moment and this hour, in that long battle Harry Truman started" (S12062). The results of the 1994 debate also echo those earlier reform periods in that health care is still a major public policy issue now several years later and that there are traces of incremental response on the issue. Indeed, national and state health care trends confirm such a view.
       It is worth noting, in very brief summary fashion, that health care rose to near the top of the American public policy agenda in the early 1990s for several good reasons. Millions of Americans lacked any insurance coverage, and even greater numbers were facing the loss of what little medical protection they did have due to policies that punished those with pre-existing illnesses and other severe medical problems. In addition, the cost of the health care crisis at the time was skyrocketing; many individuals were priced out of the insurance market and many small businesses were crippled by escalating premium rates for insurance policies. These serious problems

did not evaporate from existence when the rhetorical forces of opposition forestalled comprehensive national health care reform for a fourth time during the twentieth century.

Health care is still a significant public policy issue. Costs are, for example, still rising at a remarkable rate. Total health expenditures in 1990 were $697 billion, rising to almost $950 billion in 1994 or nearly 14 percent of gross domestic product, and they continue to increase every year (Cleverly, 1997). The human consequences of health care are also still quite dramatic. Navarro (1994) underscored such consequences by pointing to the benefits that comprehensive reform could produce: "A national health care program with single payer funding and administration would save between 47,000 and 106,000 lives annually by providing comprehensive and universal coverage, while saving $10.2 billion" (p. 1). It may well be that "the crisis we face in our health care system dwarfs these natural disasters [floods and earthquakes]" (Senator Kennedy, S11025), just as much today as it did in 1994.

It would be unfair to say that the health care crisis has received no attention from public officials or health administrators since the collapse of comprehensive reform in 1994. Indeed, incremental measures, proposals, and calls for reform have been ongoing. Issues connected to health care, such as the role of managed care or HMOs, coverage for children, portability of insurance policies, smoking concerns, and a host of other health care items have continued to populate the public policy agendas throughout the 1990s. It is possible to examine some of those incremental actions and to clearly illustrate how they are, at least indirectly, currents tied to the comprehensive reform talk of 1994.

Health care coverage and health care programs targeted to children have received considerable attention recently and they were certainly a significant component of reform talk in 1994. Senator Kennedy, for example, noted "More than 10 million children have no health coverage. They do not get the preventive care they need" (S11025). Senator Boxer made a less quantitative, but more dramatic plea when she stated: "It is absolutely immoral not to cover the children. It is also economically insane not to do it" (S11764). Additionally, it is worthy of note to recall that the first amendment offered to the Mitchell comprehensive health care reform proposal was one by Senator Dodd calling for an early phase-in of comprehensive coverage for children. Children's health care issues are, of course, closely tied to women's health issues, as Hafner-Eaton (1993) aptly noted in her analysis of prospective reform proposals early in the 1990s. Neither women's health issues nor those targeted more directly to children have fared well later in the decade. For example, it was recently reported that efforts to establish broader children's health care resources in the state of Kentucky were at a near standstill (Shameful Delay, 1999). Similarly, an initiative to establish a comprehensive women's health program was placed at the bottom of legislative priorities due to fears of a possible increase in the number of abortions in the state of Nebraska (Unicameral, 1999).

Since the failure of comprehensive health care reform in 1994, currents of the concern for children have continued to flow throughout the country. Despite the failures noted in Kentucky and Nebraska, a number of state and local jurisdictions have undertaken measures to improve the availability of preventive care and to expand overall health care access for America's youngest citizens. In addition, several HMOs and hospitals have implemented or expanded low-cost or free care programs targeted to pregnant mothers and small children. In fact, some writers have suggested that a number of such measures have been developed by both public and private health care outlets since the time of the 1994 debate (Shecter, 1996).

Managed care options, particularly Health Maintenance Organizations (HMOs), have experienced enormous growth in the past decade or so. Although the roots of HMOs and managed care extend back for decades in American society, they were of considerable importance and received enormous attention during the 1994 debate regarding comprehensive health care reform. As Randal (1993) reported, a number of those individuals and groups promoting comprehensive health care reform in the early 1990s viewed HMOs as the most efficient and cost effective means to ensure universal coverage and care for millions of Americans. During the Senate floor debate in August of 1994, Senator Packwood of Oregon was particularly noteworthy as an advocate for the free-market expansion of managed care, driven by the success of HMOs in his own northwestern corner of the United States.

Most casual observers will acknowledge that the number of and enrollment in HMOs have increased at a rapid rate in just the past few years. Indeed, many readers will likely recall being compelled to either join a managed care option or to at least make a choice between participation in an HMO or a more traditional fee-for-service option. The growth of HMOs has not occurred without serious concern by many patients and health policy makers. Media attention demonstrates that concerns have been raised regarding cost-cutting strategies by HMOs, refusal to treat some Medicare patients in managed care options, and excessive profiteering by some health care conglomerates that own HMOs. The promises of comprehensive coverage and care through HMOs have not materialized following the 1994 reform debate, but HMOs and other managed care options have remained important contemporary currents in American health care.

Issues related to managed care generally and HMOs in particular have, indeed, remained significant national currents of health care reform and policy making. In fact, HMOs were at the center of health care policy concerns at the end of the 1990s. For example, the U.S. Congress rejected a "Patient's Bill of Rights" in the fall of 1998 that was prompted by multiple cases of mistreatment of patients in managed care settings. Quinn (1998) reported that patients' rights was overwhelmed as a national issue by the impeachment of President Clinton, and that patients' rights should remain a critical health care issue as providers often offer plans that "do you wrong." Patients' rights are inherently limited in the HMO context because almost all states prohibit malpractice lawsuits against such health care organizations. In addition to malpractice and other legal aspects of health care, HMOs have been criticized for the way many of them limit access to certain types of treatment and care. That concern has recently been eased a bit as HMOs have agreed to cover costs for patients enrolled in clinical trials of new medications (Pear, 1999). Given their ever-expanding market share, HMOs are likely to remain a central focus of health care reform efforts for some time to come.

Since the mid-1960s, when the Surgeon General first issued a health warning concerning cigarettes, smoking has been a major public health current in American society. During the 1994 comprehensive health care reform debate, a number of efforts were made to capture smoking under the broad umbrella of health care reform. Many comprehensive reform advocates, both inside and outside the Senate, favored heavy taxes on tobacco as a means to help pay for universal health care coverage for millions of Americans. As I have noted earlier, the name or label, "the Tobacco Industry Protection Act," was hurled at less comprehensive proposals offered by Republicans during the Senate floor debate. The "tobacco debate" itself only intensified following the 1994 comprehensive health care reform effort. In June of 1997 a major deal was struck between several of the country's largest tobacco companies and a collection of state attorneys general who hoped to recoup losses their respective states had incurred due to the promotion and sale of cigarettes. Several weeks later, Republican-led efforts essentially extinguished any hope that Congress would provide its legislative blessing to the proposal. This current of health care reform is, however, still ongoing. The tobacco industry is still airing radio and television spots touting potential Congressional action on tobacco as "old-time, big spending politics," and promoting the election of candidates during the next election who wholeheartedly oppose federal regulation of the industry. Although a settlement had been initially reached at the state level in 1999, delays and disputes regarding use of funds from the lawsuits will continue to plague state governments for several years. Smoking is an incremental aspect of health care policy that is likely to remain a significant contemporary current for many years to come due to the health and financial consequences involved for all parties to the tobacco debate.

Roe v. Wade was the landmark Supreme Court decision regarding a woman's privacy rights and access to abortion, but it was only the first step in a long and troubled conflict on the issue. Save for those who have been in some counterfactual world where abortion is not a serious issue, everyone knows that it is still one of the most hotly contested matters on the American public policy agenda. It is important to recall that many, including Hafner-Eaton (1993), view access to abortion as an essential component in the provision of health care to America's female population. Such a medical perspective was not lost on some advocates of comprehensive health care reform in 1994. Some reform advocates touted abortion access as a necessary ingredient in any truly "comprehensive" health care package. The opponents of reform were quick to seize upon such access options as another opportunity for attack. Senator Helms, for example, raised the issue this way:

Pro-abortion groups such as Planned Parenthood, the National Abortion Rights Action League, and the Alan Guttmacher Institute, just to name two or three, have lobbied, picketed, screamed, yelled to get abortion included in the mandatory Government package and, as a political result, it is included. Could it be that these groups want to use health care reform as a means to expand the availability of abortion in this country? There is no doubt in my mind that these people want abortion in the United States to become as routine as having your tonsils taken out. (S12167)

Of course, Senator Helms need not have worried. The health care reform debate became more of a means to assault the role of the federal government, and women's access to abortion continued to be rolled back on an incremental level in state legislatures throughout the country. In addition to such policy action though, it is important to emphasize that violence against women had escalated at the end of the 1990s. Much of that violence seems to be associated a more general level of hatred aimed at the federal government. I will discuss the linkage of such hatred and violence to the 1994 comprehensive reform debate later in this chapter.

The issue of portability—the ability of an insurance policy holder to transfer that policy from job to job—was a central theme throughout the entire 1994 reform debate. Indeed, proposals offered both by Senator Mitchell and Senator Dole included some form of portability legislation. Two years after the debate regarding comprehensive health care reform, some action was taken regarding portability. Senators Kennedy and Kassebaum introduced legislation that would ensure portability of insurance policies, and in May of 1996 the full Senate passed the measure and it later became law. The legislation was designed to ensure that people could keep their health insurance when they changed jobs and that no one could be excluded from health coverage due to a pre-existing illness. Shecter (1996) reported that "The new legislation is intended to fill a few of the gaps. But its sponsors have been careful not to propose anything as ambitious as President Clinton's failed plan for health care" (p. A5). Senators Kennedy and Kassebaum learned that the Senate and the country were much more amenable to smaller, incremental action than they were to comprehensive reform.

General access issues have also remained important policy concerns related to health care, particularly at the state and local level. For example, Collier (1999) recently reported that local health care departments throughout the state of Kentucky are increasingly facing reductions in funding due to a host of other policy issues. The result, according to Collier, is that access for the working poor will be more and more limited in the years ahead. Richardson (1999) has similarly reported that access problems are escalating as local health departments lose resources, and that such disminishment of access to local health departments often forces patients to turn to hospital emergency rooms for help. Such an influx of patients into emergency rooms creates a cycle of problems—more poor patients go to emergency rooms due to lack of care elsewhere, increasing costs for hospitals, making overall medical care costs rise, and placing thousands, perhaps millions, of other citizens at the brink of an individual health care crisis. Thus, access may well remain an significant as an issue in the coming years as it was earlier in the 1990s.

One of the most significant of contemporary health care issues at the national level has been the decision to develop policies that compel millions of Medicare patients to join HMOs for their health care needs. Such actions generate implications at several levels. They help to underscore the continuing importance of federal health care programs such as Medicaid and Medicare. Further, these policies place greater value upon the role of managed care in the big health care picture. As Medicare policies encourage more individuals to enroll in HMOs, it will add to burdens on some HMO facilities, expand the overall patient population affiliated with managed care options, extend the reach of the federal government into the HMO industry, and intensify HMOs as a center of reform attention. Collier (1999), Richardson (1999), and others have also noted that an increase in HMO enrollment due to Medicare necessarily causes a decline in use of traditional facilities and therefore confounds funding and resources problems.

One market trend is also worthy of note. As it was in 1994, the U.S. health care system is an entrepreneurial, free market system. The market-driven nature of the U.S. health care system has been noted in Wall Street circles over the past few years. The number of for-profit hospitals and other health care facilitates has expanded dramatically in the past several years. The result has been a more competitive health care market, where many of the agents of action and change are more driven by profit and greed than they are by any altruistic interest in providing access to care. Schroeder (1999) recently placed this issue in perspective, based upon the personal view of a health care provider. He noted, "I personally prefer to receive my health care from an institutional provider that cares for me . . . without the distractions of generating a profit to satisfy the return of the stockholders" (p. 13A). So long as much of health care is profit-oriented, Schroeder's view will be an important acknowledgment of concerns regarding access and care.

Health care reform has, indeed, tended toward incrementalism following the 1994 debate regarding universal coverage and comprehensive reform. There is, as of this writing, still no comprehensive program designed to provide basic health coverage in the United States and there is little or no prospect for development and implementation of such a program any time in the near future. The longstanding dominance of incrementalism in the area of health care reform has been analyzed at some length in this work, and it has also been noted that periods of demand for comprehensive reform are not typically followed by total neglect; health care continues to be addressed in some step-by-step manner as has been in the case in the 1990s. The power of talk is a chief causative agent in this process. Indeed, the counterfactual is simple: Absent the power of talk to place health care reform on the nation's policy agenda, little or no action would occur. The pro-reform talk was not powerful enough to secure adherence to a proposal for comprehensive reform, but it certainly demonstrated an ability to exercise the indirect path to power that is best characterized as incrementalism.

The power of talk as defined by incrementalism extends into the closing years of the 1990s. Former Speaker of the House Newt Gingrich launched his congressional re-election campaign by stating: "I think every senior citizen should have the right to go out and have the doctor they want or go to the hospital they want" (Shipp, 1998, p. 4). Columnist Bill Shipp (1998) noted that the question of "choice" currently has little to do with abortion, but "It has everything to do with health care delivery systems and how much say-so a patient should have in selecting his or her caregivers" (p. 4). Shipp and other commentators have shed light on the recent political rhetoric and interest in patients' choice of doctor and treatment, largely due to the perception that HMOs and other managed care options have compromised those choices. Here the power of talk is rather vivid in two ways. First, the expansion of HMOs was a central theme of both Democratic and Republican advocates during the 1994 comprehensive reform debate and the ripple effect of their talk has helped to expand the use of HMOs and to raise patient concerns regarding practice within such facilities. Second, the more indirect talk among those dissatisfied with the HMO experience has helped to elevate health care to its highest level on the national agenda since 1994.

Some observers and political pundits might well tout Bill Clinton's second term as "the incremental presidency." While his first term was in many ways notable by his failure to accomplish any *major* overhaul of the health care system—or for that matter any *major* policy action that was opposed by Republicans, during his second term, President Clinton tended to embrace incrementalism to the point of virtually excluding any large-scale or comprehensive action. The President urged adoption of targeted, selective tax cuts rather than an across-the-board tax cut. Clinton issued executive orders regulating assault weapons, but did not propose a comprehensive gun control plan. He initiated several limited foreign policy actions in Bosnia, the Middle East, China, and other areas, yet there was no grand-scale "human rights" theme like that adopted by President Jimmy Carter, nor any other guiding ideological or policy beacon for the State Department to follow. These seem to be general lessons gleamed from the failure to marshall the power of talk to enact comprehensive health care reform. In fact, health care itself vividly illustrates the point. The noted scholar Paul Starr assisted the White House as it waged the political and rhetorical war for reform in 1994. Later, Starr (1994) noted: "The lesson for next time in health reform is faster, smaller. We made the error of trying to do too much at once" (p. 31). Thus, one indirect power of talk is to instruct its users how to better their efforts in the future.

Someone would most certainly point to President Clinton's signing of welfare reform legislation as a comprehensive rather than an incremental measure. That exception is certainly germane to the closing discussion of this work. One obvious point to note in connection with welfare reform is that the final legislation was largely a Republican initiative and Clinton simply did not wish to risk his 1996 re-election bid by rejecting it. Whether exclusively a Republican effort or one aided by the Democratic president, both had one thing in common—an embrace of the "big government" argument. In fact, the most dramatic power of talk that may be, at least indirectly, linked to the 1994 debate on comprehensive health care reform is that connected to the triumph of the "big government" argument—that any growth in the size and scope of the federal government is inherently evil and must be rejected, regardless of the costs entailed.

THE TRIUMPH OF THE "BIG GOVERNMENT" ARGUMENT

There can be little doubt that the United States has experienced an escalation of antigovernment rhetoric, politics, and even violence in the 1990s. Timothy McVeigh was convicted of bombing a federal building in Oklahoma City and killing 168 innocent citizens whose only mistake was to be associated with the federal government. The so-called "Freemen" in Montana refused to pay taxes or obey the laws of the land, and ultimately secluded themselves until taken into custody by government agents. And militant groups around the country have robbed banks, killed people, and generally wrecked havoc inspired by their holy war against the federal government.

A very concise summary of the "war against the government" was offered by Roszak (1995):

We are in the midst of an assault on federal power that now commands the airwaves, much of the press, a major party, the floor of Congress, and a grassroots militia movement that, though of indeterminate size, may be larger than many of us want to believe and is surely murderous enough in its intensity to be worrisome. (p. 64)

Some may claim that Roszak's assessment is a bit hyperbolic, but everyone must acknowledge the tendency of radical groups on the right, political figures, and even average citizens to voice "distrust of big government," "a dislike of federal power," "hatred of those darn government bureaucrats," or "thinking that comes from outside the beltway," on the airwaves, in campaign speeches, and in daily conversation.

All of the anti–big government efforts around the nation cannot be directly linked to the efforts to defeat comprehensive health care reform on the floor of the Senate in August of 1994. Despite the absence of an obvious empirically verifiable causal correction between the 1994 debate and more recent anti–big government actions, there can be little doubt that the opposition rhetoric in the 1994 debate is at least one significant thread in the patchwork of anti–big government rhetoric that has had the power to cause protests, bombings, and even deaths. The anti–big government argument was the largest single factor in the defeat of comprehensive health care reform.

The opponents of comprehensive health care reform made it very clear that their opposition would center around re-framing the debate as a decision process regarding expansion of both the size and scope of the federal government. I have, of course, developed that general point at some length earlier in this work. It is, however, useful to once again turn to the talk from the floor to illustrate the vividness of the anti–big government argument. The remarks offered by Senator Gorton are typical of the nature of the anti–big government argument:

[T]he challenge before the Senate is whether we will approve change that will be positive, acceptable, and affordable to the American people, or on the other hand, are we going to pursue remedies that serve Big Government political interests and endanger the very system of care on which we all depend for our families' health? (S11774)

Indeed, Senator Gorton went on to characterize "big government" as the true crisis confronting the nation:

This debate is historical because it is about nothing less than the role of Government in the most intimate decisions and fearful moments in our lives—the times at which we are in need of urgent medical care to heal ourselves and those we love. (S11774)

Perhaps the best summary of the general line of argument employed by opposition forces was presented by Senator Danforth when he proclaimed, "We think it is too big, that it goes too far" (S11766).

Considering the comments of Gorton, Danforth, and other opposition Senators, it becomes increasingly easy to accept the idea that the anti–big government argument was largely responsible for defeat of comprehensive health care reform in the summer of 1994. It may, however, be more difficult to accept that argument, or any other rhetorical stance, is in some way connected to bombings, assaults, and other outright acts of violence against the federal government. In fact, some readers will recall that there were many nationally prominent Republican figures who were among the first to condemn the Oklahoma City bombing. That is certainly true, but it is also unfortunately true that the hands of "mainstream" conservatives are not entirely clean in connection to such violence. In fact, when one closely examines the comments of comprehensive health care reform opponents during the 1994 floor debate, it becomes very clear that a pattern of talk develops that makes it not only appropriate, but necessary to hate the federal government.

Consider the comments of opposition Senators who made it vividly clear that one must *kill* such great government threats as comprehensive health care reform legislation. After recognizing that a very limited Republican proposal would not be enacted, Senator Coats noted, "I think that only leaves us with one option, and that option is to kill the President's bill" (S11678). A great many opponents of comprehensive health care reform made comments that resemble Coats's call to *kill* the legislation. Senator D'Amato was most explicit in his pleas for a slaying:

Some time ago, we had "taxasouras." I said kill the "taxasouras." That goes for this. We should kill it. We should kill it because it is a danger to the health and welfare and well-being of America and America's families. That is the monster, the Clinton-Mitchell proposal. (S12076)

D'Amato clearly wanted to put the federal "monster" to death.

The calls of Coats, D'Amato, and others to kill a piece of legislation may not be particularly alarming until one considers the line of reasoning that is established by such statements. Examine a simple syllogism:

Major premise—Big government is evil and it should be killed.
Minor premise—Comprehensive health care reform is big government.
Conclusion—Therefore, comprehensive health care reform is evil and should be killed.

This reasoning becomes quite dramatic when it is considered enthymatically. If "big government is evil and it should be killed" is considered the generalization that serves as the major premise and the conclusion to be drawn is that "agents of big government are evil and should be killed," then the risk becomes overwhelming that individual auditors might fill in or provide their own minor premise. That minor premise could easily be "an FBI agent represents big government" or "the tax system is an arm of big government" or even "my neighbor works for the big government in Washington." The possible conclusions could include "the FBI agent should be killed," "the tax system should be killed," or even "my neighbor should be killed."

The calls to kill the Mitchell proposal do not represent the only discursive line of reasoning that seem alarming and dangerous when considered enthymatically or in some extended manner. For example, Senator Durenburger's discussion regarding doctor-patient interaction is another vivid illustration: "[T]he Clinton and Mitchell bills insert the cold hand of Government into this private discussion and tells doctors and patients what sort of care will be covered what sorts will not" (S11780). By extension, Durenburger is making it seem that "the government" is not populated by warm, living beings. It should be OK to hate them, hurt them, and kill them if they are merely agents of *the cold hand of Government*.

Durenburger's remarks were not atypical comments; rather, they represented a discursive pattern during the comprehensive health care reform debate that implied that all agents of big government should be opposed and destroyed. If we continue to examine remarks drawn from the Senate floor, it is possible to further illuminate the potential power of anti–big government rhetoric. Senator Danforth noted: "This underlying bill that is before us now is never going to be amended to a point where it is not something that scares the willies out of the people of this country" (S11768). The inference could easily be that if it is OK for big government to "scare the willies" out of us, perhaps we should do something to "scare the willies" out of big government as well. It might, for example, "scare the willies" out of big government to blow up its buildings, shoot its individual agents, or refuse to obey any of its laws. The inference to be drawn from Senator Gregg's comments are even more explicit. While discussing the provision of mandatory coverage options by the states included in the Mitchell proposal, Gregg said "It is, again, a gun-to-the-head type of legislative action undertaken by the elite here in Washington" (S12052). The reverse of Gregg's view would suggest that it is necessary to put a gun to the head of that "elite . . . in Washington."

Senator Gregg extended his indictment of federal elitism. Addressing what he considered to be relatively competent legislative detail in the Mitchell proposal, Gregg said, "It is utopian elitism that runs through all of this that creates these types of documents with these huge imaginations of structure in their attempt to address problems that are humorous" (S12046). There is, of course, a common tendency to respond disfavorably to those we consider elitists. Indeed, the very term "elitist" conjures up images and connotative meanings associated with "the privileged," "the aristocratic," and so on. Such images and connotations have often been associated with the roles of federal bureaucrats in Washington. In fact, Smith (1997) reported that over 70 percent of voters and nonvoters alike do not trust the government to do what is right. Here again the power of talk may be most indirect, but it is nonetheless present.

Not only was the August 1994 floor debate replete with references to "government elitism" and the negative connotations inherent in the expression, but other speakers went even further to cast the federal government in a negative light. Senator Smith suggested that it was somehow "odd" to believe that the federal government would do anything that was logical and that made sense to the average voter. He noted: "God forbid, we do anything that makes sense around here in Washington inside the beltway" (S11436). It is striking that Smith not only condemned the government for "not making sense," but he also went to great discursive lengths to stress that the federal government was the place where such failure to reason and understand good sense resided. He stressed this in three ways. First, he said that it was odd to do anything that made sense "around here," referring to the nation's capital where the debate was taking place. Second, he emphasized that this failure of reasoning was occurring "in Washington." And finally, he worked to conjure up the worst of impressions and connotations by adding "inside the beltway." Statements such as these leave little doubt that it is appropriate to target Washington as an enemy.

Senator Smith also made it clear by inference that it is appropriate to *hurt* the federal government. He noted:

[T]here is a concern out there that the Government is going to do something to me on this issue. I think that it is coming through loud and clear, and it is a very valid concern. Rather than helping us, they are going to do something to me that may cost me my good quality health care. (S11929)

Smith did not explicitly ask people to hurt the federal government in any way, but he did say that, at least with the proposed health care legislation, the federal government may "cost" people something and it may cost them their health and well-being or their "good quality health care." Others may perceive that the federal government may "cost" them financial resources due to taxes, firearms due to gun control, or even liberty due to laws that some individuals may consider unfair. Smith went on to stress the general distrust of the federal government: "Government has proven again and again that it is not efficient, it is not compassionate, it is not thrifty; therefore, it should not be trying to provide the health care needs of people" (S11929). The track record Smith refers to would certainly not be one to instill trust. If the government "is not compassionate," then others need not be compassionate toward the government.

Senator Helms tied the lack of trust to both health care and the Postal Service. He said, "If we cannot trust the Federal Government to deliver the mail, what makes us think we can trust the Federal Government to deliver our health care" (S12167). Helms also quoted several magazine sources to bolster his argument that action on the part of the federal government is typically counterproductive because in their "eagerness to help to solve something, they sometimes make it worse" (S12167). The question that arises, then, naturally is, "Why should we trust the federal government to do anything if the government might make it worse?" Such rhetoric may cause some individuals to question their trust of the federal government; others may even fight to avoid falling into an untrusting relationship with "the Feds."

Senator Danforth's comments below demonstrate the extent of danger or threat that opposition Senators attribute to the federal government:

If we approve the Clinton-Mitchell approach, we enter a nightmare system of Government coercion, rationed health care, new taxes totaling $100 billion dollars, special punishment of Americans who have made sacrifices for good health plans, intrusion into the doctor-patient relationship, loss of jobs, reduction of wages, and harms to our nation's fiscal, economic, and medical health—a harm, Mr. President, that cannot be reversed. (S11782)

Danforth suggests that the government can employ *coercion* and *punishment* to produce irreparable harms. Certainly, some extremist elements might ask why it would not then be appropriate to use those same tactics to do harm to the great evil of the federal government.

While discussing an amendment to the Mitchell proposal that would require open meetings of all relevant health care agencies and other checks on secrecy, Senator Helms remarked that "This amendment would stop callous social engineers like Mr. [Ira] Magaziner [Hillary Clinton's chief aid on health care]who care nothing for ordinary Americans" (S12076). Here Helms implicitly draws an analogy to the most evil of all twentieth century governments—Nazi Germany. Just as Josef Mengele conducted *social engineering* experiments on unwitting Holocaust victims and just as he and other Nazi agents *care nothing for ordinary* people, the federal government in America was now engaged in similar behavior. If such an analogy does not play upon the emotions and affective states of some listeners, then it is doubtful that any language comparison does. And, once again, a natural reverse or parallel conclusion is clear: We must oppose such actions because they are evil.

As discussed at length earlier, much of the anti–big government rhetoric during the 1994 comprehensive health care reform debate was tied to the sense of narrative fidelity held by many Americans that there are inherent problems with the federal government. Late in the floor debate, Senator Mack stressed the relationship between comprehensive health care reform and general public concerns regarding the federal government:

And plain and simple, the American people did not trust the Clinton plan. They did not trust the secrecy in which it was written. They did not trust the principle that "government knows best." And, they did not trust the endless maze of new government boards and bureaucracies that would have been created. (S12083)

The sense that such risks tended to "ring true" with much of the public was stressed time and again by drawing parallels with the Postal Service. Senator Burns's remarks illustrate this:

They do not run their bureaucracies very well, and I am wondering if I want them to run my health care system. Would it end up like the Post Office? Does my time to get my hip replacement end up in a dead-letter office? I would sure hate for it to. I think Americans kind of worry about that too. (S11789)

Such a sense of narrative fidelity might best be explained as a *social epistemic*. Americans—that is, society at large—have been conditioned to see the federal government in a negative light. In fact, Senator Durenburger noted that, "The American people are sick and tired of having decisions made for them by the Federal Government" (S11779).

The creation, reinforcement, and extension of such a *social epistemic* may well be the most powerful effect of talk. Through the practice of rhetorical behavior, Americans have generally grown to think of the federal government as being an agent that should, at the very least, be used sparingly and kept in relatively tight rein. The roots of such a *social epistemic* reach back to the very creation of this nation, with checks and balances and separations of powers built into our very system of government, and to the longstanding embrace of rugged individualism. That *social epistemic* has, however, changed and evolved. The federal government in the late 1990s has come to be thought of, very often by a few and occasionally by many, as an enemy or evil that must be hated and opposed. The power of talk is expressed each time that a political figure speaks of the evils of the federal government and then, indirectly, when an extremist comes to accept such a way of thinking as a ticket for action that may be violent and deadly.

CLOSURE

Perhaps the most nagging question that some observers might pose regarding the 1994 comprehensive health care reform debate would be "Is there a way that proponents of comprehensive health care reform could have won the debate?" That is, of course, a difficult question to answer. And, in fact, there may be several possible answers. Two different responses might suggest that proponents of comprehensive health care reform could have won the debate. One response would suggest that several minor changes might have been undertaken that could have better ensured success of the Mitchell proposal. A second response would suggest that more directly refuting the anti–big government argument might have permitted proponents of comprehensive health care reform to prevail. There is also a third response that would simply say "no," the proponents of reform could not have won the debate. That response is grounded primarily in the belief that the talk of opponents was far too powerful for comprehensive health care reform to succeed. I will elaborate on each of the potential responses and stress one as the most probable.

For several years now, observers and pundits have suggested that there were several minor changes that the Clinton administration and its allies could have made in their campaign to win acceptance of comprehensive health care reforms. For example, it would have been possible to make all meetings and task force sessions regarding health care reform open to the media and to the public in order to avert charges of secrecy and "big government, behind-the-scenes" actions. It also would have been possible to propose the legislation several months earlier in an attempt to negotiate and seek compromises prior to a Labor Day recess. Furthermore, some controversial provisions, such as access to abortion or taxes on cigarettes, might have been held in reserve for future debates in an attempt to get a more acceptable measure passed by the Congress.

As noted in relation to incrementalism as a current drawn from the August 1994 floor debate, Paul Starr suggested that a leaner, smaller version of the Clinton-Mitchell plan would have fared better in Congress. In fact, Starr (1994) offered a summary list of "mistakes" that could have been corrected in an effort to implement comprehensive health care reform:

The lesson for next time in health reform is faster, smaller. We made the error of trying to do too much at once, took too long, and ended up achieving nothing. Oh, yes, I was thrilled when President Clinton waved his pen before Congress and threatened to veto anything less than universal coverage. Like many others who supported reform, I failed to appreciate the risk of losing everything. We were too confident that reform was inevitable, just as some are now too certain that defeat was inevitable. Strategy and speed matter in politics as in sports. (p. 31)

Starr, like many, saw timing and strategic changes as the answer to accomplishing reform.

Some might also argue that the very nature of the debate could have been changed if proponents of comprehensive health care reform could have been successful in directly refuting the anti–big government argument. As this work vividly demonstrates, the anti–big government argument rests at the center of the failure of comprehensive health care reform on the floor of the Senate in 1994. Proponents of comprehensive health care reform did not simply concede the big government argument and run and hide. They did, however, fail to anticipate the argument, to confront the argument directly, and to use their responses to address it as a means of pre-emption.

It might have been possible, for example, to better define the appropriate role of the federal government and to more explicitly justify that role as the Mitchell proposal was introduced. In fact, when Senator Mitchell introduced his proposal he went to great lengths to demonstrate the magnitude of the health care crisis. That crisis could have been summarized briefly and greater attention could have been focused on justifying a comprehensive federal response to it. James Q. Wilson (1989) has, for example, developed an extensive explanation of the importance of organization to the successful delivery of programs and services by government bureaucracies. Reference to such explanations do not appear in the remarks of health care reform proponents.

Although making timing and strategic changes similar to those articulated by Starr or appealing to the actual nature of successful bureaucracies within government à la Wilson might have made the debate more competitive and a lot less grueling for proponents of comprehensive health care reform, it simply would not have been enough. The talk of opponents and the *social epistemic* that it so closely connected to were far too powerful. Only absent the anti–big government argument and the general public attitude would comprehensive health care reform have succeeded in 1994.

The details of the August 1994 Senate floor debate have been developed at some length in this work. The opponents of comprehensive health care reform displayed a pattern of discourse that was both more future-oriented and more forceful in terms of potential long-term consequences than the pattern of discourse displayed by reform proponents. And, more importantly, opponents of comprehensive health care reform reframed the debate as being about a crisis of big government and not really about a crisis in health care at all. Those positions can coincided very well with a broad *social epistemic* that is still prevalent and, in fact, more exaggerated today—that we, as the public, recognize "bigness" as bad and the single most obvious agent of "bigness" is the federal government.

As long as opponents of comprehensive health care reform can engage in rhetorical behavior that identifies the federal government as an enemy or villain, comprehensive health care reform will not be passed in the United States. And, that possibility will continue to exist as long as the dominant paradigm for knowing among the public tells them that they should think of the federal government in an untrusting and suspicious light. Those who seek comprehensive health care reform and other initiatives requiring federal government actions should not, however, simply throw up their hands in defeat. Just as the current *social epistemic* has been shaped rhetorically, it is possible to reshape that *social epistemic* and engender a paradigm shift that makes the public see an appropriate and potentially helpful role for the federal government. Such a paradigm shift might well take some time, but a concerted long-term discursive campaign could go a long way toward accomplishing such a goal. It would capture the most significant instrument for change that is available. It would embrace a conclusion that could be the guide for the accomplishment of virtually any goal—talk is power.

References

Aaron, H. J. (1996). The problem that won't go away. In H. J. Aaron (Ed.) *The problem that won't go away: Reforming U.S. health care financing* (1–14). Washington, DC: Brookings.

Aday, L. (1993). Equality, accessability, and ethical issues: Is the U.S. health care reform debate asking the right questions? *American Behavioral Scientist, 36,* 724–740.

Armstrong, S. A. (1995). Arlen Specter and the construction of adversarial discourse Selected representations in the Clarence Thomas–Anita Hill hearings. *Argumentation and Advocacy, 32,* 75–89.

Auer, J. J. (1959). *Introduction to research in speech.* New York: Harper and Rowe.

Becker, S. (1995, July). Improving the nation's health: The role of communication scholars. Paper presented to the Summer Conference of the Speech Communication Association. Washington, DC.

Bellah, R. N. (1985). *Habits of the heart: Individualism and commitment in America.* Berkeley: University of California Press.

Bergthold, L. A. (1993). American business and health care reform. *American Behavioral Scientist, 36,* 802–812.

Bettingham, F. B. (1973). *Persuasive communication.* New York: Holt, Rinehart, and Winston.

Binstock, R. H. (1993). Older people and health care reform. *American Behavioral Scientist, 36,* 823–840.

Bitzer, L. (1959). Aristotle's enthymeme revisited. *Quarterly Journal of Speech, 45,* 399–408.

Black, E. (1965). *Rhetorical criticism: A study in method.* New York: Macmillan.

Borman, E. (1962). The southern senators' filibuster on civil rights: Speechmaking as parliamentary stratagem. *Southern Speech Journal, 27,* 183–194.

Borman, E. (1965). *Theory and research in the communication arts.* New York: Holt.

Bostrom, R. N., Waldhart, E. S., Shelton, M. W., & Bertino, S. (1997). *Getting there: Functional public speaking.* Prospect Heights, IL: Waveland.

Braden, W. W. (1960). The Senate debate on the League of Nations, 1918–1920: An overview. *Southern Speech Journal, 25,* 273–281.

Branham, R. J. (1991). *Debate and critical analysis: The harmony of conflict.* Hillsdale, NJ: Lawrence Erlbaum Associates.

Brockriede, W. (1972). Arguers as lovers. *Philosophy and Rhetoric, 5,* 1–11.

Brockriede, W. (1972). *Influence, belief and argument: An introduction to responsible persuasion.* Glenview, IL: Scott Foresman.

Burke, K. (1952). *A grammar of motives.* New York: Prentice Hall.

Butler, J. (1995). Carol Mosely-Braun's day to talk about racism: A study of forum in the United States Senate. *Argumentation and Advocacy, 32,* 62–74.

Byrd, R. C. (1982). Is it the *Congressional Record* or the *Congressional second-thought?* *Speaker and Gavel, 19,* 75–76.

Cahn, D. D., Pappas, E. J., & Schoen, L. (1979). Speech in the Senate, 1978. *Communication Quarterly, 27,* 50–54.

Cain, E. R. (1954). A method for rhetorical analysis of congressional debate. *Western Speech, 18,* 91–95.

Cain, E. R. (1955). Is Senate debate significant? *Today's Speech, 3,* 10–12.

Cain, E. R. (1962). Obstacles to early congressional reporting. *Southern Speech Journal, 27,* 239–47.

Camp, L. R. (1983). Treason, expulsion, and the U.S. Senate, 1862: Senator Andrew Johnson vs. Senator Jesse D. Bright, *Journal of the American Forensic Association, 14,* 226–238.

Campbell, K. K., & Jamieson, K. H. (1990). Introduction to *form and genre.* In B. L. Brock, R. L. Scott, & J. W. Chesbro (Eds.) *Methods of rhetorical criticism: A twentieth-century perspective* (pp. 343–360). Detroit, MI: Wayne State University Press.

Campion, F. D. (1984). *The AMA and U.S. health policy since 1940.* Chicago: Chicago Review Press.

Cherwitz, R. A. (1978). Lyndon Johnson and the "crisis" of Tonkin Gulf: A president's justification of war. *Western Journal of Speech Communication, 42,* 93–104.

Cherwitz, R. A. (1987). Lyndon Johnson and the "crisis" of Tonkin Gulf: A president's justification of war. In T. Windt & B. Ingold (Eds.) *Essays in presidential rhetoric* (pp. 182–193). Dubuque, IA: Kendall/Hurt.

Cherwitz, R. A., & Zagacki, K. S. (1986). Consummatory versus justificatory crisis rhetoric. *Western Journal of Speech Communication, 50,* 307–324.

Chesebro, J. W. (1976). Political communication. *Quarterly Journal of Speech, 62,* 289–300.

Chester, G. (1945). Contemporary senate debate. *Quarterly Journal of Speech, 31,* 407–411.

Chronology of Federal Involvement. (1994, October). *Congressional Digest, 231.*

Clancy, J. J. (1989). *The invisible powers: The language of business.* Lexington, MA: Lexington Books.

Clevenger, T., Jr., Parson, D. W., & Polisky, J. B. (1968). The problem of textual accuracy. In J. H. Hendrix & J. B. Polisky (Eds.). *Rhetorical criticusm: Methods and models.* (pp. 3–12). Dubuque, IA: Wm. C. Brown.

Cleverley, W. (1997). *Essentials of health care finance.* Gaithersburg, VA: Aspen Publishing.

Collier, J. M. (1999, February 21). A health care system dying of neglect. *Lexington Herald-Leader,* p. F-2.

Corcoran, D. E. (1990). Language and politics. In D. L. Swanson & D. Minno (Eds.) *New directions in political communication: A resource book* (pp. 51–85). Beverly Hills, CA: Sage.

Cousineau, M. R., & Lozier, J. W. (1993). Assuring access to health care for homeless people under national health care. *American Behavioral Scientist, 36,* 857–870.

Crable, R. E. (1976). *Argumentation as communication: Reasoning with receivers.* Columbus, OH: Charles E. Merrill.

Davis, K. (1975). *National health insurance: Benefits, costs, and consequences.* Washington, DC: The Brookings Institute.

Day, D. G. (1966). The ethics of democratic debate. *Central States Speech Journal, 17,* 5–14.

Deshler, D. (1985). Metaphors and values in higher education. *Academe, 71,* 22–28.

Dewey, J., & Bentley, A. F. (1960). *Knowledge and the known.* Boston: D. C. Heath.

Dolbeare, F. M., & Edelman, M. (1985). *American politics: Policies, power, and change.* Lexington, MA: D. C. Health.

Dryzek, J. S. (1990). *Discursive democracy: Politics, policy, and political science.* New York: Cambridge University Press.

Dunbar, N. R. (1986). Laetrile: A case study of a public controversy. *Journal of the American Forensic Association, 22,* 196–211.

Edelman, M. (1965). *The symbolic uses of politics.* Urbana: University of Illinois Press.

Edelman, M. (1971). *Politics as symbolic action.* Chicago: Markham.

Edelman, M. (1977). *Political language: Words that succeed and policies that fail.* New York: Academic Press.

Edelman, M. (1988). *Constructing the political spectacle.* Chicago: University of Chicago Press.

Edwards, G. C. III, & Wayne, S. J. (1990). *Presidential leadership: Politics and policy making.* New York: St. Martin's Press.

Ehninger, D. (1974). *Influence, belief and argument: An introduction to responsible persuasion.* Glenview, IL: Scott Foresman.

Ehninger, D., & Brockriede, W. (1963). *Decision by debate.* New York: Dodd, Mead, & Co.

Entman, R. M. (1993). Framing: Toward clarification of a paradigm. *Journal of Communication, 43,* 51–58.

Erickson, B., Lind, E. A., Johnson, B. C., & O'Barr, W. M. (1978). Speech style and impression formation in a court setting: The effects of "powerful" and "powerless" speech. *Journal of Experimental Social Psychology, 6,* 331–371.

Evans, C. L. (1995). Committees and health jurisdiction in Congress. In T. E. Mann & W. J. Ornstein (Eds.). *Intensive case: How congress shapes health policy* (pp. 23–52). Washington, DC: American Enterprise Institute and the Brookings Institute.

Fairhurst, G. T., & Sarr, R. A. (1996). *The art of framing: Managing the language of leadership.* San Francisco: Jossey-Bass.

Finlay, D. J., Holsti, O. R., & Eagen, R. R. (1967). *Enemies in politics.* Chicago: Rand McNally and Co.

Fisher, W. R. (1984). Narrative as a human communication paradigm: The case of public moral argument. *Communication Monographs, 51,* 1–22.

Fisher, W. R. (1985). The narrative paradigm: An elaboration. *Communication Monographs, 52,* 347–367.

Fisher, W. R. (1987). *Human communication as narrative.* Columbia: University of South Carolina Press.

Fitzpatrick, J. R. (1941). Congressional debating. *Quarterly Journal of Speech, 27,* 251–255.

Foley, M. (1980). *The new Senate: Liberal influence on a conservative institution 1959–1972.* New Haven, CT: Yale University Press.

Fotheringham, W. C. (1966). *Perspectives on persuasion.* Boston: Allyn and Bacon.

Freeley, A. J. (1962). *Argumentation and debate: Rational decision making.* Belmont, CA: Wadsworth.

Goodman, N. (1968). *Language of art: An approach to a theory of symbols.* Indianapolis, IN: Bobbs-Merrill.

Green, A. (1991). *Gavel to gavel: A guide to the televised proceedings of Congress.* Washington, DC: Benton Foundation.

Green, M. J., Fallows, J. M., & Zwick, D. R. (1972). *Who runs Congress?* New York: Bantam.

Griffin, C. J. G. (1994). Carter's reaction to the Iran hostage crisis. In A. Kiewe (Ed.). *The modern presidency and crisis rhetoric* (pp. 136–149). Westport, CT: Praeger Publications.

Grogan, C. M. (1991). Political theory to explain the variation in state Medicaid policy. *Dissertation Abstracts International, 52,* 9A.

Grogan, C. M. (1993). Federalism and health care reform. *American Behavioral Scientist, 36,* 741–758.

Gronbeck, B. E. (1992). Negative narrative in 1988 presidential campaign ads. *Quarterly Journal of Speech, 78,* 333–346.

Hafner-Eaton, C. (1993). Will the Phoenix rise, and where will she go? The women's health agenda. *American Behavioral Scientist, 36,* 841–856.

Hahn, D. F. (1980). Corrupt rhetoric: President Ford and the "Mayaguez Affair." *Communica tion Quarterly, 28,* 38–43.

Haiman, F. (1952). A re-examination of the ethics of persuasion. *Central States Speech Journal, 3,* 4–9.

Hanson, R. L. (1993). Defining a role for states in a federal health care system. *American Behavioral Scientist, 36,* 760–786.

Hart, R. P. (1993). Why communication? Why education? Toward a politics of teaching. *Communication Education, 42,* 97–105.

Health Care Overview. (1994, October). *Congressional Digest,* 230–232.

Health Care Reform. (1994, October). *Congressional Digest,* 225.

Heclo, H. (1996). Clinton's health care reform in historical perspective. In H. J. Aaron (Ed.) *The Problem that won't go away: Reforming U.S. health care financing* (pp. 15–33). Washington, DC: Brookings.

Hedde, W. G., & Brigance, W. N. (1955). *American speech.* Chicago: Lippincott. Hendrix, J. A. (1965). A new look at textual authenticity of speeches in the *Congressional Record. Southern Speech Journal, 31,* 153.

Heritage, J. (1984). *Garfunkel and ethnomethodology.* Cambridge, UK: Polity.

Hersey, D. R. (1986). Reagan and Mitterand respond to international crisis: Creating versus transcending approaches. *Western Journal of Speech Communication, 50,* 325–335.

Hochmuth, M. (1948). Speech and society. *Bulletin of National Association of Secondary School Principals, 32,* 17–33.

Hollihan, T. A., & Baaske, K. T. (1994). *Arguments and arguing: The products and process of human decision making.* New York: St. Martin's Press.

Hollihan, T. A., Riley, P., & Baaske, K. T. (1985). The art of storytelling: An argument for the narrative perspective in academic debate. In J. R. Cox, M. O. Sillars, & G. B. Walker (Eds.). *Argument and social practice: Proceedings of the fourth SCA/AFA conference on argumentation* (pp. 807–826). Annandale, VA: Speech Communication Association.

Iglehart, J. K. (1992). The American health care system introduction. *New England Journal of Medicine, 326,* 962–967.

Illich, I. (1976). *Medical nemesis: The expropriations of health.* New York: Pantheon.

Intriligator, M. D. (1993). A way to achieve national health insurance in the United States: The Medicare expansion proposal. *American Behavioral Scientist, 36,* 709–723.

Isaak, A. C. (1975). *Scope and methods of political science.* Homewood, IL: The Dorsey Press.

Ivie, R. L. (1986). Introduction to a special issue on the rhetoric of foreign affairs. *Western Journal of Speech Communication, 50,* 305–306.

Jaksa, J. A., & Pritchard, M. S. (1994). *Communication ethics: Methods of analysis.* Belmont, CA: Wadsworth.

Johannesen, R. (1990). *Ethics in human communication.* Prospect Heights, IL: Waveland Press.

Johnson, M. (Ed.) (1981). *Philosophical perspectives on metaphor.* Minneapolis: University of Minnesota Press.

Jorgensen-Earp, C. R., & Staton, A. Q. (1993). Student metaphors for the college freshman experience. *Communication Education, 42,* 123–141.

Kane, P. E. (1971). Extended debate and the rules of the United States Senate. *Quarterly Journal of Speech, 57,* 43–49.

Kane, T. (1995). Argumentation and the Senate: An introduction. *Argumentation and Advocacy, 32,* 57–61.

Kasper, J. F., Mulley, A. G., Jr., & Wennberg, J. C. (1992). Developing shared decision-making programs to improve the quality of health care. *QRB: Quality Review Bulletin, 18,* 183–190.

Katznelson, I., & Kesselman, M. (1975). *The politics of power: A critical introduction to American government.* New York: Harcourt Brace Jovanovich.

Kaus, M. (1994, December 5). They blew it. *New Republic,* 14–19.

Kellerman, B. (1984). Leadership as a political act. In B. Kellerman (Ed.) *Leadership: Multidisciplinary perspectives* (63–90). Englewood Cliffs, NJ: Prentice Hall.

Kendall, K. E. (1990). Political communication. In L. C. Frey, D. O'Hair, & G. L. Kreps (Eds.) *Applied communication theory and research* (225–243). Hillsdale, NJ: Lawrence Erlbaum Associates.

Kiewe, A. (Ed.) (1994). *The modern presidency and crisis rhetoric.* Westport, CT: Praeger Publications.

Klope, D. C. (1986). Defusing a foreign policy crisis: Myth and victimage in Reagan's 1983 Lebanon/Grenada address. *Western Journal of Speech Communication, 50,* 336–349.

Klump, J. F. (1981). A dramatic approach to fields. In G. Zigelmuller & T. Rhodes (Eds.) *Dimensions of argument: Proceedings of the second summer conference on argumentation.* Annandale, VA: Speech Communication Association.

Kosterbitz, J. (1991, April 27). Radical surgeons. *National Journal,* 993–997.

Kreps, G. L. (1986). *Organizational communication.* New York: Longman.

Lakoff, G., & Johnson, M. (1980). *Metaphors we live by.* Chicago: University of Chicago Press.

Lane, R. E., & Sears, D. O. (1964). *Public opinion.* Englewood Cliffs, NJ: Prentice Hall.

Levasseur, D., & Dean, K. W. (1996). The use of evidence in presidential debates: A study of evidence levels and types from 1960–1988. *Argumentation and Advocacy, 32,* 129–142.

Lieberman, P. (1991). *Uniquely human: The evolution of speech, thought, and selfless behavior.* Cambridge, MA: Harvard University Press.

Lincoln, B. (1994). *Authority: Construction and corrosion.* Chicago: University of Chicago Press.

Major Federal Health Care Programs. (1994, October). *Congressional Digest,* 233–234.

Mann, T. E., & Ornstein, W. J. (1995). Introduction. In T. E. Mann & W. J. Ornstein (Eds.) *Intensive care: How Congress shapes health policy* (1–22). Washington, DC: American Enterprise Institute/Brookings.

Matthews, D. R. (1960). *U.S. Senators and their world.* Chapel Hill: University of North Carolina Press.

McBurney, J. H., O'Neill, J. M., & Mills, G. R. (1951). *Argumentation and debate:Techniques of a free society.* New York: Macmillian.

McCroskey, J. C. (1969). The effects of evidence in persuasive communication. *Western Journal of Speech Communication, 31,* 189–199.

McKerrow, R. E. (1990). Argument communities. In R. Trapp & J. Shuetz (Eds.) *Perspectives on argumentation* (27–42). Prospect Heights, IL: Waveland.

McPherson, E. G. (1942). Reporting the debates of Congress. *Quarterly Journal of Speech, 28,* 141–148.

McPherson, E. G. (1944). Reporting of the debates in the House of Representatives during the first Congress, 1789–1791. *Quarterly Journal of Speech, 30,* 64–71.

Merriam, R. (1990). Words and numbers: Mathematical dimensions of rhetoric. *Southern Communication Journal, 55,* 337–354.

Micken, R. A. (1951). The triumph of strategy in the Senate debate on the League of Nations. *Quarterly Journal of Speech, 37,* 49–53.

Micken, R. A. (1952). Western Senators in the League of Nations debate. *Western Speech, 18,* 238–244.

Micozzi, M. S. (1996, August 16). The need to teach alternative medicine. *The Chronicle of Higher Education,* A48.

Miller, A. H. (1993). Economic, character, and social issues in the 1992 presidential election. *American Behavioral Scientist, 37,* 315–327.

Morone, J. A. (1990). *The Democratic wish: Popular participation and the limits of American government.* New York: Basic Books.

Murphy, R. (1965). Problems in speech texts. In D. C. Bryant (Ed.). *Papers in rhetoric and poetic* (70–86). Iowa City: University of Iowa Press.

Murphy, T. A. (1995). American political mythology and the Senate filibuster. *Argumentation and Advocacy, 32,* 90–107.

Navarro, V. (1994). *United States does not have a national health program.* New York: Baywood.

Neufield, J., & Greenfield, J. (1972). *A populist manifesto: The making of a new majority.* New York: Warner.

Nilsen, T. R. (1974). *Ethics of speech communication.* Indianapolis, IN: Bobbs-Merrill.

Nixon, J. P., & Ignagri, K. M. (1993). Health care reform: A labor perspective. *American Behavioral Scientist, 36,* 813–822.

Nye, J. S., Jr. (1998, January 16). Finding ways to improve the public's trust in government. *The Chronicle of Higher Education.* B6–B8.

O'Donnell, V., & Kable, J. (1982). *Persuasion: An interactive dependency approach.* New York: Random House.

Oliver, R. T. (1962). *The psychology of persuasive speech.* New York: David McKay Co.

Osborn, M. M. (1967). Archetypical metaphor in rhetoric: The light-dark family. *Quarterly Journal of Speech, 53,* 115–126.

Pear, R. (1999, February 9). HMOs expanding coverage. *Lexington Herald-Leader,* A5.

Perrin, S. G. (1987). Metaphorical revelations: A description of metaphor as the reciprocal engagement of abstract perspectives and concrete phenomena in experience. *Metaphor and Symbolic Activity, 2,* 251–280.

Peterson, M. A. (1992). Report from Congress: Momentum toward health care reform in the U.S. Senate. *Journal of Health, Politics, Policy, and Law, 17,* 553–573.

Peterson, M. A. (1993). Institutional change and the health politics of the 1990s. *American Behavioral Scientist, 36,* 782–801.

Peterson, M. A. (1995). How health policy information is used in Congress. In T. E. Mann & W. J. Ornstein (Eds.) *Intensive care: How Congress shapes health policy* (79–111). Washington, DC: American Enterprise Institute/Brookings.

Peterson, O. (1957). Judah P. Benjamin's Senate speeches on slavery and secession. *Southern Speech Journal, 23,* 10–20.

Poen, M. M. (1979). *Harry S. Truman versus the medical lobby.* Columbia: University of Missouri Press.

Pratt, J. W. (1970). An analysis of three crisis speeches. *Western Journal of Speech, 34,* 194–202.

Prosise, T. O., Miller, G. R., & Mills, J. P. (1996). Argument fields as arenas of discursive struggle. *Argumentation and Advocacy, 32*, 111–128.

Quadro, D. F. (1977). The *Congressional Record*: Another look. *Western Journal of Speech Communication, 41*, 253–259.

Quinn, J. B. (1998, December 27). Expansion of patients rights panels jeopardized. *Lexington Herald-Leader*, E1.

Randal, J. (1993, May). Wrong prescription. *The Progressive*, 22–25.

Ratzan, S. C. (1994). Communication—The key to a healthier tomorrow. *American Behavioral Scientist, 38*, 202–207.

Recent Action in the Congress. (1994, October). *Congressional Digest.* 237.

Reid, L. D. (1940). Factors contributing to inaccuracy in the texts of speeches. In D. C. Bryant (Ed.) *Papers in rhetoric* (38–45). St. Louis: Privately printed.

Reinard, J. C. (1988). The empirical study of the persuasive effects of evidence: The status after fifty years of research. *Human Communication Research, 15*, 3–59.

Richards, I. A. (1936). *Philosophy of rhetoric.* London: Oxford University Press.

Richardson, M. (1999, March 2). Public medical care put in a bind. *Lexington Herald- Leader*, A1–2.

Rieke, R., & Sillars, M. O. (1984). *Argumentation and the decision making process.* Glenview, IL: Scott, Foresman, and Co.

Rives, S. G. (1967). Congressional hearings: A modern adaptation of dialectic. *Journal of the American Forensic Association, 4*, 41–46.

Robinson, Z. (1942). Are speeches in Congress reported accurately? *Quarterly Journal of Speech, 28*, 8–12.

Roe, E. M. (1994). *Narrative policy analysis: Theory and practice.* Durham, NC: Duke University Press.

Roemer, M. (1991). *National health systems of the world: Vol. 1, The countries.* New York: Oxford University Press.

Roemer, M. (1993). National health systems throughout the world: Lessons for health system reform in the United States. *American Behavioral Scientist, 36*, 694–708.

Rosen, D. M. (1984). Leadership in world cultures. In B. Kellerman (Ed.) *Leadership: Multi-disciplinary perspectives* (39–62). Englewood Cliffs, NJ: Prentice Hall.

Rosenau, P. V. (1993a). Some reasoned utopian proposals for national health system reform in the United States. *American Behavioral Scientist, 36*, 871–886.

Rosenau, P. V. (1993b). Health system reform in the United States: Introduction. *American Behavioral Scientist, 36*, 689–693.

Rosenfield, L. W. (1968). The anatomy of critical discourse. *Speech Monographs, 25*, 50–69.

Rosenwasser, M. J. (1969). Six Senate war critics and their appeals for gaining audience response. *Today's Speech, 17*, 43–50.

Rovner, J. (1995a). "Catastrophic" attempts to fix Medicare. In T. E. Mann & W. J. Ornstein (Eds.) *Intensive care: How Congress shapes health policy* (145–178). Washington, DC: American Enterprise Institute/Brookings.

Rovner, J. (1995b). Congress and health care reform 1993–94. In T. E. Mann & W. J. Ornstein (Eds.) *Intensive care: How Congress shapes health policy* (179–226). Washington, DC: American Enterprise Institute/Brookings.

Rowland, R. C. (1982). The influence of purpose on fields of argument. *Journal of the American Forensic Association, 18*, 228–245.

Roszak, T. (1995, November/December). Mea culpa? *Utne Reader.* 64–66.

Sadock, J. M. (1979). Figurative speech and linguistics. In A. Ortony (Ed.) *Metaphor and thought* (46–63). Cambridge, UK: Cambridge University Press.

Schick, A. (1995). How a bill did not become a law. In T. E. Mann & W. J. Ornstein (Eds.). *Intensive care: How Congress shapes health policy* (227–272). Washington, DC: American Enterprise Institute/Brookings.

Schroeder, L. E. (1999, April 15). For profit hospital answers to greed, not to patients. *Argus Leader,* 13A.

Schuetz, J. (1986). Overlays of argument in legislative process. *Journal of the American Forensic Association, 22,* 223–234.

Schwartzman, R. (1995). Clarifying the role of metaphor in rhetorical epistemology. *Communication and Theatre Association of Minnesota Journal, 22,* 33–45.

Shapiro, M. J. (1981). *Language and political understanding: The politics of discursive practices.* New Haven, CT: Yale University Press.

Sharf, B. F. (1999). The present and future of health communication scholarship: Over-looked opportunities. *Health Communication, 11,* 195–199.

Shecter, J. (1996, May 24). Medical dean turned Senate aid. *The Chronicle of Higher Education,* A5.

Shipp, B. (1998, April 8). Health care next big political issue. *Statesboro Herald,* 4.

Silverman, D. (1994). *Interpreting qualitative data: Methods for analyzing talk, text, and interaction.* Thousand Oaks, CA: Sage.

Simons, H. W. (1976). *Persuasion: Understanding, practice, and analysis.* Reading, MA: Addison-Wesley.

Sinclair, B. (1989). *The transformation of the U.S. Senate.* Baltimore, MD: The Johns Hopkins University Press.

Skopol, T. (1996). The rise and the resounding demise of the Clinton health security plan. In H. J. Aaron (Ed.) *The problem that won't go away: Reforming U.S. health care financing* (34–53). Washington, DC: Brookings.

Smith, R. B. (1997, March/April). Ideology, partnership, and the new political generation. *Society,* 15–20.

Starr, P. (1982). *The social transformation of American medicine: The rise of a sovereign profession and the making of a vast industry.* New York: Basic Books.

Starr, P. (1994). What happened to health care reform? *The American Prospect, 20,* 20–31.

Tallon, J. R., & Nathan, R. P. (1992). Federal/state partnership for health system reform. *Health Affairs, 11,* 7–16.

Thomas, D. (1992). Presumption in nonpolicy debate: A case for natural presumption based on current nonpolicy paradigms. In D. Thomas & J. Hart (Eds.) *Advanced debate: Readings in theory, practice, and teaching* (220–241). Lincolnwood, IL: National Textbook Co.

Thomas, O. (1969). *Metaphor and related subjects.* New York: Random House. Thonssen, L., Baird, A. C., & Braden, W. W. (1970). *Speech criticism.* New York: Ronald Press.

Thonssen, L., Baird, A. C., & Braden, W. W. (1970). *Speech Criticism* (2nd ed.). New York: The Ronald Press.

Tompkins, P. K., & Linkugel, W. A. (1959). Speech in the Senate. *Today's Speech 7,* 30–32.

Tompkins, P. K., & Pappas, E. J. (1967). Speech in the Senate '65. *Today's Speech,* 15, 3–6.

Toolan, M. J. (1992). *Narrative: A critical linguistic introduction.* New York: Routledge.

Toulmin, S. E. (1950). *An examination of the place of reason in ethics.* Cambridge, UK: Cambridge University Press.

Toulmin, S. E. (1958). *The uses of argument.* Cambridge, UK: Cambridge University Press.

Toulmin, S. E. (1972). *Human understanding.* Princeton, NJ: Princeton University Press.

Toulmin, S. E., Rieke, R., & Janik, A. (1979). *An introduction to reasoning*. New York: Macmillan.

Unicameral: Women's health initiative fails. (1999, April 13). *Town & Country Weekly News* 3.

U.S. Department of Health and Human Services. (1990). *Seventh report of the president and Congress on the status of health personnel in the United States*. Washington, DC: Government Printing Office.

Vatz, R. E. (1973). The myth of the rhetorical situation. *Philosophy and Rhetoric, 6*, 154–161.

Voorhis, J. (1948). Effective speaking in Congress. *Quarterly Journal of Speech, 34*, 462–463.

Wallace, K. P. (1955). Rhetoric and politics. *Southern Speech Journal, 20*, 195–203.

Wasby, S. L. (1971). Rhetoricians and political scientists: Some lines of convergence. *Southern Speech Journal, 36*, 231–242.

Washburn, W. E. (1968). Speech communication and politics. *Today's Speech, 16*, 3–16.

Weaver, R. M. (1953). *The ethics of rhetoric*. Chicago: Henry Regency.

Webster's New Intercollegiate Dictionary. (1979). Springfield, MA: G. & C. Merriam Co.

Weil, T. P. (1992). A universal access plan: A step toward national health insurance. *Hospital & Health Services Administration, 37*, 37–51.

Wenzel, J. W., & Kneupper, C. W. (1981). Argument fields: Some social constructivist observations. In G. Zigelmueller & J. Rhodes (Eds.). *Dimensions of argument: Proceedings of the second summer conference on argumentation*. Annandale, VA: Speech Communication Association.

Wichert, R. (1940). A test for personal goal values. *Journal of Social Psychology, 11*, 259–274.

Wills, G. (1987). *Reagan's America: Innocents at home*. Garden City, NY: Doubleday and Co.

Wilson, J. Q. (1989). *Bureaucracy: What government agencies do and why they do it*. New York: Basic Books.

Windt, T. O. (1973). The presidency and speeches of international crisis: Repeating the rhetorical past. *Speaker and Gavel, 11*, 6–14.

Zarefsky, D. (1983). Civil rights and crisis conflict: Presidential communication in crisis. *Central States Speech Journal, 34*, 59–66.

Index

About the Author

MICHAEL W. SHELTON is Lecturer and Assistant Coordinator of Public Speaking at University of Kentucky. He maintains an active scholarly career, having published more than fifty publications, including over three dozen articles and four books and workbooks.

ISBN 0-275-96751-4

90000>

EAN

9 780275 967512

HARDCOVER BAR CODE

DATE DUE

DEC 0 6 2003			
	1 0 2010		
GAYLORD			PRINTED IN U.S.A